Visit us at

T0227139

Syngress is committed to publishing high-quality books for IT Professionals and delivering those books in media and formats that fit the demands of our customers. We are also committed to extending the utility of the book you purchase via additional materials available from our Web site.

SOLUTIONS WEB SITE
To register your book, visit www.syngress.com/solutions. Once registered, you can access our solutions@syngress.com Web pages. There you may find an assortment of valueadded features such as free e-books related to the topic of this book, URLs of related Web sites, FAQs from the book, corrections, and any updates from the author(s).

ULTIMATE CDs
Our Ultimate CD product line offers our readers budget-conscious compilations of some of our best-selling backlist titles in Adobe PDF form. These CDs are the perfect way to extend your reference library on key topics pertaining to your area of expertise, including Cisco Engineering, Microsoft Windows System Administration, CyberCrime Investigation, Open Source Security, and Firewall Configuration, to name a few.

DOWNLOADABLE E-BOOKS
For readers who can't wait for hard copy, we offer most of our titles in downloadable Adobe PDF form. These e-books are often available weeks before hard copies, and are priced affordably.

SYNGRESS OUTLET
Our outlet store at syngress.com features overstocked, out-of-print, or slightly hurt books at significant savings.

SITE LICENSING
Syngress has a well-established program for site licensing our e-books onto servers in corporations, educational institutions, and large organizations. Contact us at sales@syngress.com for more information.

CUSTOM PUBLISHING
Many organizations welcome the ability to combine parts of multiple Syngress books, as well as their own content, into a single volume for their own internal use. Contact us at sales@syngress.com for more information.

SYNGRESS®

Techno Security's Guide to Securing SCADA

Jack Wiles Lead Author

Ted Claypoole
Phil Drake
Paul A. Henry
Lester J. Johnson Jr.
Sean Lowther
Greg Miles
Marc Weber Tobias
James H. Windle

Foreword by Amit Yoran
Chairman and CEO of NetWitness Corporation

KEY	SERIAL NUMBER
001	HJIRTCV764
002	PO9873D5FG
003	829KM8NJH2
004	BPOQ48722D
005	CVPLQ6WQ23
006	VBP965T5T5
007	HJJJ863WD3E
008	2987GVTWMK
009	629MP5SDJT
010	IMWQ295T6T

PUBLISHED BY
Syngress Publishing, Inc.
Elsevier, Inc.
30 Corporate Drive
Burlington, MA 01803

Techno Security's Guide to Securing SCADA

Printed and bound in the United Kingdom

Transferred to Digital Print 2011

ISBN 13: 978-1-59749-282-9

Publisher: Andrew Williams   Page Layout and Art: SPI
Acquisitions Editor: David George   Copy Editor: Michael McGee and Jill Batistick
Developmental Editor: Matthew Cater   Indexer: SPI
Project Manager: Andre Cuello   Cover Designer: Michael Kavish

For information on rights, translations, and bulk sales, contact Matt Pedersen, Commercial Sales Director and Rights, at Syngress Publishing; email m.pedersen@elsevier.com.

Lead Author

Jack Wiles, (PPS, IAM, IEM) is a Security Professional with over 30 years experience in security related fields. This includes computer security, disaster recovery and physical security. He is a professional member of the National Speakers Association and has trained federal agents, corporate attorneys and internal auditors on a number of computer crime related topics. He is a pioneer in presenting on a number of subjects that are now being labeled 'Homeland Security' topics. Well over 10,000 people have attended one or more of his presentations since 1988. Jack is also a co-founder and President of The TrainingCo., producers of the Annual Techno Security Conferences and the popular Techno Forensics conferences. He is in frequent contact with members of many state and local law enforcement agencies as well as Special Agents with the U.S. Secret Service, FBI, U.S. Customs, Department of Justice, The Department of Defense and numerous members of High-Tech Crime units. He was also appointed as the first President of the North Carolina InfraGard chapter that is now one of the largest chapters in the country. He is also a founding member and 'official' MC of the US Secret Service South Carolina Electronic Crimes Task Force.

Jack is also a Vietnam veteran who served with the 101st Airborne Division in Vietnam in 1967–68. He recently retired from the U.S. Army Reserves as a lieutenant colonel and was assigned directly to the Pentagon for the final seven years of his career. In his spare time, he has been a senior contributing editor for several local, national and international magazines.

This is the fifth book published by Syngress that we have been a part of in the last 18 months. I'm in our friend Johnny Long's camp in acknowledging that I can do nothing without the help of my Lord and Savior, Jesus Christ. I dedicate my small part of this book to Him, my wonderful wife of 30 years (long years for her) Valerie, and my son Tyler as he heads off to college. I'm very proud of you son. My partner Don Withers is like a brother to me in every way. For ten years now, we have been fortunate to produce our Techno Security and our popular Techno Forensics conferences, which have had attendees register from over 45 countries around the world. I wish that I had space to thank all of the other authors of this book. I know them all well, and have known some of them for more than two decades. These are some of the most respected and talented security minds in the world, and I am honored to have my work in the same book as theirs. And last, but certainly not least, I'd like to thank the thousands of friends who have become Techno groupies at our annual events. Many of them have traveled from half the world away to spend a few days with us each year. THANK YOU! – Jack

Jack wrote Chapter 1, "Physical Security: SCADA and the Critical Infrastructure's Biggest Vulnerability."

Contributors

Ted Claypoole is a Member of the law firm Womble Carlyle Sandridge and Rice, in Charlotte, North Carolina, in the Intellectual Property Transaction group, and a senior member of its Privacy and Data Management Team. He has long concentrated on the business and legal implications of information security and computer crime, first as in-house corporate counsel for CompuServe, Inc. and as assistant general counsel for Bank of America. He now advises business clients and information security companies on contracting for data protection, allocating risk in digital certificate infrastructures and reacting to electronic threats. He has served on a U.S. Justice Department computer crimes task force and the Information Protection Committee for the Banking Industry Technology Secretariat. He has presented talks at the RSA Security Conferences in 2007 and 2008, including a talk on the ethics of pervasive biometrics.

Ted wrote Chapter 8, "Biometric Authentication for SCADA Security."

Phil Drake is Communications Manager for the Charlotte Observer in Charlotte, N. C. The Observer is a daily newspaper that serves readers throughout North and South Carolina. In addition to the newspaper, the Charlotte Observer produces specialty magazines, voice information, and Internet services.

Phil is responsible for all aspects of communications at Observer operations in both Carolinas, including telephone and data communications, wireless systems, conventional and trunked two-way radio, and satellite systems. He is also responsible for business continuity and disaster response planning and related budgeting. He is responsible for providing emergency communications facilities for reporters and photographers covering breaking news stories.

His background includes photojournalism, mainframe computer support, network management, telecommunications planning and management, and business continuity planning. Phil is a former chairman of the Contingency Planning Association of the Carolinas and currently serves as a Board Advisor of the organization. He is a Certified Business Continuity Professional with the Disaster Recovery Institute International.

Phil speaks to public and private sector groups and has been interviewed by and written for a number of national publications on a wide range of emergency communication issues, and business/homeland defense planning. He leads business continuity training seminars for both the public and private sectors, and he has provided project management in business continuity. He has advised major national clients in emergency planning, workforce protection, threat assessment, and incident response for a number of large national corporations.

He enjoys backpacking and spending time in the outdoors. He also has taught outdoor living skills to youth group leaders. He was appointed by the North Carolina Secretary of the Department of Environment and Natural Resources as a voting member of the NC Geological Survey Advisory Committee.

Phil wrote the Appendix, "Personal, Workforce, and Family Preparedness."

Paul A. Henry, (MCP+I, MCSE, CCSA, CCSE, CFSA, CFSO, CISSP, ISSAP, CISM, CISA, CIFI) is the Vice President of Technology Evangelism at Secure Computing®.

Paul is one of the world's foremost global information security experts, with more than 20 years experience managing security initiatives for Global 2000 enterprises and government organizations worldwide.

At Secure Computing, Paul plays a key strategic role in launching new products and re-tooling existing product lines. In his role as Vice President Technology Evangelism, Paul also advises and consults on some of the world's most challenging and high-risk information security projects, including the National Banking System in Saudi Arabia, Department of Defense's Satellite Data Project, USA, and both Government as well as Telecommunications projects throughout Japan.

Paul is frequently cited by major and trade print publications as an expert on both technical security topics and general security trends, and serves as an expert commentator for network broadcast outlets such as NBC and CNBC. In addition, Paul regularly authors thought leadership articles on technical security issues, and his expertise and insight help shape the editorial direction of key security publications such as the Information Security Management Handbook, where he is a consistent contributor.

Paul serves as a featured and keynote speaker at network security seminars and conferences worldwide, delivering presentations on diverse topics including network access control, Cyber crime, DDoS attack risk mitigation, firewall architectures, computer and network forensics, Enterprise security architectures and managed security services.

Paul wrote Chapter 2, "Supervisory Control and Data Acquisition."

Lester J. Johnson Jr. is employed by the SCANA Corporation, a $ 9 Billion, Fortune 500, energy–based holding company, headquartered in Columbia, South Carolina. Mr. Johnson serves in the Corporate Security and Claims Department as a Manager with responsibility for Investigations and Crisis Management. Mr. Johnson leads a staff of professional investigators who conduct investigations of internal corporate compliance issues, criminal violations against the corporation's property and personnel, executive protection, background investigations and risk reduction efforts on behalf of the Corporation. The Crisis Management Department is responsible for the development and continual assessment of security risk management and reduction plans for the critical infrastructure operated by the Corporation. These risk management and reduction plans include the assurance of compliance with the various governmental agencies with oversight responsibilities for the critical infrastructure. Business continuity and emergency procedure planning are also a major component of the crisis management group.

Mr. Johnson is a retired Deputy to the Assistant Director of Investigative Services for the South Carolina Law Enforcement Division. He was responsible for the delivery of all investigative services, which included general investigations, bomb and arson, tactical, computer crimes, special victims, executive protection, behavioral science, public corruption, and insurance fraud.

During his twenty–eight year career Mr. Johnson received numerous awards and commendations, including the Strom Thurmond Award of Excellence in 2004. Mr. Johnson is a graduate of the FBI National Academy and has served as an adjunct instructor for numerous organizations.

Mr. Johnson is married to the former Laura Whelchel of Cordele, Georgia and resides in Lexington, South Carolina with his two children.

Lester wrote Chapter 5, "Working with Law Enforcement on SCADA Incidents."

Sean Lowther is the President and Founder of Stealth Awareness, Inc., www.stealthawareness.com.

Sean is an independent consultant who brings years of experience designing and implementing information security awareness programs at the highest level. He founded Stealth Awareness, Inc. in 2007.

Sean worked at Bank of America for over seven years, managing the enterprise information security awareness program. The program received the highest rating from its regulators and was consistently rated "world class" by industry peer groups.

Sean has worked with BITS, the Financial Services Roundtable Task Force on Privacy, prior to the enactment of the Gramm-Leach-Bliley Act. He produced the video "It's Not If, But When" for the Financial Services Sector Coordinating Council in partnership with the U.S. Treasury Department with the goal to improve critical Infrastructure protection and Homeland Security. Sean was recognized by senior government officials and business executives for his "work to defend our nation's critical infrastructure."

Sean is a sought after speaker for a variety of events and meetings. Most recently he spoke at the Computer Security Institute's annual 2007 conference in Washington, D.C., the Contingency Planning Association of the Carolinas, and the 2008 Charlotte ISSA annual conference.

Sean lives in the Charlotte, North Carolina area.

Sean wrote Chapter 4, "Developing an Effective Security Awareness Program."

Greg Miles, (Ph.D., CISSP#24431, CISM#0300338, IAM, IEM) co-author of Security Assessment: Case Studies for implementing the NSA IAM (Syngress Publishing, ISBN 1-932266-96-8), Network Security Evaluation: Using the NSA IEM (Syngress Publishing, ISBN: 1-597490-35-0), and Security Interviews Exposed: Secrets to Landing your Next Information Security Job (Wiley Publishing, ISBN-10: 0471779873) is the President, and Chief Financial Officer of Security Horizon, Inc. Security Horizon is a Global, Veteran-Owned Small Business headquartered in Colorado Springs, Colorado. Security Horizon provides global information security professional services, training, and publishes The Security Journal, a quarterly online publication. Greg is a U.S. Air Force Veteran and has been supporting the technology and security community for the last 22+ years. Greg's background includes work with NSA, NASA, and DISA. Greg has supported efforts covering security assessments, evaluations, policy, penetration testing, incident response, and computer forensics.

Greg holds a Ph.D. in Engineering Management from Kennedy Western University, a master's degree in Management Administration from Central Michigan University, and a bachelor's degree in Electrical Engineering (with a concentration in Control Systems and Power Systems) from the University of Cincinnati. Greg is a member of the Information System Security Association (ISSA) and the Information System Audit and Control Association (ISACA). He is also Adjunct Faculty for the University of Advancing Technology (www.uat.edu).

Greg would like to thank his family and friends for the incredible support provided to him. Greg has two incredible, loving children, Kirstin and Justin, that provide a great deal of enjoyment. Also at home is another incredible kid that just adds to the fun, Brennon. He would also like to thank his soul mate, Tania, for teaching him what it means to love once again.

Greg wrote Chapter 3, "SCADA Security Assessment Methodology."

Marc Weber Tobias is an investigative attorney and security specialist living in Sioux Falls, South Dakota. As part of his practice, he represents and consults with lock manufacturers, government agencies and corporations in the U.S. and overseas regarding the design and bypass of locks and security systems. He has authored six police textbooks, including *Locks, Safes, and Security, (ISBN 978-0398070793),* which is recognized as the primary reference for law enforcement and security professionals worldwide. The second edition, a 1400 page two-volume work, is utilized by criminal investigators, crime labs, locksmiths and those responsible for physical security. A fourteen-volume multimedia edition of his book is also available online. His website is security.org.

As a former prosecutor and Chief of the Organized Crime Unit for the Office of Attorney General, state of South Dakota, Marc supervised many major investigations and prosecutions. He continues to work investigations for government and private clients, mainly involving technical fraud issues.

Marc is a member of a number of professional security organizations, including the American Society of Industrial Security (ASIS), Association of Firearms and Tool Marks Examiners (AFTE), American Polygraph Association (APA) and American Association of Police Polygraphists (AAPP).

Marc has lectured extensively in the United States and Europe on physical security and certain aspects of criminal investigations and interrogation techniques. He holds several patents involving the bypass of locks and security systems. Marc contributes a column to engadget.com and has been featured in many publications as well as radio and television stories around the world.

Marc wrote Chapter 6, "Locked but Not Secure: An Overview of Conventional and High Security Locks."

James H. Windle is employed as a Police Sergeant in Charlotte, North Carolina, where he serves as a certified bomb technician and is assigned as the Bomb Squad Commander and Arson Supervisor. He is certified as a North Carolina Law Enforcement Instructor and has advanced instructor training in Specialized Police Driving, Firearms and Hazardous Materials. He is an instructor of the United States National Domestic Terrorism Preparedness Program and delivered terrorism training to numerous governmental agencies both police and military as well as private security.

Jim began his experience in explosives from his service as a member of the United States Marine Corps providing training in mines and booby traps domestically and with NATO forces overseas. As a police bomb technician he graduated from the F.B.I.'s Hazardous Devices School at Redstone Arsenal and ATF's Advanced Explosives Destruction Techniques, Advanced Post Blast Investigation and Home Land Security Live Agent WMD School. He is also crossed trained as a Hazardous Materials Technician. He has worked site security and threat assessment in conjunction with the U.S. Secret Service and U.S. State Department for domestic and foreign dignitary protection missions. He was sent to Israel to train with Israeli bomb technicians on countermeasures for suicide bombers and vehicle bombs and this year was sent to England to work with London Met Police and Royal Navy EOD squads.

He is an active member of the International Association of Bomb Technicians and Investigators (IABTI) and also a member of the High Technology Crime Investigation Association (HTCIA). Both groups are highly respected international organizations whose primary mission is to share information, train, and help in the prevention and prosecution of high technology and terrorist crimes.

Jim wrote Chapter 7, "Bombs, Bad Guys and your Business."

Foreword Contributor

Amit Yoran is the Chairman and CEO of NetWitness Corporation, the leading provider of next generation network security monitoring solutions. Prior to serving at NetWitness Corporation, Mr. Yoran acted as the Director of the National Cyber Security Division of Homeland Security, and as CEO and advisor to In-Q-Tel, the venture capital arm of the CIA. Mr. Yoran was the co-founder of Riptech, the market leading managed security services company, and served as its CEO until the company was acquired by Symantec in 2002. He served as an officer in the United States Air Force in the Department of Defense's Computer Emergency Response Team.

Mr. Yoran has served as an independent Director on the boards of several innovative security technology companies such as: Guardium, Trust Digital, Digital Sandbox, and Guidance Software (GUID). He previously served on the board of Cyota, until the company's acquisition by RSA in 2006, and as an advisor to Intruvert Networks, until the company's acquisition by McAfee in 2003.

Mr. Yoran received a Master of Science degree from the George Washington University and a Bachelor of Science degree from the United States Military Academy at West Point.

Contents

Foreword xxiii

**Chapter 1 Physical Security: SCADA and the Critical
Infrastructure's Biggest Vulnerability** 1

Introduction 2

Key Control. 3

Check All Locks for Proper Operation 4

A Little More about Locks and Lock Picking 5

The Elephant Burial Ground 12

Dumpster Diving Still Works. 18

Employee Badges 20

Shredder Technology Has Changed 22

Keep an Eye on Corporate or Agency Phonebooks 23

Tailgating. 24

Building Operations—Cleaning Crew Awareness 25

Spot-Checking Those Drop Ceilings 28

Checking for Key Stroke Readers 28

Checking Those Phone Closets 31

Removing a Few Door Signs 32

Review Video Security Logs 32

Motion-Sensing Lights 33

Let's Go to Lunch 34

Fun in Manholes 37

Internal Auditors Are Your Friends. 40

Always Be Slightly Suspicious 40

Getting Every Employee Involved 41

Summary. 42

Solutions Fast Track 42

Frequently Asked Questions (and Special Interviews) 45

Chapter 2 Supervisory Control and Data Acquisition. 61

Introduction 62

Just What Is SCADA?. 62

SCADA Systems and Components 65

Remote Terminal Units (RTUs). 65

Programmable Logic Controllers (PLC) 65

Discrete Control 65
Continuous Control 65
Human Machine Interface (HMI). 66
Distributed Control Systems (DCS) 66
Hybrid Controllers 67
Event Loggers 67
Common SCADA Architectures 68
SCADA Communications Protocols 70
How Serious Are the Security Issues of SCADA? 71
Determining the Risks in Your SCADA System 75
Risk Mitigation for SCADA 76
Firewall Considerations for SCADA 78
Negative and Positive Security Models in Firewalls 79
Multi-Network Connectivity 79
Reactive and Proactive Solutions 80
Firewall Inspection Methods. 82
Static Packet Filter 82
The Stateful Packet Filter 83
The Circuit-Level Gateway 84
Application-Level Gateway (Proxy). 85
Intrusion Prevention Gateway. 87
Deep Packet Inspection 88
Unified Threat Management (UTM) 89
Summary. 90
Solutions Fast Track 90
Frequently Asked Questions 93
Chapter 3 SCADA Security Assessment Methodology 95
Introduction 96
Why Do Assessments on SCADA Systems? 96
Assessments Are the Right Thing to Do. 97
Assessments Are Required. 97
Information Protection Requirements. 97
National Institute of Standards and Technology (NIST) Guidance 98
North American Electric Reliability Council (NERC) Critical
Infrastructure Protection (CIP) Standards 99
Water Infrastructure Security Enhancement (WISE). 99
The Critical Infrastructure Information Act of 2002. 99
An Approach to SCADA Information Security Assessments 100
Pre-Project Activities 102

Vetting the Assessment Request. 102
Gaining Buy-In from Management and Technical Personnel. 102
   Management Buy-In 103
   Technical Staff Buy-In 103
Researching the Organization. 104
Researching Regulatory and Policy Requirements. 105
Determining if this Is a Baseline Assessment or a Repeat Assessment. 106
Making a Go/No-Go Decision. 106
Pre-Assessment Activities 106
Determining the Organizational Mission 107
Identifying Critical Information 107
   Example: Information Criticality 108
      Business Description 108
      Mission Statement. 108
      Critical Information for OOPS 109
Identifying Impacts. 109
   Example Continued: OOPS Impact 110
The Information Criticality Matrix. 110
   Using the Impact Definitions 111
   Organizational Criticality. 111
   Example Continued: OOPS OICM 112
Identifying Critical Systems/Networks 113
   OOPS Example Continued 113
Defining Security Objectives. 116
Determining Logical and Physical Boundaries 117
   Physical Boundaries 117
   Logical Boundaries 117
Determining the Rules of Engagement, Customer Concerns,
   and Customer Constraints. 117
   The Rules of Engagement 118
      Levels of Invasiveness. 118
      Testing Machine Addressing. 118
      Time Frames for Scanning and Interviews 119
      Notification Procedures. 119
      Scanning Tools and Exclusions 119
   Customer Concerns. 119
   Customer Constraints. 120
Legal Authorization 120
Writing the Assessment Plan. 120

Components of the Assessment Plan 120
On-Site Assessment Activities 122
 Conducting the Organizational Assessment 122
  Documentation Review. 123
  Interviews 123
  System Demonstrations 124
  Observation. 124
 Conducting the Technical Assessment 124
  Enumeration Activities. 125
  Vulnerability Identification Activities. 125
  Tools. 127
  Communication. 127
Post Assessment Activities 127
 Conducting Analysis. 127
 Final Report Creation 128
Resources 129
Summary. 130
Solutions Fast Track 131
Frequently Asked Questions 134

Chapter 4 Developing an Effective Security Awareness Program. 137
Introduction 138
Why an Information Security Awareness Program Is Important 140
 We Fail to Recruit Our Employees into the Company's
  Security Program 141
 We Need to Take the Issue Seriously. 142
How to Design an Effective Information Security Awareness Program 143
 Seven Times, Seven Different Ways 146
 Show Me the Money!. 148
 Two Important Keys to Implementing an Effective Program. 150
 To Print or Not to Print. 152
 Online Training Programs. 154
 Your In-House Web Site. 154
How to Implement an Information Security Awareness Program 155
 What We Have Here Is a Failure to Communicate. 157
  Communicate, Communicate, Communicate! 157
  Other Touch Points 157
  Manager's Quick Reference Guide. 158
  Let's Talk about Alliances 159
  Audit. 159

Legal 159
Privacy 159
Compliance 160
Training and Communications 160
Personnel 160
Information Security Consultants 161
How Do You Keep Your Program a Successful Component of Your
    Company's Mindset? 162
How to Measure Your Program 163
Summary 167
Solutions Fast Track 167

Chapter 5 Working with Law Enforcement on SCADA Incidents 171
Introduction 172
SCADA System Overview 172
Secure Network Management 175
Securing Wide Area Network Perimeter 175
Controlling Access 176
Performing Network Backup and Recovery 176
Transmitting Legacy Non-Routable Protocol Securely 176
Dial-Up Access to the Remote Terminal Units (RTU) 178
Vendor Support: Dial-Up Modem/VPN Access 178
IT Controlled Communication Gear 178
Corporate VPNs 179
Database Links 179
Poorly Configured Firewalls 180
Business Partner Links 180
Managing Security Events 181
Conduct Routine Assessments 182
Examples of Common Attack Techniques 182
Man-In-The-Middle Attacks (MITM) 182
Key-Logger Software 183
Summary 184
Solutions Fast Track 185
Frequently Asked Questions 187

Chapter 6 Locked but Not Secure: An Overview of
Conventional and High Security Locks 189
Introduction 191
Conventional Pin Tumbler Locks 192
The Origins of the Modern Pin Tumbler Lock 194

A Review: The Essentials of Pin Tumbler Lock Design. 196
Security Enhancements for Conventional Locks. 197
    Anti-Bumping Pins 197
    Security Pins 198
    Keyways and Related Designs. 199
    Bitting Design 199
    Design of the Key 200
Standards for Conventional and High Security Locks. 201
Transforming a Conventional Cylinder to High Security 202
Deficiencies in the UL 437 Standard. 204
    Failure to Specify Real World Testing 204
    Pick and Impressioning Resistance 205
    Complex Forms of Picking 206
    Forced Entry Resistance. 206
    Issues Not Addressed by UL 437. 206
    Bump Keys 207
    Decoding Attacks. 208
    Key Control 208
    Mechanical Bypass of Locking Mechanisms. 209
BHMA/ANSI Standards: 156.50 and 156.30 210
    BHMA/ANSI 156.50 210
    High Security Locks and the BHMA/ANSI Standard 210
The Concept of Security 211
BHMA/ANSI 156.30 High Security Standard. 212
    Key Control 213
    Destructive Testing. 213
    Surreptitious Entry Resistance 214
Deficiencies in the 156.30 Standard. 214
Security Vulnerabilities of Conventional Locks: Why High Security Locks
    Are Supposed to Offer More Protection Against Methods of Entry. 215
Conventional Pin Tumbler Locks: Security Vulnerabilities and Their
    Compromise. 216
    Lock Control Procedures 217
    Key Control and Key Security 218
    Key Security 218
    The Concept of Key Control As It Applies to Security 219
    The Importance of Key Control and Key Security 219
    Rights Amplification 220
    Replication, Duplication, and Simulation of Keys and Key Blanks 221

Gathering Intelligence About a System from Its Keys. 221
Covert Entry Techniques: Manipulation of Internal Locking Components 222
Bumping 223
Picking 223
Impressioning. 223
Extrapolation of the TMK. 223
Mechanical Bypass 223
High Security to High Insecurity: Real World Attacks 224
Summary. 226
Solutions Fast Track 226
Frequently Asked Questions 228

Chapter 7 Bomb Threat Planning: Things Have Changed **231**
Introduction 232
The Day Our World Changed 233
Insider Information:
Where Do These Guys Get This Stuff? 234
The Terrorist Profile. 236
Potential Terror Targets 237
Statement Targets 237
Infrastructure Targets. 238
Commercial Targets 239
Transportation Targets 239
What Should I Be Looking For?. 239
The Container 240
The Power Source 240
Switches. 240
Initiators 241
Main Charge 242
Searching: What Am I
Looking For and Where?. 244
Recommendations for Target Hardening 245
Outside. 245
Employee Identification 246
Cameras 246
Deliveries 246
Interior 246
Mail rooms 247
Evacuation Plans 249
Summary. 251

Chapter 8 Biometric Authentication for SCADA Security. **253**

Introduction 254

Understanding Biometric Systems and How They Are Best Used for
  SCADA Security 255
  Footprints to DNA Readings 255
    Human Measurements Can Slow Machines. 255
    Biometric System Imperfections Are at Odds with Perception 256
  What is Biometric Authentication? 256
    Multiple Factor Authentication. 257
    What Parts of You Can Be Measured for Security Purposes? 257
    Common Measurements for Current Biometric Authentication. 257
  How Does Biometric Comparison Work? 258
  Where Are Biometrics Used in SCADA Systems? 260
Choosing the Best Form of Measurement for Your System. 261
  Biometric Measurements Trigger Recognition. 261
  Biometric Measurements Useful in SCADA Security Processes. 262
  Identify Your System Priorities Before Choosing a
    Biometric Application. 264
Where are Biometric Authentication Regimes Vulnerable?. 266
  Tricking the Biometric Capture Device. 266
  Electronic Manipulation of the Authentication Process. 268
  Identity Theft with Biometric Files: Capturing Your Essence. 269
    Presumptions of Accuracy 270
    How Can We Replace That Finger? 270
    Measuring Minutia Can Be Safer Than Storing a Whole
      Biometric Photograph. 271
Anticipating Legal and Policy Changes That Will Affect Biometrics 272
Summary. 274
Solutions Fast Track 274
Frequently Asked Questions 276

Appendix **279**

Index. **319**

Foreword

The safeguarding of supervisory control and data acquisition (SCADA) systems is a paramount cause for concern for the national security of our country and for its security professionals. SCADA systems control power, water, oil, gas, chemical, telecommunications and several other different critical and sensitive operational infrastructures that are absolutely vital to the machinery of our nation and the conduct of our day to day lives. If these essential systems were compromised and became inoperable for even a short time, the results could be costly, both in terms of financial repercussions, and the impact upon our quality and way of life.

Similar to all computer systems over the last four decades, SCADA systems have evolved. In the 1960's, there was a time when most of these control systems were stand-alone, at a point when the network protocols and the control applications used in SCADA systems were considered to be proprietary. During those early days, a so-called "security by obscurity" aided in providing a palpable layer of cyber security defense and a general feeling of immunity from the kinds of nascent network security problems that began to emerge in the mid-1980's, beginning with the notorious Morris Worm.

However, with the global standardization of government and corporate networks on the TCP/IP communications protocol, and during the last 20 years, with the migration of stand-alone proprietary SCADA systems to interconnected grid networks, the security risks have increased geometrically. Security managers can no longer rely on the isolated nature of these systems to provide protection. It still may be tempting to imagine that proprietary software applications provide a layer of secure abstraction, but these mission-critical applications may have unknown and untested security weaknesses. If the organization is not running home-grown/propri-etary applications, in many cases, they already may have well-known and well-publicized vulnerabilities resulting from the use of off-the-shelf commercial software.

Unfortunately, the security of SCADA systems has not kept pace with advances in computer technology and the technical capabilities and intentions of adversaries. According to a 2003 report by Sandia National Laboratories, security for SCADA is typically five to ten years behind typical information technology systems. From a threat perspective, the adversarial pool has widened to include not only domestic and foreign terrorists, but nation-state actors, disgruntled insiders, organized crime, and even inter-national competitors. This volatile convergence of globally pervasive computer network-ing, and the critical weaknesses in operating system and application software, is well understood by the adversaries. While a catastrophic failure is unlikely, unchecked, these risks could be highly problematic and cause disruptions in essential services and billions of dollars of losses. The SCADA world is very complex, however. No one can simply say, "Charge forward and by next year, fix all security problems and you'll be protected!"

All is not gloom and doom, however. Some key public and private sectors have had to step up to face these seemingly daunting challenges and threats before. For example, the financial services industry moves billions of dollars each day over the public Internet, with relatively few losses or disruptions in service. Online retail organizations such as Amazon.com, eBay, and many others facilitate a steadily grow-ing percentage of all retail transactions in a multi-trillion dollar a year industry. Many federal, state, and local governments provide rich transaction-based services to their citizens securely over the Internet. Within this framework of a set of strong business requirements to provide valuable networked services, and the backdrop of a challenging threat environment, informed security managers develop processes for assessing risk, create strategies and plans, and implement the right security control structures. This same lifecycle approach applies to the protection of SCADA systems and the work facing SCADA security managers.

I am pleased to provide this foreword to "Techno Security's Guide to Securing SCADA," because I believe that this book takes important steps forward in arming today's SCADA security manager with the tools and information needed to achieve a higher level of information assurance within these critical and essential control systems. While there is no silver bullet technology or security plan that can anticipate all threats or situations, I urge you to take to heart the strategic and tactical ideas in this volume, and adapt them to your own environment.

—*Amit Yoran*
Chairman and CEO of NetWitness Corporation

Physical Security: SCADA and the Critical Infrastructure's Biggest Vulnerability

Jack Wiles, *(PPS, IAM, IEM) is a Security Professional with over 30 years experience in security related fields. This includes computer security, disaster recovery and physical security. He is a professional member of the National Speakers Association and has trained federal agents, corporate attorneys and internal auditors on a number of computer crime related topics. He is a pioneer in presenting on a number of subjects that are now being labeled 'Homeland Security' topics. Well over 10,000 people have attended one or more of his presentations since 1988. Jack is also a co-founder and President of TheTrainingCo., producers of the Annual Techno Security Conferences and the popular Techno Forensics conferences. He is in frequent contact with members of many state and local law enforcement agencies as well as Special Agents with the U.S. Secret Service, FBI, U.S. Customs, Department of Justice, The Department of Defense and numerous members of High-Tech Crime units. He was also appointed as the first President of the North Carolina InfraGard chapter that is now one of the largest chapters in the country. He is also a founding member and 'official' MC of the US Secret Service South Carolina Electronic Crimes Task Force.*

Jack is also a Vietnam veteran who served with the 101st Airborne Division in Vietnam in 1967–68. He recently retired from the U.S. Army Reserves as a lieutenant colonel and was assigned directly to the Pentagon for the final seven years of his career. In his spare time, he has been a senior contributing editor for several local, national and international magazines.

Introduction

Please don't let my opening chapter's title make you think that I'm starting this book off in a negative light. Believe me, I'm not. There are many positive things we can all do to help secure our most critical applications and resources. Some of the things I will discuss in this chapter have been on my mind since the mid '70s. I believe it's time that I put them in writing, and present my thoughts on what I believe could be the biggest potential hole in any security plan: Physical Security!

This chapter (as well as the rest of the book) isn't meant to be read as a complete story from beginning to end. I'm writing it as a collection of experiences and learned lessons from 30-plus years of working in the fields of physical and technical security. Some of the subject matter in this chapter is partially covered in chapters of mine in our other *Techno Security's Guide* series of books. I do believe that the readers of this book will most likely come from a different group of specialists than the readers of our other books. Throughout the book, you will also notice that several of our authors will address similar topics from their perspective and experience level. A good example of this will be the discussion of locks, keys, and bypass methods. I first became a locksmith in 1970 and worked in a locksmith shop for several years learning the trade. I'll share a lot of my thoughts on this critical subject throughout my chapter. Unlike the technical world where most things sitting on your desk are already obsolete, many of the locks used in our buildings (and in our homes) haven't changed at all in many, many years. Most of what I learned in the early '70s is still very applicable today when it comes to the common locks found on about 95 percent of the doors on the planet.

The reason that I rambled a little about locks at the beginning of my chapter is to let you know that some of the other authors in this book will have their own opinions and suggestions regarding these critical pieces of hardware. Marc Weber Tobias wrote one of our chapters, where he goes into great detail on High Security Locks and their possible vulnerabilities. Without question, Marc is considered one of the most gifted experts in the world today in understanding and researching the security offered by many types of locks. We are honored to have his work in this book. Be sure to read his chapter carefully, because some of the locks you're relying on to protect critical information and equipment might not be as secure as you think.

I'll be addressing a number of risks, threats, and countermeasures (there's that risk management talk again) throughout this chapter. Let's go ahead and get my thoughts on locks out there as my first in-depth topic on physical security.

Key Control

The types of keys used in most buildings have remained virtually unchanged since Linus Yale invented them in 1861. Just about all of our homes and most businesses still use his pin tumbler locks for their primary physical defense. I have no way of knowing how often the master, grand master, and possibly great-grand-master key systems in buildings are changed. I do suspect that it's not very often. This can be an expensive process. Recently, I walked into a public rest room in a large office building and saw a full set of keys, including the building master key, hanging from the paper towel dispenser. I suspect that the janitor had just filled the towel rack and left his keys hanging there. Should they fall into the wrong hands, the person could own the building.

While using our social engineering skills during each penetration test, our team always tried to make friends with the cleaning crew. Sooner or later, we would need to ask a favor and borrow their keys for a few minutes. (Typically, their keys would open all of the doors on that floor and sometimes the entire building.) That was all it took for us to make a copy with the portable key machine we brought with us in a small bag. Very few people have any idea how keys (and the locks that they open) work. This is another area of physical security that has changed greatly during the past few decades. I became a bonded locksmith back in the '70s and found it fascinating. Back then, I couldn't even purchase lock picks or key blanks until I graduated from a credited locksmithing school and had proper identification. Now, about 30 years later, we have much more at risk in general, and anyone can purchase lock picks at several local hardware stores or from Internet-based stores, with no questions asked.

Regarding the use of lock picks to get into buildings and rooms, I don't suspect that many "casual" social engineers use them. They require a lot of that "practice, practice, and more practice" stuff that's required for any social engineering skill. The availability of these devices for anyone to purchase is something that corporate security specialists must consider as they plan their countermeasures.

Tip

Attempt to set up some form of key control if you don't already have a system in place. It is very important to know who has the keys to your kingdom as well as how many doors can be opened by each. It is very seldom a good idea to have one key that opens everything in the building. It may be convenient for certain things, but it creates the security concern of controlling who has those keys and how easily they can be duplicated.

Master keys are an additional concern if you rent space in a large building or office park. You might have a very strict policy of your own for your company, but if the management company that handles the building rentals isn't as careful with their master keys, the entire building is at risk. Unless the keys are of a high-security design like the Medico line, they can be duplicated anywhere. Even if the disgruntled building maintenance person turns in his keys upon being fired, there is no way to be sure he didn't have copies made. You should ask the building manager about his/her policy regarding the security of the master keys. It will let them know you are aware that there are keys to your office that are not under your control.

Install special locks on critical doors. Highly pick-resistant Medeco locks are some of the most effective. In addition to providing additional security, they add another level of due diligence should you need to document your attempts to prevent intrusions.

Conduct special employee awareness training for everyone who works the evening and night shifts. That's when I took our team into their buildings most of the time. We used our social engineering skills to befriend these people and to the best of my knowledge, we were never reported by any of them.

Another prime target during our evening and night visits was the janitorial team. The main reason we always tried to befriend the people on the janitorial team is that they usually had those important keys that we were trying to get our hands on. These are some of the most important people in your company when it comes to protecting your buildings when most people are gone. They spend some time in just about every room in the building each week. If you train no one else in your company, these people must be well trained on how they can help. They should be made aware of your security policies and what they can do if they see anything suspicious. This would include strangers, suspicious packages, doors that are opened which should be locked, and so on. They are one of your most valuable resources. Tell them that and teach them how they can help.

Check All Locks for Proper Operation

On every one of our penetration tests, we found at least one lock (either interior or exterior) in the building that wasn't functioning properly. This provided us with easy access to buildings and rooms that we shouldn't have been able to get through so easily. If employees are trained for just a few minutes on how to check to see if the locks on the doors that they use every day are working properly, this vulnerability can be all but eliminated. Building maintenance teams should also take a close look at all locks at least twice each year. Slightly misaligned strikes on the doorframes are the most common problem that we find. This is a serious problem, in that it defeats the purpose of the dead bolt feature of the lock. It takes me less than a second with my trusty finger nail file to see if a particular lock has this problem. If it does, I'll know (and have the door opened) instantly.

TIP

Don't forget to check those locks and doors at home. We also recommend that the lock combinations (keys) be changed immediately after occupying a new home, or after moving into a home that was owned by someone else. Keys are easy to duplicate, and you have no way of knowing how many copies are already out there, even in a brand new home. I'd also recommend changing the codes to your garage door openers as well. This is a very easy thing to do for most modern openers.

WARNING

If you have a garage door opener installed, do not leave it set to the default code (frequently 000000 or something very generic). This could make you vulnerable to another form of war driving where the bad guys simply drive around neighborhoods with generic openers trying to see if any doors begin to open as they drive past. This gives them a very nice potential future target for a break-in later. Also, many houses that have whole house alarms do not have the garage door alarmed. The keypad for turning the alarm on or off for the house is frequently located in the garage.

If you ever find your garage door opened and you didn't open it, I'd recommend immediately changing the door opener (and receiver) code.

A Little More about Locks and Lock Picking

Locks have fascinated me for almost 40 years now. In many ways, they are the hardware versions of the passwords and authentication devices that we use to gain access to our computers. They are also what I like to call the low-hanging-fruit of your perimeter security. Unfortunately, many times, they are the place where we spend the least amount of money. I'm going to try to convince you to spend a little more for a whole lot more protection when selecting locks for your office or home.

In preparation for this part of my chapter, I visited several chain stores just as school opened to watch people. Johnny and I both do a lot of people watching while we are out and about. It's fascinating. As I was looking around at the locks available in different stores, I watched as several people came over to the area and quickly picked up a lock or two for school. Most of them chose a Master brand combination lock that has been a standard for decades. That didn't surprise me. I also watched as several people purchased padlocks with keys. What every one of them did wasn't a surprise either: They purchased the CHEAPEST lock they could find. I watched this over and over again. Little do they realize that they got what they paid for.

Most of them picked up either a warded padlock, or a cheap pin tumbler padlock, none of which costs more than $5. These locks looked as strong as the better locks on the outside, but anyone who knows even a little about locks knows that these cheap locks aren't even going to keep the honest people honest. How about a quick lock awareness war story to give you an example of how easily the wrong type of lock can be bypassed:

Case Study

A Lock Awareness War Story

Our penetration team had been inside their building for about four hours when we came across a row of filing cabinets that must have contained some important documents. About ten tall filing cabinets stood in a row, and each of them had a vertical bar attached to the cabinet with a padlock securing the bar to the cabinet. This was more security than we normally saw on these kinds of cabinets.

When we were working on the inside of a building, we tried to look at everything we thought could be a vulnerability. I took the time to quickly examine every lock on these filing cabinets. It wasn't surprising to me to find one that looked the same as the others on the outside, but that was drastically different on the inside. Someone had replaced one of the pin tumbler padlocks with a warded padlock. In less than ten seconds, I opened the lock, taped my business card on the INSIDE of the filing cabinet to prove we had been there, and closed the lock again. The bad guys could have accessed the entire contents of that file cabinet just as quickly.

Continued

Why was this one lock different from the rest? I suspect that someone either lost the key to the original (more secure) lock, or lost the lock itself. If that happened, they could have simple gone to the hardware section of their local store and purchased a lock that looked like the rest of the locks on those file cabinets. If they went with the mindset of most people that I watched purchase locks, they would have purchased the least expensive lock they could get, as long as it looked as strong as the original lock.

Let's look at a few types of locks to help you learn which ones are better than others:

Figure 1.1 shows a pin tumbler Master brand padlock. It's the exact kind of lock we saw on most of the filing cabinets. Pin tumbler locks are also the most common type of lock we see on doors in homes and office buildings. These locks *can* be picked, but I've never been very successful with such endeavors.

Figure 1.1 A Pin Tumbler Master Brand Padlock

The warded padlock (shown in Figure 1.2) that we found on one of the filing cabinets looked about the same, but it had a different keyway.

Figure 1.2 A Warded Padlock

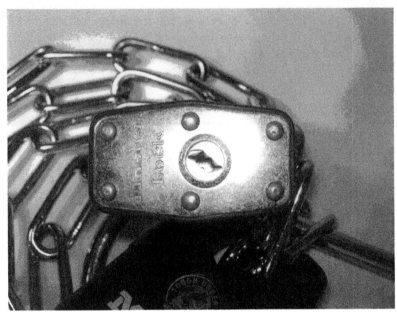

I was able to open this one in less than 10 seconds, and you could, too. Opening locks like this isn't even lock picking in my opinion. The pick sets for these are more like master keys.

In Figure 1.3, the key on the left is the key to the pin tumbler lock. The one on the right is to the warded lock. This is really basic information for anyone familiar with locks. My experience has been that most people aren't even a little familiar with what makes a lock reasonably secure (or very insecure). If they were, they wouldn't be out there buying the cheapest locks they could find as long as it looks strong.

Figure 1.3 A Few Keys

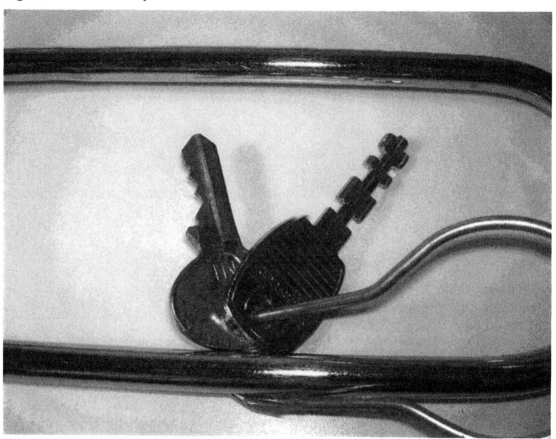

So, are there any padlocks that are reasonably secure and not terribly expensive? My favorite has always been a lock that looks a little different, but has a lot of leave-me-alone features (see Figure 1.4). This lock, the Abus Diskus No. 24, is made in Germany and is quite secure for its $25 price tag. It's a pin tumbler lock with all five of its pins being mushroom-type bottom pins. There *are* people out there who *can* pick it, but I've never successfully picked a lock with any mushroom pins, much less one with all five pins being mushroom pins.

Figure 1.4 The Abus Diskus No. 24 Lock

If we want to talk about the grand-daddy of all high security padlocks (in my humble opinion, and I'm not alone), we need to take a look at a lock that has been at the top of the list for several decades. My winner here would be my favorite (I have five of them myself) combination lock, the Sargent & Greenleaf 8077AD. It's a 1.5-pound fortress in so many ways. From the outside, it doesn't look all that impressive, but it is! Just enter the name S&G 8077 in Google, and countless articles will pop up about their strength and reliability. Just like anything else in life, you get what you pay for. These are not your $5 combination locks, however. The non-government model is still available in many places on the Internet, at prices ranging from $165 to $325 (or more). I do see them frequently on eBay at great prices and they're worth every penny. Figure 1.5 shows one of mine.

Figure 1.5 The Sargent & Greenleaf 8077AD

Now, let's talk about due diligence a minute. This was something I explained to all the groups that hired us to perform penetration tests during our exit interviews. Regarding locks, there's no way to keep a determined and knowledgeable "bad guy" from getting past whatever security measures you place in their way. Even the best burglar-resistant safes are rated according to how many minutes it would take an educated thief to open it. Your task is to show you did whatever you could to make it as difficult as possible for someone to get to your valuables. A simple example of improved due diligence would be to replace the locks (even the pin tumbler locks) on most of the filing cabinets in the earlier war story, with locks like the Abus, or the S&G 8077 combination lock. The difference in cost for the entire row of ten filing cabinets would be less than $200 TOTAL for the Abus locks and about $3,500 max for the S&G locks. These locks will be protecting some pretty important stuff, so isn't it worth an extra $200 to $3,500 to gain some considerable security while at the same time increasing your due diligence efforts? I don't think for a second that an additional $200 (or even $3,500) would make a difference as far as expense goes. Most of the firms I was involved with during these penetration tests wished to prevent millions of dollars in possible espionage losses. They simply didn't know that this small change could make such a big difference for their company. It may have prevented the event that had us in there in the first place. That's why books like this one are so valuable. One or two "techno-tidbits" as I like to call them can make a huge difference in your overall security posture. While this book is titled *Techno Security's Guide to SCADA Security*, in my mind, its real value is in explaining how to prevent a lot of bad things from happening to anything that is important to you even if it doesn't impact our nation's critical infrastructure.

The Elephant Burial Ground

I've been making a simple statement at presentations for the past ten years. "A new computer is a wonderful thing, but as soon as you buy it, it's already obsolete." Technology continues to change at a rate that few of us even notice. My statement isn't meant to be negative in any way. It's just that the computer is doing exactly what those new calculators did 35 years ago. They simply get faster, better, and cheaper as soon as you walk out of the store with your brand new one. I'm not suggesting that you don't buy a new (soon-to-be-old) computer, you just need to realize that you're going to most likely need a new one in about two years.

What happens when that "elephant" you purchased a few years back finally dies or becomes too old to do any work for you? I'll bet it gets moved to your elephant burial ground with the rest of the electronic equipment that still looks new and valuable, but isn't fast enough to keep up anymore. You can't simply put it out for the trash man to pick up, so there it sits, sometimes for years.

This burial ground was a prime target for our penetration teams as we conducted our vulnerability tests from inside our clients' buildings. We frequently used our social engineering skills to find out where the old computers were stored. If it was in a locked room, we would find a way to either get someone to open the door for us, or we would use our lock picks or pick gun to open the door.

Figure 1.6 offers some examples I found on the Internet, showing a set of picks very similar to the set I've owned the last 30 years. LockPickShop.com is the company where we buy our locksmith supplies for our training classes. Their outstanding response and customer service, and their quality products, have kept us coming back for years. Figure 1.7 shows a pick gun that's also similar to mine. Pick guns don't take a lot of practice to learn how to use. If you are thinking about running out and buying some of these tools, please be sure to read the warning I have included with the pictures. I don't want to have to include you in a future war story about what *not* to do with lock-picking equipment.

Figure 1.6 The LockPickShop.com Web Site

Figure 1.7 A Lock Pick Gun at LockPickShop.com

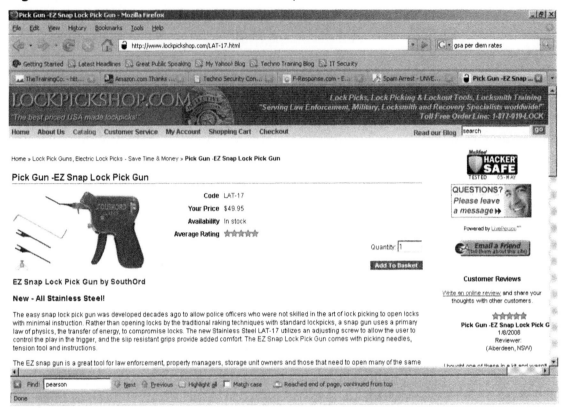

Once we found a room that obviously contained some outdated equipment, we knew we were going to leave with some very valuable intellectual property. All we did was open a few computer cases, remove the hard drives, and neatly close the cases back up. How valuable was the information on that drive, and how soon would you know that the drive itself was now missing from the elephant burial ground?

Most likely, you will never know that the disk drives are gone. Our experience has been that these older computers are seldom powered on again by the organization that owned them. They may get powered on by whoever eventually winds up with them at some junk auction or thrift store where they were donated. If they sit in some onsite location for any length of time, the chances of anyone ever knowing that the entire computer is missing, much less the hard drive itself, are very slim. It's likely the crime could go completely undetected.

How valuable was the information on the old drive? Our experience has been that about 80 percent of the information on the old drive may still be of value to the "bad guys." If you think through the process of how that computer wound up in the burial ground, you will see what I mean. If the data on the old drive were properly backed up as a part of your disaster recovery plan, then it would most likely be restored to the new computer prior to retiring the old one. As soon as everything looked fine on the new computer, the old one may never be powered up again.

Technical issues are associated with each of the processes I just described, of which I didn't go into detail here. Nevertheless, here's the bottom line from my experience with these old drives: If they weren't properly wiped clean, and if the drive itself was operational, we were able to get to the data on them without any problem.

TIP

Old disk drives will be an area of concern for years to come. Terabyte drives will soon be available at stores like Office Depot for anyone to purchase. Less than ten years ago, I was thrilled to be able to purchase a 200MB disk drive for $200. I was the first person in my circle to own a drive this size for a mere $1 per megabyte. Now, I'm seeing 200GB disk drives on sale for around $50 (after rebates). That's about 25 cents per gigabyte, which means that the same $1 per megabyte I paid (actually worth less today) would buy me 4 gigabytes or 4,000 times as much storage space for the same dollar spent.

The advice here is to be careful with those old disk drives. This applies to the computers at home as well as at the office. There is much valuable data on them, and the risk grows as the storage capacity of every drive rapidly climbs each year. Let me share some of the most effective tools I have seen for *really being sure* that your valuable proprietary information is gone when you dispose of a broken or outdated hard drive.

The first of these is a device called Digital Shredder sold by DestructData (www.DestructData.com), which insures that your valuable information is gone from the drive before it is reused or destroyed (Figure 1.8). Once Digital Shredder has done its job, the disks can be reused (knowing for sure that all data has been removed) or they can be completely destroyed using a device that I found most interesting for complete drive destruction.

Figure 1.8 Digital Shredder from DestructData

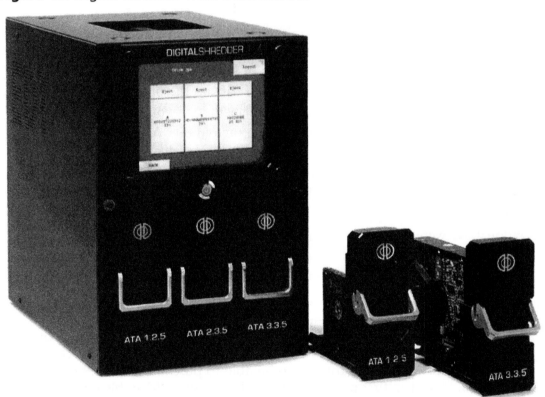

The second device will render the drive completely unusable by punching a large hole thru the middle of it. Figures 1.9 and 1.10 show a destroyed disk drive and the machine that destroyed it. And here's the URL to the Web site of the only company I'm aware of that offers the complete destruction of obsolete hard drives: www.edrsolutions.com.

Figure 1.9 A Destroyed Disk Drive

Figure 1.10 EDR's Disk Destroyer

Dumpster Diving Still Works

"Dumpster diving" is one of the easiest ways to find out information about a company or its customers. This is sometimes referred to as "trashing," and there have been a number of articles discussing what worked and what didn't for some experienced "trashers." One article discussed "advanced trashing" and ways to talk yourself out of a confrontation if you get caught. I'd be willing to bet that a very small percentage of "dumpster divers" ever get caught. As simple as this problem seems, it isn't one that is given much attention by most companies.

What kinds of things can you find in a company's dumpster? You would probably be shocked if you started to look through your own dumpster occasionally. (I highly encourage you to do just that.) There may be old company phone directories (still quite accurate and very valuable for use in "social engineering"), pieces of scrap paper with phone numbers and possibly passwords written on them, last month's customer lists that were discarded when the new list was printed this month, employee lists with home addresses and Social Security numbers listed on them, and so on, and so on.

It doesn't take much imagination to think of all the potential problems that could have their beginnings right there in your trashcan. Someone who is trying to pretend they work for your company can use the old company directories. Most names in the directory, their work locations, and their titles remain the same from update to update. These discarded directories are some of the most prized finds of the "dumpster divers" looking to get information about your company. The discarded scraps of paper with the passwords on them are also prized finds. Many times, they are discarded just because they were no longer sticky enough to stay on the terminal they were attached to, so a new one was written and the old one thrown in the trash. Last month's customer list will probably wind up in the hands of your competitor if the wrong person gets his hands on it. The employee list with the home addresses and Social Security numbers on it will cause different problems if it winds up in the wrong place.

What can you do about this problem? For one thing, we can all be a little more careful about what we throw in the trashcan. Management commitment to correct this problem and employee awareness of the problem will help correct it. The commitment usually involves the shredding or burning of all-important documents. If a company is going to invest in their own shredder, I always recommend a crosscut shredder over a strip cut shredder. Strip cutting is better than nothing, but crosscutting is much more secure. It turns the documents into confetti instead of long strips. I guess it's theoretically possible to reassemble a crosscut shredded document, but if it falls into a bin with a large number of other crosscut shredded documents, it will create the world's most difficult jigsaw puzzle.

Old habits die hard, and this one will probably be no exception. As a country, we have been throwing away just about everything since the end of World War II. During the war, security was on everybody's mind, and each person encouraged their friends and neighbors to be careful about what they said and what they threw away. (I wasn't around during World War II, but I was the product of a happy home after the war.) As individuals and companies, we need to bring back just a little bit of that thinking. We need to become aware of this problem and encourage each other to be more careful with assets by being more careful with our trash.

TIP

Many of the topics presented for thought in this chapter, and throughout the entire book, are just as appropriate in our homes as they are in our offices. This is especially true of our home office computers, networks, and trash!

Most of us are inundated with snail mail at home as well as at work. I have a policy in our home that nothing stays in our trashcan that clearly has any family member's name on it. This requires a little extra effort to destroy a single page of a credit card offer each time I receive one. If it has a name and address on it (obviously everything that arrives at my home does), I destroy that part of the document. Every little thing I can do to protect my family from things like identity theft and credit card fraud helps me sleep at night.

Employee Badges

I know employee badges can be faked, but I still think it's much better to have some form of visible identification worn by every employee at all times. Most of the companies that hired us did not have a policy requiring employees to wear their corporate ID badges all the time. This made our social engineering attempts much easier. Once we were inside the buildings, it was as if everyone just took it for granted that we belonged there. Not only were we inside their buildings, but we were also inside their firewalls and intrusion detection systems.

Employees can be somewhat trained to even detect fake ID badges. I was working for a large company that did require employees to always wear their ID badges when they were on company property. This was back in the days when color printers were just starting to show up in homes and offices. I created a fake ID that was intentionally made without any thought of quality control. The first time I wore it into the building instead of my real ID, I suspected I would immediately be stopped and questioned about it. This was a security project, so I was prepared to explain myself. To my initial amazement, I never had to explain anything because it was never questioned. For the next three months, I wore it everywhere and not one person noticed it was fake. During one of our security meetings, I told everyone in our group about my little experiment and most were quite surprised it was never detected.

Part two of my experiment offered the most interesting results to me. I created a picture showing my two IDs side by side. The fake one was quite obvious when seen next to the real article. We began to teach people how to take a slightly closer look at the IDs people were wearing as they walked through our buildings. From that time forward, I only wore my fake ID when I was conducting security awareness training for a group of employees. I was amazed at the number of my friends, who after a training session, spotted the fake ID as I passed them in the hall. Some would see it from ten feet away. These were the same people who, before the training, hadn't even noticed it while sitting three feet from me in my office. AWARENESS TRAINING WORKS!

WARNING

Tailgating, frequently called piggybacking, is simply following someone into a building after they open the door with an access card or by entering a door code. The "bad guy" will often pretend to be searching for his or her access card while waiting for someone to enter with a legitimate card. If there is no guard at the entrance, the "bad guy" will probably go unchallenged and unnoticed. You really need to think about this one before you decide how you want to solve it. You can't place a legitimate employee in the position of having to challenge the "bad guy" to ask for identification.

The legitimate employee probably didn't come to work for you to be a security guard. On the other hand, you don't want "bad guys" just walking into your building. This problem is as old as dirt, but the solutions just keep getting more complex and expensive. Some companies employ cameras that photograph everyone who enters the building. Others are now employing biometrics scanners and other high-tech devices. As with everything else in the security field, you need a system that is appropriate in cost to what you are trying to protect.

At a minimum, you can make your employees aware of this threat and have them notify their immediate superior that someone followed them in and note the time and date of the incident. This same employee awareness session should instruct all employees to display an ID so fellow employees, who may not know them, don't think they are "tailgating" as they walk in behind them.

Shredder Technology Has Changed

As with everything else these past few high-tech years, shredder technology has changed considerably. Our team had gotten very good at putting strip cut papers back together again. We used to take bags of it back to our office during the test. Frequently, it was sitting outside in or near a dumpster where we simply picked it up and put it in our vehicle. Most of the time, documents that are strip cut shredded all fall neatly into place in the bag or box where they are stored, waiting to be disposed of. Our team was able to reassemble many of these documents within a few minutes. We would even take a document and paste the strips on a piece of cardboard in the shape of a Christmas tree, spreading the strips out as they were glued to the cardboard. Even with up to an inch between strips, the documents were still easily readable once reassembled. We never even attempted to reconstruct a document that had been sent through a crosscut shredder.

Tip

If you have too much invested in your strip cut shredders to replace them, at least consider purchasing some of the small crosscut shredders and place them directly in the offices of people who have especially sensitive documents that should be destroyed. These small crosscut shredders are very inexpensive and durable if you keep them oiled with the special oil available for shredders. I have a small one that cost $39 and it creates a very small particle that would be next to impossible to reassemble. I have tried to wear it out for about six months and it just keeps on working. I'd also recommend encouraging all employees to get one for home use. Once you start doing this, it will become second nature and you'll never have to worry about anyone seeing your personal information once it leaves your home. Especially since identity theft is on the rise as well.

Outdated but still sensitive documents should also be disposed of securely. When I worked at the Pentagon during the final seven years of my military career, we were required to place certain sensitive (not classified, simply sensitive) documents into a safe containing a burn bag. Burning them would then destroy these items. To this day, I still use a burn bag at home for documents that I need to destroy that are too bulky for my shredder. It's a great way to clean out the barbeque grill on a cold sunny day. I feel good every time I destroy sensitive personal documents rather than simply throwing them in a trashcan. Left unshredded or unburned, they become possible fuel for the most rapidly growing white-collar crime in the country: identity theft!

Keep an Eye on Corporate or Agency Phonebooks

When conducting a test, the first thing we went for were corporate and agency phonebooks. Once we got our hands on a corporate directory, the social engineering began. Most corporate phone books are laid out in a way that conveniently shows the entire corporate structure as well as the chain of command, building addresses, and department titles. That kind of information also lets us know the order in which to try entering the various buildings, if there were several. Wherever the Human Resources department was located was usually where we went last. Here's why.
As we tried to enter all of the other buildings by simply walking in the door like we belonged there, we were frequently challenged by a receptionist and asked where we were going. Our social engineering answer was always the same. "We were told that this is where Human Resources is located and we're here to fill out a job application." In every case, the receptionist simply sent us in the right direction. We thanked her or him and walked out the door and directly into the building next door to try the same con. The phonebook even gave us the Human Resources manager's name to drop if we needed to be a little more convincing that we belonged there but were simply lost. It also gave us the names and titles of the rest of the important people in the organization whose names we could drop if we were challenged further. In addition to the names in the directories, most contained the physical location and chain of command ranking for the most important person in each department. It was often their offices, filing cabinets, and trashcans that we spent the most time in during our nightly visits.

Employee awareness of how important a corporate directory is will help greatly with this one. Old directories are still quite accurate, especially regarding buildings and department locations. They should be burned or shredded rather than simply thrown into the dumpster (we might even get hit if you throw them in while we're there looking for goodies).

If paper directories can be eliminated altogether, that would make our job a little tougher. Everything you do to make it a little harder for the bad guys will make you a less likely target since they're looking for an easy mark. Online directories are better only if you don't let the social engineers get into your building. Once we were inside, we began looking for a monitor with the infamous sticky note on the side with the person's login ID and password scribbled on it. Once we logged onto the network as them, we could usually get to an online company directory if there was one.

Let me address one additional countermeasure while I'm on the subject of sticky notes with login IDs and passwords. Maybe this doesn't happen where you work, but we found at least one person who had done this on every job we were hired to do. There is another reason we like to use someone else's login ID and password to get onto their networks. If we are able to do that, not only are we on their network on the inside of any firewall, but everything that we do will show up in some log as being done by the person who let us log in as them. Many larger companies now use at least some form of two-part authentication that employs either biometrics or a handheld authenticating device of some type to attain two-part authentication. Fortunately, some forms of biometric access control are becoming very reasonable in price. So, everything you do in the way of authentication will greatly reduce your vulnerability to this form of instant identity theft.

Tailgating

Tailgating was one of our most successful entry techniques, regardless of a building's security procedures. For some reason, people in the outside smoking areas never questioned our being there or walking in behind them as they returned to work. We found that many corporations had good security at their main entrance points, but were lacking at other entry and exit points, allowing us to gain access on several occasions through parking deck or garage entry points that required card access. We would simply follow someone who was headed to the door and walk in behind them as we pretended to search for our imaginary access cards.

TIP

Here again, companywide awareness training and a strong security policy can go a long way in preventing this type of entry. These outside break, lunch, and smoking areas are frequently places where there are no security guards or receptionists to ask for proper ID as someone passes through the door. As mentioned earlier, having every employee wear an ID badge would make this type of entry a little more difficult should someone try to walk in without an ID.

WARNING

The countermeasures for this vulnerability really aren't as simple as we might think. Most employees who enter a building aren't security people. They are simply trying to return to work. Even though someone trying to enter a building using the tailgating or piggyback method should be challenged, challenging them is an uncomfortable situation for most people. Unless there is a strong corporate policy requiring all employees to challenge anyone they can't identify, this is a difficult problem to deal with. At an absolute minimum, employees should be trained on when and how to notify security if they suspect an unauthorized person has followed them in.

Building Operations—Cleaning Crew Awareness

I can't emphasize enough the need to train all of your second- and third-shift employees, and especially your janitorial services people, about the threats of social engineering. Obviously, pre-employment screening and possibly bonding is essential for any outside firm you allow inside your buildings at any time. This is especially true for building access outside the normal 8 to 5 Monday thru Friday standard work schedule. Frequently, these people have access to the master keys for a large section of the building and sometimes the entire building. They need awareness training to better prevent them from becoming victims of bad-guy social engineers who would like to borrow their keys for a minute or get them to open a certain room.

This team should also immediately know whom to contact if they see anything suspicious that should be reported. If there is no immediate supervisor on duty during the evening or night shifts, everyone on that shift should know how to quickly contact their security forces. It can be very dangerous for them to approach a stranger themselves in an attempt to get them to leave.

This suggestion may not seem to fit in the context of this book, but let me mention it anyway. There is another very good reason to train your janitorial team (at least the team supervisors) to be extra watchful during the evening and night shift work hours. I have been teaching bomb recognition classes for the past ten years. These same social engineering skills and physical building penetration methods could apply in any situation where the collective "bad guys" are trying to get into your building. The eyes and ears of the people who work in your building every day are critical when it comes to detecting anything, or anyone, unusual in the vicinity of the building. Bomb recognition training for key individuals and having an effective bomb incident plan are another countermeasure that can be employed with considerable effect.

Case Study

Bomb Threats in Chicago

This is a good time for a little side story that will let you see how the many risks, threats, vulnerabilities, and countermeasures overlay in the worlds of physical and technical security.

Several years ago, I received a call from a friend in the Chicago area asking for help. He said his company had office locations in several cities throughout the country and one office outside it. A series of bomb threats called into their corporate headquarters was causing them to lose a little sleep. They just wanted our team's suggestions about what they should do. This meant a trip to Chicago for us in February. (Being the warm-blooded person from the sunny South that I am, this was a bit like a trip to Iceland in mid-winter. We went anyway.)

Prior to going, I decided to look on the Internet to see if I could find anything out about his company. It could also provide a possible hint as to why someone would call in these bomb threats that fortunately were only threats, so far!

The company flew in their senior managers from around the country and we suggested that their corporate attorneys and risk managers attend the training as well. They were going to learn everything they wanted to know but were afraid to ask about bombs and bomb threats.

We arrived a day early, and we asked if they would like for us to take a look around their corporate headquarters building to see if we saw any glaring physical vulnerabilities that could allow someone to easily place a bomb in or just outside their building. The outside perimeter was about as close to perfect as I had ever seen in a building of that size. As we were looking at the various locations from the inside, my eyes kept being drawn to their newly installed access control system. Each employee had been issued an ID card that would allow him or her to enter certain doors at specific times of the day. The system also kept track of the times they entered and left the building. It was impressive.

When I stated that a simple metal coat hanger might be able to compromise the entire system, my fellow team member gave me a strange, "you've done it now" kind of look. I was about to be put to the test as we approached

Continued

the next set of outside access doors in that part of the building. The person that had hired us was standing there with a metal coat hanger and handed it to me.

Keep in mind, we were walking around inside the nicely heated building without our coats. On the other side of the doors that I had been asked to break in through, it was still like Iceland in February. I politely said that I would go outside (without my coat!) and try for a few minutes to gain entry. All that I asked was that If I started to turn blue, to please please *please* "open the door from the inside and let me back in."

In the end, it was an unnecessary request. I was back inside in less than 30 seconds as everyone looked on with that patented deer-in-the-headlights look, after I'd calmly breached a quarter-of-a-million-dollar security system with no indication that I'd ever touched it. This was not the first time I'd seen this issue with an improperly adjusted access control system. The system was one that, detecting motion from the inside, automatically unlocked the door as someone approached it to exit. I had noticed that it detected us walking past the door from a considerable distance away. It was just too sensitive. I also noticed that the locking mechanism opened only one of a pair of double doors and that the motion sensor was mounted dead center between the double doors. The only thing protecting the opening between the double doors was a thin piece of weather stripping. While I was standing outside briefly freezing to death, it was a simple matter of taking my thin metal coat hanger and sliding it between the two doors while rapidly moving it up and down. Within seconds, I heard the familiar "click" I was hoping for. The security system thought I was inside because that's where it saw the motion of my coat hanger.

For another insight into this vulnerability, be sure to read Johnny Long's chapter as well.

All of the senior managers, attorneys, risk managers and security team members were in a training room the following morning for their day of Bomb Threat Training. I opened the meeting by letting them know that this was most likely a low probability threat, but that they were smart to decide ahead of time to learn as mach as they could about what they should do concerning these threats. We were going to spend the rest of the day learning about bombs, bomb threats, bombs in buildings, bombs outside of buildings, and all kinds of other scary things. It was going to be a fun day.

As I was finishing up my introduction, I walked around the room and placed a small packet consisting of one to three pages in front of four of their most important people. As the four targeted people started to look through the papers placed in front of them, I simply stated that this was your their probability threat and something they needed to address immediately in our opinion.

Continued

The papers contained just about everything we would ever need to know about these people. Where they lived, how they most likely traveled to work, in some cases where they went to college, where their children went to school, and much more. All of it was gained from a few social engineering phone calls and about an hour of searching the Internet for information about them. Much of the information about these people (and possibly about you) was out on the Internet. It's not easy to find, but every consumer search engine has an opt-out capability, letting you remove your name and contact information from their databases. Just type the words "people search engines" into Google for the most recent list of these services. You should put your name in some of them to see what information is out there about you. You will most likely be surprised at how many places your name pops up.

Spot-Checking Those Drop Ceilings

On several occasions, we used our social engineering skills to get into buildings and then install a sniffer in the telecommunications hub for that floor. I recommend that all companies have their building maintenance teams perform a spot check above all suspended ceilings at least twice each year. We have been amazed at some of the things we found up there while we were conducting the penetration test. You may even stumble into a security vulnerability you weren't even aware of.

This suggestion would also be one I'd make if considering places to hide things like bombs. We walk under drop ceilings day after day and normally have no reason to think about what might be up there. Usually, there is at least a foot of clearance between the grid work holding the drop ceiling in place and the ceiling itself. I have seen as much as three feet of clearance. You would may be amazed at what you find hidden up there (hopefully it's not ticking!).

Checking for Key Stroke Readers

Some of our favorite tools are the software and newer hardware versions of keystroke readers. These can make a good social engineer's job a lot easier. If we wanted to find out what a certain individual in the company was doing on their computer during a certain time frame, we would install a keystroke reader on their workstation during one visit and retrieve the results on a second visit.

By far, the most effective keystroke loggers we have used are the Key Ghost hardware loggers being sold as security devices (www.keyghost.com). When these are installed between the keyboard of a workstation and the keyboard socket on the back of the computer, they look like they belong there to the casual observer. The one we used looked like the induction coils we used to see on some of the older parallel printer cables. It just doesn't look like anything you need to worry about.

If you didn't put it there, you better worry, because it's logging every single keystroke you type in!

The version we used could hold about 500,000 characters or a half a megabyte. That might not sound like much, until you consider that the Word document that eventually became this entire chapter took up only about 20,000 characters (16,000 characters for the text and about 4,000 backspace key strokes to correct all my typing errors). That would only be about 4 percent of its capability. By the way, those backspace keys would show up as ASCII characters (control H for you techies) as would any other nonprinting character entered as part of a password or whatever. It only records keystrokes, so it holds a lot more information than you might think. We have left them connected to target computers for up to three weeks and still the user's activity only filled up about 80 percent of their capacity.

Here's something else to consider if you feel safer entering information into your Web browser over a secure socket connection (https). The encryption happens between your browser and the server that is receiving your sensitive information over the Internet. That's a good thing if you're entering your credit card number or bank account access information. But here's the problem with that warm fuzzy: The keystroke reader is reading your keystrokes before they get to your browser, meaning everything will be in the clear when someone (hopefully only you) looks at the data that your keystroke reader collected.

How do you know if you have one connected to your workstation or home computer? You don't, unless you physically look back in the rat's nest that lives behind most computers and see if anything looks strange. Unless you have been made aware of what they look like, it probably won't look strange to you even if you do see one. I pass one around for people to see at every one of my security training classes. Statistically, I've read that people are 27 times more likely to remember something if they can see and touch it. I usually ask my attendees for a show of hands by those who have never seen one. Almost every time, more than half of the hands go up. How can you defend yourself against something you don't even know exists? (Another subtle hint for more awareness training.)

Here's a quick awareness training class using one of my workstations as the target computer. Figure 1.11 shows the workstation in a minimum configuration with only a monitor, mouse, power cord, and keyboard connected to the motherboard. Take a look at that little bulge about three inches from the end of the cable that goes into the monitor. It's the only cable that has a bulge of the four that you see. That's an induction coil and you may see one or more of these on cables found behind most workstations.

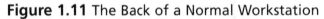

Figure 1.11 The Back of a Normal Workstation

Let's take a look at this same workstation after I have installed my keystroke reader between the keyboard and the motherboard socket where the keyboard was connected (see Figure 1.12). Of the two cables in the center next to each other, the keyboard cable is the one on the right.

Figure 1.12 With a Keystroke Reader Added In

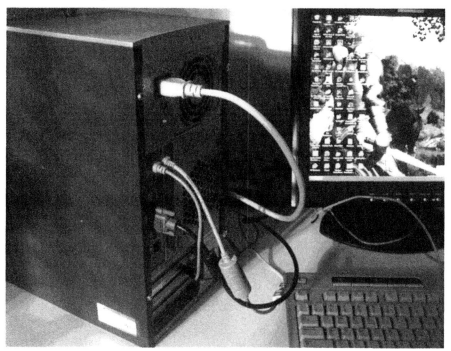

Now what do we see when we look back there? The keystroke reader looks like a second induction coil and would be very hard to detect if you didn't know what one looked like. I didn't try very hard to hide it, and normally, there are more wires back there than this. There is no way that the computer would know it's there. It uses virtually no power, and doesn't require any software to be installed to make it work. When I finally remove it and take it back to check out the internal log, the computer (and you) would never know it was gone again.

This device can be used as an excellent security instrument if you suspect someone is using your computer when you are not there. It is sold primarily for that purpose. This is a good thing, as long as you know it's there.

Checking Those Phone Closets

If your building is in a rented space, or in a multi-tenant building, it's a good idea to have someone perform a thorough check of your hard wiring for the phone lines. You don't know who was in there before you were, and old wiring is sometimes not removed when new tenants move in. On more than one occasion, our teams found old phone cable wiring still in place and being used in an inappropriate manner by inside employees. While we are on the subject, techno security also comes into play when considering the corporate PBX. This is the Private Branch Exchange, which is the internal phone company for larger corporations. It may still have a modem for remote maintenance needs, and the phone number for that modem may be written on the wall right near the modem. We found many PBXs that we "visited" in the evenings to be very social-engineer friendly.

Removing a Few Door Signs

It always amazes us to see rooms that have a sign over them saying *Computer Room* or *Phone Closet*. Obviously, the people who work there know where it is, and there's no reason for anyone else to know what's inside. It's all right for the room to have a number on the door that building maintenance would understand, but there's little reason to make it so easy for the bad guys to know where their best target is on that floor. This may sound like I'm getting a little too picky, but I'm not. The more difficult you make it for people who don't have a need to know about these critical rooms, the more secure you will be.

TIP

If you are going to have high security locks on any doors in your building, dedicated computer rooms, and phone closets would be high on my list of rooms needing the most secure locking mechanisms.

Review Video Security Logs

Normally, after we have completed our mission and have taken all of the "evidence that we have been there" out to our vehicle, we would re-enter the building and try to be seen by the building security cameras that we knew were there. Hopefully, there were some we didn't know about. We would even jump up and down waving our arms just to see if anyone would eventually report us. As far as we know, we were never reported as being seen on the tapes recorded by those cameras, so one of three things must have happened. Either the cameras weren't working (unlikely), or the people looking at the playback of the video missed seeing us on the tape (probably unlikely), or they were simply never looked at (most likely). I'd recommend that someone in the company periodically test this process. If there were internal auditors in the company, this would be a good audit step. That entire expensive surveillance system is worthless if whatever is captured on tape isn't ever seen by a human who can do something about it.

This is another area where I believe that the people responsible for the techno security of the systems need to talk to the people responsible for physical security. Cameras and lights have always been countermeasures that I like to see in and around buildings and personal homes. They can scream "Go find an easier target!" to the bad guys of the world. There may be areas where additional cameras could be recommended to help improve the security of critical areas or rooms. The team responsible for overall physical security might not know about these areas unless you tell them. They may already be monitoring areas you aren't aware of, which could help you if you have an incident.

The reason I mentioned personal homes several times throughout this chapter is that this can be another area of vulnerability for physical penetrations or social engineering attempts to gain specific information. Many people now do much of their work from home on workstations connected to the Internet at high speed. I employ as much physical security at my home office as I have at every other office where I've worked. The technology associated with home security products has increased significantly while the prices for that security have dropped, along with the cost of the latest computers.

I recently installed a number of digitally controlled security cameras around the perimeter of my home as well as motion-activated security lights in all approach areas. This may sound a little paranoid, but I know that I am much more protected than most of my neighbors and my family feels very safe knowing that it would be difficult to attempt anything around our home without someone knowing about it. The security cameras are also motion-activated, so the only thing I see is recorded activity where movement was detected by the software. With the rapid advances in technology, these kinds of sophisticated security systems are very affordable and powerful.

Motion-Sensing Lights

Most of our social-engineering-based inside penetration tests would have been much less successful if the companies that hired us had motion-sensing light controls installed in every office in their buildings. These are not the same kinds of light controls that I installed around my home. Those would help on the outside of any building. What I am talking about here are the motion sensors that turn on the lights inside an office or room when someone walks in. These same sensors turn the lights off after a pre-set time once the final person leaves the room.

Every penetration test that we were hired to conduct had several buildings of opportunity for us to attempt to enter, and every one of them had at least a few lights on all night long. While we were conducting our initial surveillance of the buildings, that was one of the first things that we noted. Are there lights left on at night, and if so, were they the same lights every night. In most cases, with a building having about 15 floors, there would be six or eight lights left on. Our assumption was that whoever was assigned to that office was either still there, or they forgot to turn the light off when they left. Either way, it created a good situation for us. If a random number of lights were left on each night, the security forces would not have any easy way to decide if everything was "normal" at any given time.

As they patrolled from the outside (we were watching them do this from the outside and from the inside once we got into the building), they really had no reference for what would be a normal building profile. As we became bolder towards the end of a penetration test, we would even turn certain lights on just to see if security would become suspicious of this activity. No one ever did.

Several of the buildings we penetrated didn't have anyone working in them at night. If motion-sensing lights had been used throughout these buildings, we would have looked for softer targets. If we had entered a room in a completely dark building, the light coming on would have been very abnormal for any security team member who saw it.

There is another good reason to install these sensors. Over time, the energy saved by having the lights automatically turn off when there was no human around needing light could eventually pay for the additional cost of the sensor.

Let's Go to Lunch

This little problem remains high on my list of things we should all be considering every time we go out for a meal in a public place. Many of our office buildings have public restaurants either in the building itself, or close-by within walking distance. Here's what I think happens all too often. We're at work discussing something important, and someone realizes that it's time for lunch. Out we go to the local fast-food restaurant of choice that day. There's no reason to let lunch slow down our train-of-thought for the project we're working on. The in-depth conversation about that new marketing scheme or the great new product we're about to announce continues as if we were still back at the office.

You would be shocked at how many of these kinds of conversations I've heard over the years in public places. Things were discussed in the open, among total strangers, that should never have left the corporate boardroom. It just seems like we are all too busy to stop and think about security, and controlling who has access to our proprietary information. I occasionally get a chuckle from my friends when I remind them of a time when the national security message was "loose lips sink ships." (That was during World War II, which was just a little before my time, and I do mean *just* before.) Judging by the conversations I have had with some of the people who were alive during that time, pretty much everybody took security seriously. Why has that changed so drastically in our high-tech world just 60 years later? We certainly don't have less at risk than they did then. If anything, we have much more at risk, especially in the world of technology. People were careful and concerned that there could be spies anywhere. Has that threat gone away? I don't think so.

There couldn't be a better example of No Tech Hacking than simply sitting in a crowded restaurant on a typical day, in a typical city, and listening. The technology that exists today for helping people hear things a little better didn't even exist in the "loose lips sink ships" days. These are legitimate devices that can help anyone with a hearing problem hear MUCH better. I'm not talking about hearing aids; I'm talking about amplified listening devices that are available just about anywhere. A couple of them are shown in Figures 1.13 and 1.14.

Figure 1.13 An Amplified Listening Device

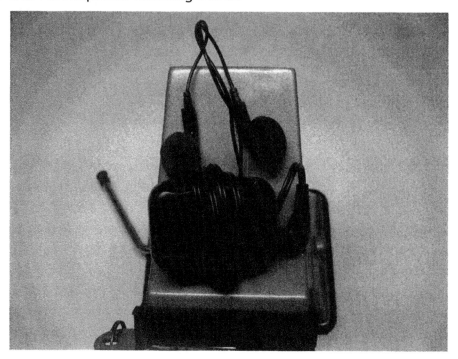

This is the smallest sound amplification device that I found at my local Radio Shack. This picture was taken with the device sitting on the anvil (back) portion of my portable vice. I've left a key in the device (visible at the bottom of the picture) to give you a reference as to the size of the device. It's pretty small. The sound amplification is amazing considering that this device only costs around $10. Let's take a look at a higher-end version of the same component.

Figure 1.14 A RadioShack Amplified Listener

The one in Figure 1.14 is a little more expensive and uses a single AAA battery that is easily replaced. The quality seemed to be about the same as the smaller, less expensive model. It cost about $25. With so many people today using MP3 players and other small devices with earphones, you need to be aware that these devices might not be noticed in a crowded public or private meeting space. My purpose in describing these kinds of devices is to make you aware of how available they have become at a very low cost. They have plenty of valuable and legal uses. You just need to be aware that some people could use them for other purposes. Have a nice lunch....

Fun in Manholes

This is certainly not a new topic, but it is one that I suspect most people don't ever think about. Those of us who work in major cities, and even in small cities, walk over manholes every day. That's certainly nothing to be concerned about, but do we ever consider what's under those small circles of metal? While most companies don't own the manhole covers (and what's under them) surrounding your building, it's still a good idea to check on their security. The extent of the infrastructure that exists below the streets of most cities is incredible. Figure 1.15 a boring picture of a boring manhole on a boring street. Pretty neat, huh?

Figure 1.15 A Boring Manhole Cover

Things get more interesting when we take a brief look at what's under some of them (see Figure 1.16).

Figure 1.16 A Ladder to Trouble

Figure 1.16 shows a ladder on the underside of a manhole and it's about 10 feet long from top to bottom. I wouldn't want to fall into that one if someone removed the cover on a dark quiet night. If you enter the words "manhole security" in Google, you'll find a few interesting articles about how manholes can now be protected, as well as a few stories that discuss the problem in some cities with manhole cover theft.

One of my fondest memories of a manhole in the movies was seeing Mother (Dan Aykroyd) working away in a nearby manhole at the beginning of the movie *Sneakers* in 1992. His penetration team was hired to test the security of a bank. The story was pure fiction, but the vulnerability of what could be accessed from within certain manholes was real. Figure 1.17 shows a manhole cable vault that Mother would have been proud to work in. This picture was taken from the base of the ladder shown in Figure 1.16.

Figure 1.17 A Manhole Cable Vault

Most manholes like this have long since been secured, especially since 9/11. That doesn't mean you shouldn't become aware of any manhole that could be used to access your building. This is even truer for multi-tenant (that's most of them) buildings in large cities.

Internal Auditors Are Your Friends

Just about everything I have mentioned in this chapter would make a good spot check audit point for an internal auditor. Someone on the good-guy side of the fence needs to check for these possible vulnerabilities and insure that the proper countermeasures are employed before they are exploited and become security incidents.

My experience with auditors over the years has been that things usually happen once *they* have made a suggestion for improvements in a certain area. Many of the larger corporations have information system auditors, who have the primary responsibility of looking after the technical world within a corporation. That's a lot to keep up with.

Most mid-sized corporations have internal auditors who are responsible for IS in addition to their usual audit tasks.

Always Be Slightly Suspicious

The number one countermeasure for the threat of social engineering is to be just a little more suspicious than we normally are as good friendly trusting Americans. This holds true for social engineering attempts that come by way of a phone call, or a visit from a friendly salesman. The same principle will help all of us be more aware of possible terrorist planning activities as well. We all need to be just a little bit more aware of what is going on around us and who is possibly trying to pretend to be other than who they really are as they use that age-old skill of social engineering to try and breach our security.

Unfortunately, this is a difficult countermeasure to continue to implement. We simply just stop being concerned about things that happened only a few years ago. I suspect this has something to do with our wonderful freedom from most of the things that people live with every day in other parts of the world. We can never afford to become complacent again. If we do, it will make life much easier for future bad guys, social engineers, and even terrorists. This and most of the countermeasures suggested in this chapter help to mitigate all of these threats.

Getting Every Employee Involved

I've been saying this over and over for close to two decades now. I don't care what kinds of sophisticated security devices are employed for physical access control or network access control with intrusion detection, firewalls, incident response, and so on, there will always be a large hole in a security plan if it doesn't get all of its employees involved with the overall protection process. I know that I'm not the only one who has ever mentioned this.

Summary

I've thrown a lot at you in this combination of risks, threats, vulnerabilities, and countermeasures associated with SCADA security concerns. What I have tried to address in this extended chapter are what I consider the low-hanging fruit that the bad guys of the world are very aware of. Most of the vulnerabilities mentioned are fairly easy to fix once you know about them. Most of you who read this book won't even be responsible for correcting many of the vulnerabilities, but you might be able to get this book to someone in your organization that can correct them.

Security will always be a long-term team effort. This is true for every size company as well as every size family at home. If you have a computer in your home and you access the Internet to pay your bills or check your bank statement, you need to consider security every time you do so. Even though we are in a very technical world that will do nothing but get technically more complex, we should never forget about physical security at home and at work. If you become a victim of identity theft, you will spend about two years getting your financial life back in order. Prevention is your absolute best countermeasure for most, if not all, of these possible threats.

Solutions Fast Track

How Easy Is Social Engineering?

☑ Social Engineering is something that anyone could easily fall victim to.

☑ Knowledge of the threat and employee awareness are the major countermeasures.

☑ Unfortunately, it is still way too easy to con someone out of proprietary information regarding physical access.

Human Nature—Human Weakness

☑ The threat of social engineering is a risk management issue.

☑ Most people are way too trusting of friendly strangers.

☑ Always be just a little bit suspicious until you know for sure whom you are interacting with in person, or on the phone.

Physical Security and Social Engineering Countermeasures

- ☑ Employee awareness training explaining social engineering and how to become a less likely victim.

- ☑ Role play (it can be fun) to show examples of social engineering.

- ☑ Conduct little internal social engineering tiger team attacks and share the lessons learned (or not learned the first time through) with employees.

Dumpster Diving Still Works

- ☑ It's amazing what we still find in dumpsters. Much of it should have been shredded.

- ☑ Crosscut shredders are now very inexpensive and effective at home and at work.

- ☑ Consider crosscut shredders at every desk where important papers could accidentally be thrown in the trash.

- ☑ Shred EVERYTHING that comes into your home with anyone's name on it. You don't need to shred the entire document or magazine, just the pages where a name or address appears.

Beware of Tailgating

- ☑ Most of us kindly hold the door open for someone walking in behind us.

- ☑ Security policies should be clear as to what employees should do if they suspect that someone who doesn't belong in the company has followed them into their building.

- ☑ Avoid potential workplace violence incidents by following your security policy.

Check for Keystroke Readers

- ☑ Hardware keystroke readers are very hard to detect.

- ☑ News reports indicate that these are now being found in public access workstations.

- ☑ This threat is another employee awareness issue to be covered with all employees.

Check All Locks for Proper Operation

- ☑ Check all locks at home and at work. Report malfunctioning locks.
- ☑ Don't prop doors open and report any that you find propped open.
- ☑ Change the lock combinations (have them re-keyed) when you move into a new or used home. You never know who has that extra key.

Let's Go to Lunch

- ☑ Be extra careful what you talk about in a public restaurant.
- ☑ Be aware of the people around you or sitting close by.
- ☑ Also be careful what you talk about on elevators. You never know who is listening and why.

Fun in Manholes

- ☑ Be sure that someone in your company knows just what's under your building.
- ☑ If you spot a potential building entry point, report it to your security group.
- ☑ Every major city has a considerable infrastructure underground with access through manholes.

Frequently Asked Questions (and Special Interviews)

Writing chapters in books isn't easy. This is the fifth book in the Syngress/Elsevier library that I have had a hand in the past 18 months. Even writing a single chapter is really time-consuming hard work. Many internationally known experts are long-time personal friends and acquaintances of ours, and most of them have a lot of experience to share with us on some critical subjects. Unfortunately, most don't have the time available to write a complete chapter in one of our books, but I still wanted them to share something with us. The solution to this dilemma was to include some of their knowledge as a special section in this opening chapter, substituting (in a way) for our books' usual end section of frequently asked questions. Here, *I* will conduct a series of interviews, and ask the questions, prodding the experts about their respective areas of skill. So, let's dive into the interviews!

Critical Infrastructure Emergency Communications

Special Interview with Phil Drake, Telecommunications Manager, The Charlotte Observer, Charlotte, North Carolina

Jack: The ability to continue to communicate is certainly critical to keeping our entire critical infrastructure secure. Share with us some of your thoughts on ways to continue to communicate in emergency situations.

Phil: The first step is to have a plan to be able to communicate in *any* situation. Having the most modern equipment and the best responders are of no value unless you can deploy them when and where needed. If you can't communicate with your assets, you are part of the problem, not part of the solution. Have an emergency communication plan, test it routinely, and be certain that everyone understands it.

Jack: If a department or agency does not have a plan specifically addressing what to do when their communications links fail, where do they begin the planning process?

Phil: Plan to communicate under any circumstances. Approach planning with a "what if" attitude and expect the worst. If one system fails, for whatever reason, have another system or plan ready to take its place. If the primary system fails, what's your backup? If the backup fails, what's next? I know of a number of agencies who have well-designed plans and multiple layers of communications links but in testing they still can't communicate with some of their key assets. The reason? The people in the field didn't remember what to do or were never told. Have a plan, document it, test it, and be sure everyone understands it.

Jack: In emergency communications, what's the number one concern?

Phil: People. That's not the answer you expected, but it's the most important. Every company and government agency must ensure that its people (work force) have the necessary plans, training, and equipment so they can respond to an emergency when needed. This includes the day-to-day "onsite emergencies" and it's especially true for a natural disaster or other event that affects the employee's home life. A major part of this readiness is personal and family disaster preparedness. If an employee's family is safe, he or she will return to work much quicker and can focus on their job. My employers feel that this level of preparedness is not their concern; it's a serious mistake.

Following workforce preparedness, electrical power is the major concern and dependency. Commercial electrical power may be unavailable for days or possibly longer periods following a disaster. We have some of the greatest communications technology imaginable, but it still is totally dependent on "old fashioned" electricity. You've got to power your equipment, and whatever communications infrastructure you depend on must have power to support your communications needs. The majority of large agencies and businesses have backup generators powering uninterruptible power supplies (UPSs) for fixed and wireless communications equipment. Smaller businesses tend to avoid the expense of this protection and "take their chances." It's important to understand the impact of a power outage on the operation and its ability to continue to provide the products and/or services that are expected.

The majority of cellular carriers provide backup power at many (but not all) cell sites. Public safety and most business radio systems have emergency power. Our dependency on wireless keeps growing, so talk with your service providers about their backup power plans. Here are a few questions to ask:

- Is the entire system protected by backup power?

- Will the system "footprint" or coverage area be decreased in a power outage?

- Is the emergency power provided by a generator, batteries only, or a UPS (uninterruptible power supply)?

- What's the "run time" on emergency power before the batteries need recharging or the generator needs refueling?

- While operating on emergency power, will the system support normal traffic levels? (In an emergency, communications systems will carry more traffic than during normal conditions.)

Backup power is so important that the FCC has mandated that every telephone central office, commercial two-way radio system provider, and cell site have eight hours of backup power by early 2009. The "land line" phone companies have operated on battery power backup up with generators since the start of the industry. That's not the case for the wireless or land mobile industry. There are over 210,000 cell sites in the U.S., plus all those other operations just mentioned. So while it's a great idea, it's not going to happen anytime soon. The cost, space requirements for battery banks and generators, plus the wireless industry attorneys will slow the implementation down to something more realistic.

Now let's switch to the "end users"—the responders or field personnel depending on the communications system to save lives and/or serve their customers. In a protracted emergency, can the users charge their handheld radios and cellular phones without commercial power? Is a supply of alkaline (non-rechargeable) batteries available for two-way radios? Does every cellular phone and laptop PC have a 12-volt cigarette lighter adaptor cable?

Twelve-volt inverters are another excellent investment that will provide emergency power from your vehicle's battery. These small boxes plug into the cigarette lighter outlet (now called the 12-volt power outlet) and provide 110-volt AC power. They come in various sizes and technologies, so shop around and get a model that will supply your needs. Large inverters connect directly to the vehicles' battery, smaller ones plug into the 12-volt outlet. A decent one will power a laptop, a TV, or charge radio and cellular batteries.

Other 12-volt or low voltage D.C. solutions include an increasing number of products hitting the market with "hand crank" power supplies. A minute or two of cranking supplies enough power to operate an AM/FM radio, lantern, or even charge cellular batteries.

Small inverter generators are also an option. These generators produce DC voltage first, and then convert it to 110 volts AC. The conversion process produces very clean voltage that is well suited for communications and computer use. These tend to be more expensive than the normal gasoline-powered generator, but are worth the extra cost. Buying a brand name will provide a much quieter generator and that's an important consideration in any communications operation. While power may be our number-one communications concern, safety is always our ultimate concern when operating any mechanical or electrical equipment. Read and follow all instructions. Gasoline is dangerous in normal conditions, and especially so when conditions aren't normal. So be careful.

Jack: You've used solar power in the past to power some of your emergency equipment. Are you still doing that?

Phil: Absolutely. The technology has advanced dramatically in the past few years. We now have fold-up solar panels that can charge and power radios and satellite phones. These panels are formed onto high-density flexible material that's very tough and waterproof. A 25-watt, 1.5-amp panel measuring 8 × 11 × 1.5 inches unfolds to a little less than 2 × 4 feet and weighs less than a pound. Currently, they are a bit pricey but worth the money as they are non-polluting and very compact and totally quiet.

Jack: You once told me that you used two telephone companies for critical locations. Why?

Phil: Using two "local telephone companies," the incumbent telephone company (for example, a Bell company) and a "CLEC" or "competitive local exchange carrier" eliminates a single point of failure and allows you to take advantage of some new creative pricing arrangements offered by the competitive companies.

This is not a complicated process. Your company or agency can simply use one phone company for outbound calls and another company for inbound calls. You may want to split your range of telephone numbers and let one company provide inbound services on half of the numbers and another carrier to carry the other half. Lowering the costs of communications and doubling the diversity will make every-one happy.

You may ask: Why bother? Well, we live in interesting times and the communications infrastructure is a target of those who would do us harm. The big telephone companies are big targets in this new arena of terrorism. They take extraordinary steps to protect their facilities and services. Your workplace or agency should take protective steps too, to improve your chances of surviving a service interruption.

Jack: I know you used satellite links extensively during Hurricane Katrina. What's new in that technology?

Phil: Portable/mobile satellite phones and service are almost common now for any organization tasked with disaster communications. Hurricane Katrina certainly proved the value of satellite service for any company or agency that was there and had to stay operational. Mobile, stationary, and handheld units have dropped in size and price. One newer entry is BGAN (Broadband Global Access Network), which is

IP-based and allows users to connect to the Internet and conduct voice calls simultaneously. These units are also available in small (about the size of a laptop computer) and smaller (about half the size of a laptop). Higher bandwidth is available and comes with larger antennas, power requirements, radio equipment, and, of course, larger prices.

Satellite links for SCADA installations are becoming much more common and affordable. Security of the data, higher link speeds, and reliability are major justifications for considering replacing traditional communications links with satellite where appropriate.

"Ham" radio operators have a saying: "When all else fails, amateur radio works." I have yet to find an EOC (Emergency Operations Center) that does not have an amateur radio station onsite or access to one nearby. Emergency management agencies, the American Red Cross, and the Salvation Army partner with amateur radio clubs to ensure reliable communications when disaster strikes. The private sector too can benefit from knowing which of their employees have "ham" licenses as they can provide emergency communications to provide health and welfare reports between employees and their families when the need arises. A private sector enterprise, for example, may provide products and services that would help the recovery process in a disaster. Having trained radio operators capable of communicating with emergency management officials will benefit the enterprise and the community.

There are a number of organizations within the ranks of amateur radio that train ham operators in emergency operations and traffic handling. These skilled volunteers spend many hours training in sometimes-primitive conditions to duplicate disaster situations.

Annual "Field Day" exercises allow "ham" operators to test their emergency skills under simulated disaster conditions. It's also a great opportunity for the public to see first-hand what critical services this "hobby" provides. These unpaid volunteers have a long history of providing critical communications when the need arises.

Jack: Most offices have a centralized telephone system. Are there any "preparedness points" for companies or agencies to check?

Phil: Is the system protected by a UPS and is the UPS backed up by a generator? If so, is the generator routinely tested and serviced? Are the UPS batteries replaced when recommended by the manufacturer?

As mentioned earlier, having carrier and central office (where your local communications circuits originate) diversity is very important. If one carrier or central office suffers an outage, the other will most likely be unaffected.

If the phone system (PBX for Private Branch Exchange) stops working for whatever reason, is there a plan in place to provide communications in the most critical areas? Most phone systems are installed with a "power fail transfer" switch. This small device senses if power to the PBX and related equipment fails and then bypasses the affected equipment by using a limited number of "outside" lines. These lines are automatically connected (on a one-for-one basis) to extensions (telephones, fax machines, or modems) in the facility. These extensions should be marked as "emergency phones" and their use explained.

Another preparedness method is to have a number of outside lines ready for use that can be manually switched to nonfunctioning extensions in a PBX failure. A two-position toggle switch can be used to switch the extension between the PBX for normal operation, and the outside lines during a service interruption.

If your "PBX" is now a server in a VoIP (Voice over Internet Protocol) installation, there are additional concerns if the LAN (local area network) fails. In these systems, the voice communications are carried over the LAN, not telephone wiring as in the traditional PBX system. Most system designers and vendors provide a number of "failsafe" phones (these are generally analog or "POTS" telephone sets) that are hard-wired the old-fashioned way to protect them from a network failure. Again, it is important to clearly mark these extensions and [make sure] everyone knows their locations.

Jack: Is cellular an infrastructure or "tool" that you recommend for emergency use?

Phil: Yes, but with some reservations. Public safety and service operations, industry, and the general population so depend on cellular technology today that during an emergency, there simply isn't enough cellular capacity to go around. Businesses particularly need to keep this in mind if their "emergency communications plans" depend entirely on cellular phones—which many do unfortunately.

When we mention cellular, we immediately think of the standard flip phone, but one very good cellular "tool" to consider is fixed cellular. These special cellular devices are excellent backup for critical landlines that might experience an interruption in service, or for use in a remote location where phone service for alarms or monitoring are unavailable. These cellular transceivers operate on 110-volt power and use an antenna, which is usually mounted outside the facility. These units have the ability to sense a telephone line failure and automatically provide a cellular "dial tone" to the telephone set or other device until service is restored.

Public safety and government, who are huge cellular users, faced the same problem of "system overload" during emergencies and needed a solution. Enter the National Communications Service (a federal government agency) and their WPS (Wireless Prioritization Service). This service allows certain key leaders (local, state, and federal) plus others who are authorized, to have cellular access at a higher priority than general users. A W.P.S. user will be able to make and receive calls while others will get fast busy signals. Anyone with key leadership or emergency response duties should investigate this service.

Cellular providers not only provide cellular telephone and "walkie-talkie" voice services, they have some very robust data services that anyone who needs to stay connected should investigate. This cellular-based Internet access is generally delivered via a PCMCIA card, "ExpressCard," or a USB modem. Simply plug the card or modem into your laptop, or if it's built in, just click on the icon, and in less than a minute, you have broadband Internet access almost anywhere. In an emergency when voice channels are overloaded, the data services continue to carry traffic at near normal levels. This is due in large measure to engineering and the fact that there are still more voice users competing for finite resources.

BlackBerries and other PDAs are the largest users of cellular data services. These devices provide access to e-mail, the Internet, and a host of applications that make the mobile user very productive regardless of location. In addition to the traditional communications methods (e-mail, voice, and text messaging), BlackBerries have the ability to text message unit to unit, bypassing the organization's exchange server, BlackBerry Enterprise Server, or the Internet, which may be inoperable during disasters or other more localized emergencies. Using only the unit PIN (personal identification number—each BlackBerry device has its own) and the cellular data network, this BlackBerry-to-BlackBerry communication can provide a critical link to key personnel during a crisis.

Jack: You just mentioned WPS, which is a federal program to help communications keep flowing during an emergency. Are there other programs that may help our readers?

Phil: Here are two others that may be considered:

GETS (Government Emergency Telephone System). This telephone communications network is managed by the NCS (National Communications System) and is a workaround for a congested or damaged public switched network. Government employees, emergency responders, and certain private sector businesses can qualify for GETS. Users are issued access cards, which contain an access telephone number and a personal identification number. Dialing the access number and entering the PIN allows the user to place a telephone call over a highly protected telephone network.

TSP (Telecommunications Service Prioritization) is a registration system for listing critical telephone and other communications circuits. In a disaster or other emergency situation, these registered agencies or companies will receive priority repair and restoration service from the local telephone companies and long distance carriers. Any company, agency, or organization that provides critical support for the public or government will probably qualify. This program also falls under the National Communications System.

One of the most reliable and cost-effective communications methods for emergencies or any other time is conventional or trunked two-way radio. A private radio system or simply a number of two-way radios on commercial frequencies provides a quick and simple method of directing resources. If a private system is financially out of reach, there are numerous radio system providers in most metropolitan areas who provide the system infrastructure and radio equipment for a monthly fee.

Trunked radio systems are multi-frequency computer-controlled radio networks that provide voice, data, and telephone service to hundreds or thousands of radio units on a single system. These systems use "repeaters" (receiver/transmitter radios) mounted on high towers, buildings, or mountains that receive a radio signal and retransmit it automatically. This allows a low power radio signal to travel many miles. The majority of public service agencies around the world use this technology. "Trunking" allows the creation of virtual channels so that one group of users cannot hear or interfere with other system users even though they share the same frequencies and may be talking at the same time.

Conventional (radio-to-radio communications without computer control) radio users share the same channel or frequency even if using "select tones" or other techniques that afford users the ability to silence the radio when the information does not directly affect them. Any users can bypass the select tone and listen to all conversations much like a conference call. Conventional radio systems may also use "repeaters" to extend the range of coverage, but many do not.

A caution about two-way radio. Anything you say "over the air" can be heard by someone else. Thousands of "short-wave listeners" monitor scanners—short-wave radios—that can receive any radio frequency. Government and some public safety systems use digital signaling, encryption, and frequency hopping technology to avoid being overheard. That technology, as you might guess, is very expensive and out of reach for the majority of radio users.

Jack: Do you have any low-tech low-cost emergency communications tips to share?

Phil: I'm glad you mentioned "low-tech" because when a major disaster or incident takes away our "high-tech" infrastructure or systems, we are forced to get back to basics. Those simple low-tech tools can help us recover. Here are some tips that I share with both public and private audiences.

S.A.M.E. Alert Radio (Specific Area Message Encoding) Having an alert radio is as important as having a smoke detector in your home or office. These radios sit quietly on a shelf until dangerous weather or other local emergencies cause officials to issue public warnings. They can be programmed for "specific" counties or even smaller geographic areas to alert when conditions warrant. These radios have battery backup so if the power is off, the radio still keeps watch. Frankly I wish there was a law that every home, office, school and public building was required to have a S.A.M.E. radio. We would all be much safer.

Pagers One and two-way alphanumeric pagers are often overlooked but are still solid communications tools in an emergency. The infrastructure supporting these devices has gained capacity as customers have moved to cellular and PCS. Pagers don't depend on the Internet or e-mail to deliver messages unit to unit and the power is generally a single AA battery. So for low-tech low-power requirement communications, these are hard to beat.

Payphones Public pay telephones are harder to find these days, everyone has a cellular phone, and so the "payphone" industry has almost disappeared. While the (almost) bulletproof case may be larger and the inner workings more complex, these are still simple old "POTS" lines that operate on phone line power. If there are payphones in or around your facility, record their numbers and make them part of your emergency communication plan.

Over-the-Counter Radios These multi-channel FRS (Family Radio Service) radios are intended for family recreation but provide excellent communications over short distances of a quarter to half mile. Using these to stay in touch with family or neighbors in a community in an emergency situation can be very helpful. They are available in electronics, discount, and home supply stores. Most FRS radios do not use rechargeable batteries, instead using easily obtainable AA batteries.

GMRS (General Mobile Radio Service) These radios are intended for personal use, but require a license purchased from the Federal Communications Commission and are more expensive than FRS radios. However, they have higher power and are manufactured to higher-quality standards than FRS radios. A number of GMRS radios use rechargeable batteries, which of course require electrical power to recharge. Check to see if the model you may be interested in can use AA batteries as well.

A number of commercial radios are also available "over the counter" in many electronics stores and, of course, through the Internet. These also require a license purchased from the FCC and operate on commercial frequencies with less chatter. Commercial radios generally use rechargeable batteries only, so keep some extra charged batteries on hand.

<u>Pre-Paid Long Distance Cards</u> With a prepaid LD card and a payphone, you can stay in touch with local or long distance contacts.

<u>Citizens Band Radio</u> It's still alive and doing well—in fact, it's better now that several million users have left CBs to truckers and some hard-core hobbyists. This license-free group of radio channels can provide mobile and base station communications over distances of roughly ten miles, but this can be increased if the mobile or base is higher than the average terrain (hill or mountain for instance).

<u>POTS Line (Plain Old Telephone Service) and Phone</u> Few things can beat the reliability of a single telephone line and a wired telephone (an old-fashioned plug-in phone set with a corded handset). Power to operate the phone is provided by the telephone company central office. Employees need to be reminded that all those cordless phones at home stop working in a power failure (some do have battery backup, but they are rare and the batteries drain quickly).

Special Interview with
J. Michael Gibbons, Principal, Deloitte

J. Michael (Mike) Gibbons is a Principal in the Enterprise Risk Services organization of Deloitte & Touche LLP, where he oversees security services to both commercial and government agencies nationally.

Following a 15-year career with the FBI and seven years leading security practices for another "Big 4" consulting firm and an international systems integrations company, Mike joined Deloitte in 2006. During his tenure with the FBI, he was chief of computer crime investigations and established the National Infrastructure Protection Center. He was an investigating special agent in the "Hannover Hackers" case detailed in the best-seller, *The Cuckoo's Egg*, and was involved in the first Internet worm case in the late-1980s.

Jack: What is the criticality of SCADA/Industrial Control Systems (ICS) compared to other important IT systems?

Mike: Even before 9/11 the government was concerned about SCADA as the world was becoming more available. Using wireless, Internet connections, and riding other network backbones, SCADA became available for inspection, interception, and subterfuge. Not all SCADA were affected, and those that managed risk according to government standards and industry best practices kept ahead of outsiders attempting to take control of them. In some cases—for example, where wireless or remote access was introduced—there were more attacks due to this new way to access the systems. Closed-end systems were inherently secure, but they actually had to be in a proven closed-loop. Outside access was the new vulnerability, in many cases introduced without the knowledge that it introduced new vulnerabilities.

Jack: Have we seen an increase in attacks on SCADA? If so, why?

Mike: If not an increase, we have seen enough to make us worry both in the public and private sector.

Insecurity of SCADA/ICS is not a theory. Several popular recent attacks on SCADA/ICS systems demonstrate the "powder keg" state of SCADA/ICS insecurity, a few being listed next:

- In 1992, a former Chevron employee disabled its emergency alert system in 22 states, which wasn't discovered until an emergency happened that needed alerting.

- A cyber-security breach occurred at the Salt River Project, a major water and electricity provider in Tempe, Arizona in 1994.

- In 2000, in Maroochy Shire, Queensland, Vitek Boden released millions of liters of untreated sewage using a wireless laptop, apparently taking revenge against former employers.

- In 2000, the Russian government announced that hackers succeeded in gaining control of the world's largest natural gas pipeline network (owned by Gazprom).

- In 2002, hackers disabled PLC components during a national unrest and general workers strike, crippling the country's main port in Venezuela.

- In 2003, cyber-attacks penetrated the Israel Energy Corporation using DoS attacks but failed to shut down the power grid.

- In Ohio, the Davis-Besse Nuclear Power Plant safety monitoring system was offline for five hours due to the slammer Worm in January 2003.

- In January 2003, a Romanian pair hacked into the computers at the Amundsen-Scott South Pole Station that controlled the life support for the 50 scientists there. The attackers demanded money.

- In 2003, the east coast of America experienced a blackout, while not the cause, many of the related systems were infected by the Blaster worm, causing damages of US$50 billion.

- In 2005, 13 U.S. Daimler-Chrysler manufacturing plants were shut down due to multiple internet worm infections.

- A malware-infected HMI system disabled the emergency stop of equipment under heavy weather conditions at an international energy company in 2005.

- In 2005, ARP spoofing attacks shut down a port signaling system at a Middle East sea port.

- Extremist propaganda was found together with text files containing user-names and passwords of control systems at an international petrochemical company in 2006.

Given the preceding list of recent attacks, coupled with the sensitivity of information being used for communication, it is clear that attacks on SCADA/ICS systems have grown. The personal and political motivations for the attacks vary widely. In the future, the free availability of data and the weaknesses in the SCADA/ICS infrastructure could be exploited by cyber terrorists and the damage due to such attacks could be beyond our current ability to predict.

Jack: How critical are interdependencies between SCADA, and are they connected?

Mike: In the same way that critical infrastructures are interdependent, the control systems have the same vulnerabilities. Many are not yet known, as the interconnections are exceptionally complex. The evolution of SCADA to their third generation today has continued to open attack vectors still protected by obscurity alone.

The data that flows on a third-generation (WAN-based) SCADA/ICS network includes sensitive information not limited to:

- Data from remote field devices

- Activity data

- Financial data

- Real-time monitoring data

- Access control data

- Logs of access (logical and physical)

- Backup data

- Report data for various regulatory compliance

- Data used in business projections

- Human resource data

- Configuration data

- Equipment maintenance data

- Archived data (real-time data is archived)

- Historical data

- Graphs and pie charts

- User manuals

The combination of complex systems, sensitive data, and known vulnerabilities cry out for scientific exploit. Only by establishing a broad framework of protection and controls can the controls themselves be safe.

Special Interview with Kevin Manson, the Original Cyber Cop, Extranet Secure Portal

Jack: The ability to share information over the Internet securely is always a hot topic. Tell us a little about the robust security afforded by the Cyber-Cop portal. And is it just for cybercops?

Kevin: First, a bit of context or background. I have long considered myself an online community builder or "architect." When the Internet was little more than a text medium (BB – Before Browsers), I was running a BBS on my personal computer for the Treasury Department (Federal Law Enforcement Training Center), which was connected to my home phone line, and I was "tossing" mail off USENET. This was what came to be known as the Cybercop BBS. The term "cybercop" is one which I coined in the late 80s. The mission of the Cybercop BBS was to create an online community where law enforcement could share primarily open-source information without regard to traditional "stove pipes" or jurisdictional boundaries that had long hampered information sharing in law enforcement.

Law enforcement has traditionally kept its networked communications in a closed environment because of the sensitive information that police and investigators handle. Sensitive shared or networked communications are obviously not unique to law enforcement. 9/11 brought the critical interdependencies of industry and law enforcement to the forefront, especially what we now call "critical infrastructures," such as the power grid, telecommunications, transportation, water, and so on.

Jack: How did this series of events lead to secure collaboration over the Internet?

Kevin: Presidential Decision Directive 63 had a large impact on my world view and I was determined to help build a secure online community where law enforcement, industry, the DoD community and academia could collaborate in a secure fashion. It was a great stroke of luck that I ran into a DARPA security professional, Bob Dowling, who introduced me to a DARPA manager, Matt Donlon, and a techno code writing wizard, George Johnson (with a background at the Software Engineering Institute at Carnegie-Mellon). These folks had built a secure online community prototype for industry security professionals called the Extranet for Security Professionals.

At that time, I was also serving as a moderator for the National Cybercrime Training Partnership on the FBI secure online system called LEO (Law Enforcement Online), created by a friend, Gary Gardner. LEO was successfully serving law enforcement, and the XSP was likewise serving industry security professionals. Recognizing the tremendous benefits that each of these systems brought to their users, I approached Matt Donlon and asked if he would be willing to help build a synergistic collaborative system for both law enforcement AND industry. Over a handshake, the Cybercop Secure Portal was built. Eight years and 11,000 users later, Cybercop is now fulfilling the dream of securely linking law enforcement and industry in pursuit of homeland security.

www.cybercopportal.com

Shortly following 9/11, I was approached by a friend and colleague who asked if the Cybercop Portal could help disseminate information to the WatchList community of more that 150 industry groups and businesses. Within 48 hours, all of those communities were enabled with their own secure compartment in the larger Cybercop Portal community.

Jack: How does a secure online system like the Cybercop Portal serve to enhance our nation's security?

Kevin: As former National Security Advisor Richard Clarke has observed, "Security is community." Retired FBI Profiler, Bill Tafoya, and I filled in at the last minute for Richard Clarke for the keynote address at the Blackhat conference two months before the 9/11 tragedy. During that keynote, we invited the industry-heavy audience to join with law enforcement in protecting our nation's infrastructure. We emphasized that the "elite" are not those who attack and wreak havoc on the Internet, rather it is those who protect and defend the Net.

Conferences like TechnoSecurity (www.TechnoSecurity.com) bring a strong security-oriented community together for a week or so each year. The Cybercop Portal extends the collaboration reach of security professionals far beyond the fixed and rigid bounds of time and location. It's effectively a 24/7 security community with a memory, and the ability to create secure compartments within the larger community within a matter of minutes.

Chapter 2

Supervisory Control and Data Acquisition

Paul A. Henry, (MCP+I, MCSE, CCSA, CCSE, CFSA, CFSO, CISSP, -ISSAP, CISM, CISA, CIFI) is the Vice President of Technology Evangelism at Secure Computing®

Paul is one of the world's foremost global information security experts, with more than 20 years experience managing security initiatives for Global 2000 enterprises and government organizations worldwide.

At Secure Computing, Paul plays a key strategic role in launching new products and re-tooling existing product lines. In his role as Vice President Technology Evangelism, Paul also advises and consults on some of the world's most challenging and high-risk information security projects, including the National Banking System in Saudi Arabia, Department of Defense's Satellite Data Project, USA, and both Government as well as Telecommunications projects throughout Japan.

Paul is frequently cited by major and trade print publications as an expert on both technical security topics and general security trends, and serves as an expert commentator for network broadcast outlets such as NBC and CNBC. In addition, Paul regularly authors thought leadership articles on technical security issues, and his expertise and insight help shape the editorial direction of key security publications such as the Information Security Management Handbook, where he is a consistent contributor.

Paul serves as a featured and keynote speaker at network security seminars and conferences worldwide, delivering presentations on diverse topics including network access control, Cyber crime, DDoS attack risk mitigation, firewall architectures, computer and network forensics, Enterprise security architectures and managed security services.

Introduction

Within the time span of the author's career, process controls have evolved from pneumatic systems to analog, and then again from analog to digital. Today's digital controls are predominately referred to as Supervisory Control And Data Acquisition (SCADA) systems.

Early pneumatic and analog control systems were isolated from organizations' business systems. Simply putting the integration of process control data into the business decision-making process was a labor-intensive task. Control system data loggers and variable recorder chart data were typically read by an operator or supervisor and then manually entered into business systems.

Current-technology SCADA systems integrate directly with organizations' business systems. Control system data are immediately available to specialized business systems that can optimize SCADA system set points and parameters to better meet the immediate business needs of the organization. It is the integration of SCADA systems and the organizations business systems that pose the greatest risk in SCADA security today.

Just What Is SCADA?

Supervisory Control and Data Acquisition (SCADA) systems provide for the supervisory control, management, and monitoring of process control and manufacturing automation systems through the collection and analysis of real-time data. The prevalence of SCADA systems has grown to the point that our national infrastructure today depends, to a large degree, on SCADA systems.

Today SCADA systems play important roles in several industries (Table 2.1):

Table 2.1 Industries Where SCADA Plays an Important Role

Aluminum	Boilers
Automotive	Chemical
Electric Power	Nuclear Power
Chemical	Oil and Gas Transportation
Flight Simulation	Paper Manufacturing
Food Processing	Specialized Petrochemical
Fossil Fuel Production	Rubber Manufacturing
Glass Production	Steel Manufacturing

SCADA system capabilities have evolved from that of simply replacing lights and push buttons to handling very complex process control and critical safety shutdown systems. The intelligence of SCADA systems has advanced to the point where their automated operation requires fewer operators: less human supervision than previous control system methodologies. Today, common applications for SCADA systems include, but are not limited to, those shown in Table 2.2.

Table 2.2 Common Applications for SCADA Systems

AC efficiency test standards	Batch process controls
Bearing temperature monitor	Boiler and turbine controls
Boiler controls	Burner management systems
Boiler data acquisition	Sequence of Events (S.O.E.)
Boiler water treatment controls	Brick kiln controls
Bulk resin dispensing	Carburetor test standards
Clay manufacturing controls	Continuous polymer manufacturing
Continuous welding SPC monitoring	Desulphurization and acid processing
Dynamometer controls	Electric power T&D monitoring
Extruder controls	F16 and F117 flight simulation
Fiber optics filter manufacturing	Floating dry dock controls
Food preservation	Fore hearth controls
Fuel injector test standard	Fuel oil handling system
Fuel pump test standards	Furnace controls
Gas processing	Glass furnace controls
H_2O chemistry controls	Hazardous chemical waste controls
High-flux research reactor controls	Hydroelectric load management
Incinerator controls	Material handling and finishing
Meteorological monitoring	Military data acquisition
Nuclear plant DAS	Nuclear plant full-scope simulators
Nuclear simulators	Offshore platform oil/gas separation
Paper mill wet end process controls	Petroleum pilot plants
Plant energy management	Plant monitoring
Power distribution monitoring	Process controls

Continued

Table 2.2 Continued. Common Applications for SCADA Systems

Process simulators	Product distribution monitor
Radwaste monitoring	Reactor and plant monitoring
Reactor core temperature monitoring	Reactor monitoring / reactor plant DAS
Refrigerator efficiency test standards	Resin mixing
Rod drop monitoring systems	Rolling mill controls
Rotating equipment monitoring	Safety parameter display systems
Ship controls development systems	Shipboard LNG controls
Solder manufacturing controls	Spool-winder temperature monitoring and controls
Steam control systems	Submarine diving simulators
Tank controls	Target ranges
Textile finishing range controls	TG monitoring
Tritium processing	Turbine controls
Turbine generator fuel test cells	Turbine monitoring
Utility monitoring	Virtual annunciator panels
Waste tank controls	Waste water monitoring
Water chemistry monitoring	Weapons release simulators
Whole body calorie monitoring	Compressor surge controls
Wind tunnel controls	

Tools & Traps...

Greatest Benefit—Causes the Greatest Risk

The greatest benefit of current technology SCADA is its ability to integrate directly with back-end business systems. No longer are SCADA systems an island unto themselves. It is the integration of SCADA into the business system that causes the greatest concern. By integrating the SCADA system into the business systems of the enterprise, you are inadvertently increasing the risks within the SCADA system by adding those of the enterprise network and often those of the public Internet as well.

SCADA Systems and Components

While exceptions exist, such as self-contained and stand-alone SCADA systems that are purpose built for a given application, most SCADA systems are comprised of several components that communicate across a network.

Remote Terminal Units (RTUs)

An RTU (Remote Terminal Unit) provides intelligent I/O collection and processing, such as reading inputs from switches, sensors, and transmitters and then arranging the representative data into a format that the SCADA system can understand. The RTU also converts output values provided by the SCADA system from their digital form into that which can be understood by field-controllable devices such as discrete (relay) and analog outputs (current or voltage).

Programmable Logic Controllers (PLC)

The PLC can be regarded as the "brain" of the SCADA system. The actual control program for a given process or its control systems is executed within the PLC. A PLC can either work with local physically connected inputs and outputs or with remote inputs and outputs provided by an RTU. Typical PLCs can provide for two different types of control: discrete and continuous.

Discrete Control

In discrete control applications, the PLC works with inputs and outputs that have defined states (on/off) and can perform actions based on time, events, or a particular sequence (for example, turn on an output at a given time, turn off an output after the input from a field device, such as a limit switch closes; turn on a series of outputs in a given sequential order).

Continuous Control

In continuous control applications, the PLC typically works with analog input and output devices and uses special algorithms to maintain a steady operating state. For instance, the PLC has a set point that is provided by the SCADA system for the desired temperature of a given process. It receives an analog input value of 0 to 100 percent, representing the process temperature. The PLC uses specialized algorithms (such as PID algorithms) to generate an analog output value of 0 to 100 percent that is then used to position a valve or to control the speed of a motor in an effort to continuously keep the temperature at the desired set point.

Combinations of both discrete and continuous control are often used in what is referred to as batch control. In batch control applications, both discrete control and continuous control are used together. In the simplest of terms, discrete operations could be used to mix the given ingredients of a recipe and place the batter in a pan in the oven, while continuous control would be used to maintain the oven at a specific temperature to create the finished product—the cake.

Human Machine Interface (HMI)

The HMI (Human Machine Interface) is the means by which the user (operator) interacts with the SCADA system. Simply put, the HMI provides a clear and easy-to-understand computer representation of what is, in fact, being controlled or monitored by the SCADA system. Further, it provides for interaction, either in the form of a touch screen, a specialized keyboard, or both.

Current-generation SCADA HMIs are not just a replacement for push buttons and pilot lights of the past. In fact, they provide a simpler user interface for even the most complex SCADA systems. The "usability" of the HMI is the measure by which a user can effectively interact with the SCADA system. HMI implementations that offer high levels of usability provide SCADA systems that are intuitive, efficient, and effective. A good and effective SCADA HMI design makes the interaction with the SCADA through the HMI seem natural to the operator—in other words, clear and easy to understand, with no need for explanation.

The International Engineering Consortium (IEC) has defined a standard ISO 9241 that provides a definition for the quality of use for an HMI. The ISO 9241 standard defines three components of quality of use applicable to the design of an HMI:

1. Effectiveness—Does the product do what the users require? Does it do the right thing?

2. Efficiency—Can the users learn the HMI quickly? Can they carry out their tasks with minimum expended effort, including a minimum of errors? Does it improve the productivity/effort ratio? Does it do things right?

3. Satisfaction—Do users express satisfaction with the product? Does the new product reduce stress? Do end users now have a more satisfying job?

Distributed Control Systems (DCS)

Historically, the term DCS could best be defined as a dedicated control system that did not rely upon a single central computer to control a given process, was comprised of multiple computers, did not require operator intervention, and afforded for inter-action between those computer systems to provide for the total control of a given manufacturing or process control system.

The distinction between DCS and SCADA systems has become difficult since SCADA systems have evolved to become more powerful and capable with many SCADA solutions today offering DCS-like capabilities. In fact, vendors of SCADA systems today would argue that the current-generation SCADA system gives the distributed control capability of a large DCS system, while still affording the ease of use found in a SCADA system. At the same time, of course, DCS vendors are today claiming that their DCS systems are able to handle much more complex processes with the ability for operator interaction through an HMI that rivals the ease of use found in a SCADA system.

Looking toward the future, it is not hard to imagine that SCADA systems will continue to become more powerful and capable and, in fact, may one day replace the traditional DCS, at least in the form that we know them today.

Hybrid Controllers

Hybrid controllers are specialized devices that provide for capabilities not found in standard discrete and continuous control modules for PLC systems. Capabilities such as adaptive control, artificial intelligence, and fuzzy logic are afforded by typical hybrid controllers.

The capability of hybrid controllers is one of the primary mechanisms that is blurring the line between SCADA and DCS systems. Benefiting from Moore's Law (computing power nearly doubles every 18 months), the most complex control algorithms and intricate mathematical capabilities previously reserved only for powerful DCS systems are quickly finding their way into today's increasingly more powerful hybrid controllers for SCADA systems.

A SCADA system may utilize multiple hybrid controllers distributed as needed to perform the tasks at hand across a given process while still operating under the supervisory control of the SCADA system.

Event Loggers

Event loggers provide for the capturing of events as they happen within a SCADA system and provide time/date stamping, which affords a complete audit trail of the events that have occurred in the SCADA system. Typically, time within a SCADA system event logger provides for usable resolution down to 1/10 of a second.

While this is more than fast enough for many typical applications, it is not suitable for applications where multiple events can happen only milliseconds apart, such as in the switch gear for power distribution systems and safety shutdown systems for critical processes. In these applications, specialized event loggers that can capture events occurring perhaps just milliseconds apart are typically required.

In SCADA systems that utilize the integrated event logging capability of multiple individual components, it is critical that the time across the SCADA system be synchronized. Hence, it is not uncommon today for a SCADA system to use a single time reference such as that found in a Global Positioning System (GPS) satellite receiver as a time-synchronizing source to assure that all real-time and historical data timestamps are accurate across all HMIs, PLCs , hybrid controllers, and other devices within the SCADA system.

Tools & Traps...

SCADA Is Often Deployed in Distributed Environments

The processing power of SCADA has increased dramatically. They are more capable of complex tasks than ever before and have closely followed the overall trends in computer architectures. Current technology SCADA systems like current technology computer networks are most often architected in a distributed model. While individual components perform complex tasks, data are shared between components in order to optimize the overall process that is under SCADA control.

Common SCADA Architectures

Early SCADA systems used proprietary event–driven operating systems and some form of rudimentary/proprietary serial communications typically based on R232/ RS422/RS485. One could perhaps argue that early SCADA systems benefited from the "Security by obscurity" that was afforded by their specialized operating systems and communications.

Today, SCADA system components utilize purpose built event-driven operating systems, commercial operating systems (for example, Windows/Linux as well as hybrids), and commercial operating systems with real-time extensions. While SCADA systems for critical processes are available with fault-tolerant networking, most have evolved to take advantage of UDP/TCP over Ethernet communications.

In a SCADA network (Figure 2.1), field devices are typically connected to the PLCs across an independent network using specialized protocols such as Fieldbus, HART, or MODBUS.

Figure 2.1 A SCADA Network

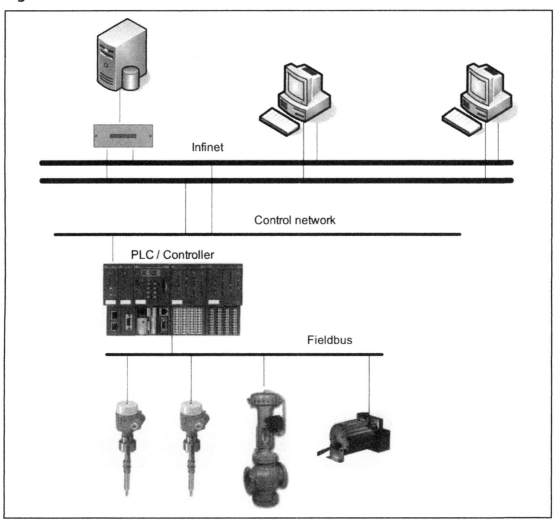

The PLCs are on a separate network and Communicate to the system's HMIs, hybrid controllers, and event loggers using protocols such as InfiNET.

If the preceding example were the extent of connectivity to the SCADA system, they would be relatively secure. However, it is common today (Figure 2.2) for the corporate IT network to typically connect to the InfiNET network with a bridge to allow for the collection of production data, and SCADA vendors are typically allowed to connect to PLCs or hybrid controllers in order to facilitate vendor support of the SCADA system.

Figure 2.2 A Typical Network Bridge

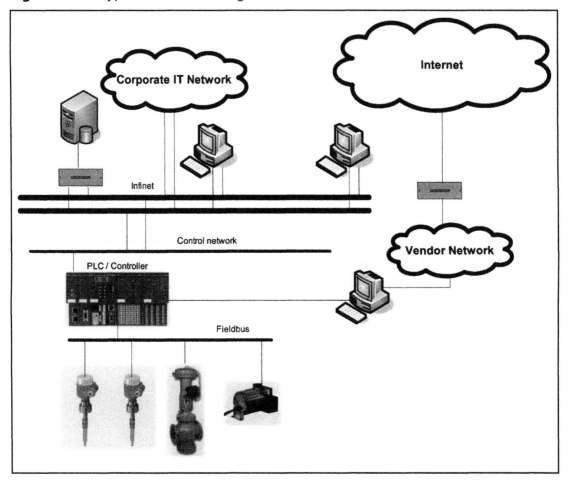

SCADA Communications Protocols

In the early years of SCADA systems, few if any communications standards existed, hence individual SCADA equipment vendors each created their own exclusive proprietary protocols. It has been estimated that at one point there were between

150 to 200 different proprietary SCADA protocols in use. The high number of protocols in use along with their proprietary nature actually afforded a degree of security through "security by obscurity."

As the SCADA industry matured and vendors began to adopt open standards, the total number of SCADA protocols commonly in use was reduced to a small number of popular protocols that were being promoted by industry professional organizations, which included, but were not limited to, the following:

- MODBUS
- Ethernet/IP
- PROFIBUS
- ControlNet
- InfiNET
- HART
- UCA
- Fieldbus
- Distributed Network Protocol (DNP)
- Utility Communications Architecture (UCA)
- Inter-Control Center Communications Protocol (ICCP)
- Telecontrol Application Service Element (TASE)

How Serious Are the Security Issues of SCADA?

Data within the British Columbia Institute of Technology (BCIT) report titled "The Myths and Facts behind Cyber Security Risks for Industrial Control Systems" issued in 2004 indicates that there has been a ten-fold increase in SCADA incidents since 2000. Of those organizations surveyed within the report that placed a dollar value on the losses associated with a SCADA attack, 50 percent reported financial losses of $1,000,000 or more.

The BCIT report includes 100 or so recent SCADA incidents, but unfortunately this only uncovers the tip of the iceberg. The problem is in the reporting (or lack thereof) of SCADA incidents. Out of the 200 Fortune 500 companies that are considered to be part of our critical infrastructure, only 14 currently report anything on SCADA issues to authorities. Simply put, if the incident is not reported to authorities, then it is not included within the Industrial Security Incident Database (ISID). The next issue in reporting SCADA issues is that those 14 organizations that do report to ISID are considered to be the leading edge, hence they are using more current technology perhaps than a typical SCADA operator and would perhaps naturally see lower incident numbers. Security companies have published white papers that suggest a more probable number of annual SCADA incidents is actually 2,000 to 3,000.

At a recent SANS security seminar, featured speaker CIA Analyst Tom Donahue noted that recently declassified information had revealed that cyber criminals had in fact disrupted electrical power in several regions outside of the US and further noted that the goal of the attacks was extortion.

Tools & Traps...

Are SCADA Issues Under-reported?

The most relied upon database of SCADA vulnerabilities, BCIT includes only 100 or so reported incidents. Only 14 of the 200 Fortune 500 companies that are recognized as part of our national infrastructure actively report SCADA incidents. Security companies dismiss the 100 or so incidents noted in the BCIT database as inaccurate and estimate that the actual number of incidents is closer to 2,000 to 3,000 incidents per year.

Early digital SCADA systems were designed for performance, and little if any regard was given to the proper error handling normally associated with network protocols. Hence, many times only a portion of the given protocol was ever properly implemented. Simply put, saving a few bytes of code was considered more important than properly handling protocol errors. After all, SCADA was a closed system and the normal errors associated with network protocols would be nonexistent. Hence, most of the current installed base of SCADA systems in use today utilize protocols that are either inherently insecure by design or that by-and-of themselves are not necessarily insecure but are poorly implemented by the SCADA product vendor, which results in SCADA insecurities. It should come as no surprise that a simple port scan of a SCADA network could in fact cause the entire network to crash because of the lack of proper error handling.

TCP/IP Error Handling Absent in Early SCADA Systems

Imagine living in a world where a common cold could easily kill you—Welcome to the world of SCADA. A simple Port-Scan as typically run within most enterprise networks to determine what ports are open on a SCADA component has the potential of causing the SCADA system to crash due to the improper support of TCP/IP error handling.

Unfortunately, in order to reap the full financial benefits of a SCADA system, interconnection to the enterprise network is necessary to provide real-time process data to enterprise back-end systems. It is this interconnection of SCADA systems and the enterprise network that is the weakest link in SCADA system security.

The first step in understanding the risks associated with SCADA while operating in today's digital world is to accept that SCADA systems have always been designed to operate in closed environments. While most organizations claim that their SCADA system is not connected to their enterprise network it has been estimated that, in reality, 80 to 90 percent of SCADA systems are in fact connected to the enterprise network. It is that connection to the enterprise network that opens the door for Internet hackers to attack SCADA systems.

Interconnection of SCADA and Business Systems Are a Weak Link in SCADA Security

Many believe that it is the interconnection of SCADA and business systems across the enterprise network that poses the greatest risk to SCADA. In other words, SCADA systems were not initially intended to operate within the enterprise environment. At issue is the inability within SCADA components to deal with the exposure to viruses, worms, and malware that are commonplace today within the enterprise network.

Basically, SCADA systems have no inherent ability to cope with the issues commonly found plaguing today's enterprise networks. Connecting the SCADA system to a corporate network dramatically increases risks poised by traditional malware.

A common denominator among most SCADA protocols is that they were nearly always based on a given vendor's proprietary standard and were almost always designed to pass data accurately and quickly between devices with little if any direct regard to security.

Further in some implementations only a portion of a given protocol was implemented in the SCADA device in order to save development time, and perhaps memory and CPU cycles. Unfortunately, it is not uncommon for a SCADA system protocol implementation to have improperly implemented error handling within the given protocol. Hence most of the current installed base of SCADA systems in use today utilize protocols that are either inherently insecure by design or that by-and-of themselves are not necessarily insecure but are poorly implemented by the SCADA product vendor, which results in SCADA insecurities.

Typical high-level weaknesses found in SCADA systems today include:

- Does not require any authentication.
- Does not require any authorization.
- Does not use encryption.
- Does not properly handle errors and exceptions.

These high-level weaknesses open several potential attack vectors:

- Data interception
- Data manipulation
- Denial of service
- Address spoofing
- Unsolicited responses
- Session hijacking
- Protocol / packet fuzzing
- Modification of log data
- Unauthorized control

These attack vectors can lead to potentially disastrous results, such as:

- Altering or otherwise affecting the HMI display screen, which may cause the SCADA operator to take incorrect corrective actions.

- Permitting an unauthorized person to assume control of the SCADA system.

- Disrupting the process that is under the control of the SCADA system.

Tools & Traps...

Typical SCADA High-Level Weaknesses

The lack of authentication, authorization, encryption, and error handling are regarded as the typical high-level weaknesses in SCADA.

Determining the Risks in Your SCADA System

First, a word of caution: Determining the risks within your SCADA system is not as easy as it may first seem. The traditional methods used in determining if vulnerabilities exist within an IT network can wreak havoc within a SCADA network. The simple task of port scanning can bring down a SCADA system if the network error handling was not properly implemented by the manufacturer. Further, care must be taken not to overwhelm the SCADA network with traffic in testing since many SCADA controllers rely upon data passed across the network to continue safe operation. In fact, many SCADA controllers are designed to failover to a safe manual value if they do not receive a set point or other controller variables within a predetermined time period. Hence, it is critical that only technicians that are knowledgeable of the shortcomings inherent to SCADA systems be used for any vulnerability assessment.

Active scanning considerations:

- Use a lab environment first, not a production network, to determine the impact of scanning.

- Be sure the scanning software that is utilized simulates vulnerabilities by testing version levels and so on, rather than simply executing known vulnerabilities.

- Any devices more than five years old should not be targets of any vulnerability scan.

- Be sure that any back-up devices are operational and ready for failover should a primary controller fail during scanning.

- Be sure control system operators are fully informed of the potential for SCADA system failures before any scanning begins.

Passive scanning considerations:

- Passive scanning does not generate any network traffic within the network being tested and is considered a safer alternative to active scanning.

- The rate of passive network discovery is determined by the amount of network traffic and the number of SCADA nodes that are talking.

- Passive scanning can discover hosts, services, and versions that can then be mapped to potential vulnerabilities.

Tools & Traps…

Active Scanning of SCADA Can Itself Pose Serious Risks

The lack of proper and/or complete TCP/IP error handling in early SCADA components can cause disastrous results when the SCADA component is actively scanned. Simply put, if your SCADA system is over 5 years old, active scanning should first be tried in a closed lab environment to determine the risks imposed by such a scan.

Risk Mitigation for SCADA

While most enterprises have a security policy to deal with the operation of the enterprise network, few have policies that address the SCADA environment specifically. With SCADA systems operating today within the inherently insecure world of TCP/IP and often interconnected to the enterprise network and public Internet, a SCADA security policy is a crucial first step in securing the system.

Tools & Traps...

The First Step in Risk Mitigation
Is the development of a SCADA Security Policy

Once policies are in place, they must be continuously updated and monitored to account for changes in the SCADA network, SCADA component software updates, and (as with any enterprise network) the addition and subtraction of users (operators).

A SCADA security policy should (at the least):

1. Require the development and maintenance of a list of all SCADA components and version levels.

2. Require the development and maintenance of diagrams for data flows within the SCADA network and just as importantly between the SCADA network and the enterprise network.

3. Require use of the latest stable software release for all SCADA components.

4. Disable all unnecessary servers and services on SCADA components.

5. Establish a password policy, eliminate the use of shared passwords, and utilize one-time passwords wherever possible.

6. Require the development and maintenance of a policy for a Rule of Least Privilege across the entire SCADA system.

7. Require the use of all available auditing capabilities across the SCADA system.

8. Regularly test all SCADA components for vulnerabilities.

9. Approach security and the hardening of all SCADA workstations and database servers as if they were connected directly to the public Internet.

10. Utilize firewalls to both separate the SCADA network from the enterprise network and segment the SCADA network.

11. Encrypt all communication between enterprise applications and the SCADA system.

Tools & Traps...

Security Considerations for SCADA Servers

When considering the security requirements for servers within the SCADA network, they should be approached as if they were facing the very same risks as that of a server within the enterprise network being directly connected to the public Internet.

With a SCADA security policy in place, the next step in risk mitigation would be the incorporation of technical safeguards to enforce the security policy.

Firewall Considerations for SCADA

A firewall by-and-of-itself is not the Holy Grail, and simply installing one to isolate the SCADA network from the enterprise network and walking away does not fix all the problems. The firewall is a tool where vigilance is required. Risks do not magically go away when you flip the switch on your firewall. While a good firewall offers some security and functionality out of the box, the administrator must take security to an even higher level. The firewall is, in effect, a necessary tool that is part of an overarching approach and philosophy of security. It is a gateway tool for implementing an all-encompassing security policy that defines your entire network's level of access and services when connecting with other networks like the Internet. The following three items are important in making your firewall work for you:

1. Create an appropriate set of perimeter access and content inspection policies.

2. Implement the right type of firewall that is capable of most effectively automating the enforcement of your perimeter security policies.

3. Properly configure the firewall.

Given the right approach and a good understanding of firewall fundamentals, you can stop attacks from crossing into and impacting your SCADA network.

Negative and Positive Security Models in Firewalls

Even before the Internet and Web 2.0 ushered in our current era of threats, network-based systems were still a target, and firewalls evolved very quickly to mitigate the risks. The concept was simple: create a device that prevents undesirable elements from entering the network, while still allowing legitimate access. As such, the firewall's basic task is to control traffic that flows between computer networks. The firewall has evolved considerably, and today there are usually multiple zones of trust, each one with different levels of access. Most early firewalls, and some that are still being offered, work on a "negative" security model that identifies undesirable traffic and prevents it from entering. It's very much like having a list at a country's port of entry, which identifies known criminals. When people travel into the country, their passports are checked against this list, and if they are not on it, they are allowed in. This design is effective to the degree that it catches known criminals, but what about those who have not yet committed any acts of terror, or have not yet been caught for their crimes, or who should also be considered a risk because of their associations or reputation? In fact, it is not always possible to determine whether somebody, or in the case of the network, a particular packet of traffic, is undesirable based on known parameters. The most effective security policy revolves around one statement: "Trust no one." That's why the best firewalls operate on a "positive" security model, which denies all access unless it is explicitly allowed.

Multi-Network Connectivity

At its most basic, think of a firewall as a "control point" computer with two interfaces (typically Ethernet) that is located between two separate networks. A cable connects the first network to the firewall, and a second cable connects the firewall to the second network. All traffic is then blocked, and is not allowed to pass to the other network unless the firewall computer decides, based on its preconfigured rules and policies, that it should be allowed.

Because the firewall has two or more physically separate network interfaces, it is a multi-homed device. This is why firewalls are unlike most other networked devices. Other networked devices, such as servers, workstations, and printers, are connected to networks with only one physical connection (or wireless port), which passes all needed traffic coming and going in both directions, simultaneously. Some vendors and industry observers claim that it is possible to build a network firewall with only one physical interface, but that architecture would have serious limitations and has never been accepted by the market, and it would not be recommended by any serious security practitioners as a primary firewall device.

A firewall should "know," by way of configured policies and rules, which networks to trust more than others. The Internet, for example, is not under the control of the company deploying the firewall, and the content is completely unknown. As such, the Internet is a zone that should be attributed no trust at all, and the firewall that is connected to the Internet should have the highest level of defenses established. But firewalls do far more than just protect internal networks from the perils of the Internet, and the firewall must still be used even to separate traffic flowing between internal networks, even if they are not connected by the Internet. Not all attacks are Internet-based, and internal attacks are unfortunately quite prevalent. As a result, large enterprises usually deploy multiple firewalls, with one for each department, division, or branch. Not only does the firewall protect the company's Internet server from the external Internet, it also protects each departmental sub-network from any risks that may already be inside.

However, an internal departmental network is under control and its content is well known, so it should be a zone with a higher level of trust. The ultimate goal is to provide high-speed, reliable, and tightly controlled connections between networks of differing trust levels, while enforcing a "deny all unless explicitly allowed" security policy.

While some firewalls are more intuitive than others, they still require proper configuration and skill to maintain. Some administrators get a false sense of security because they have a firewall and mistakenly believe it can be plugged in, powered on, and forgotten. In fact, an improperly configured or neglected firewall is more dangerous than having none at all. The firewall is a key component when implementing policy. As such, the firewall itself should be useful in designing that policy, but it is the policy itself that guides how the firewall is used and how effective it becomes.

Reactive and Proactive Solutions

Within the framework of the firewall, and in the case of a Unified Threat Management environment (all of the associated protections such as anti-virus, anti-spam, URL filtering, SSL scanning, and IPS/IDS), the firewall appliance must take both a reactive *and* proactive approach. In many of the first- and second-generation firewalls, it became obvious that being limited to reactive security provided some, but not enough, protection. An example of reactive security is signature-based anti-virus databases, which keep track of known virus signatures to prevent them from entering the network. Similarly, URL filters that rely exclusively on categorized lists prevent users from accessing Web sites that are known to be harmful.

Proactive security comes from several different angles. First and foremost, proactive security comes from the "deny everything that is not explicitly allowed" philosophy. This approach to proactive security is exemplified in the Sidewinder firewall's deeply aware and deeply configurable application-specific security proxies. Proxy-based Web and mail security gateways from numerous companies have recently emerged into the market as well to (basically) plug the holes in traditional firewalls protecting most corporate networks today. Deeply configurable application-specific proxies will eliminate most attacks that have not yet been detected and defined by simply sloughing them off as superfluous to the use of the company's applications (in other words, not needed) or because they violate the fundamental use of the applications when checked against the Internet RFCs. An extra layer of proactive security comes from the inclusion of a reputation-based system, which acts as a sort of virtual credit agency to determine a precise reputation score for every sender.

Reactive signature-based systems are quite good at catching malware attacks that have already been detected and included in signature databases, and these sorts of systems play an important role in unified threat management. However, there is a growing body of malware that has not yet been detected, and in such cases, signature-based reactive solutions must themselves be secured within a more comprehensive and proactive security software environment. Attacks that have not yet been catalogued, known as "zero-hour" attacks, are on the increase. Signature engines simply cannot keep ahead of large instantaneous malware outbreaks spewing out of zombie networks today. Zombie machines (PCs connected to the Internet that can be remotely controlled at will from across the Internet by the bad guys) are responsible for the majority of spam, viruses, and "for profit" schemes like phishing attacks on the Internet today.

Criminal elements lease access to thousands or tens of thousands of zombie PCs to create malicious networks of computers called botnets. These botnets are used to distribute whatever the criminal or hacker wants them to distribute and pose a serious threat to SCADA systems. With hundreds of thousands of computers being silently hijacked and turned into zombies on a daily basis, corporate networks suffer a constant stream of unwanted and dangerous traffic. To combat this threat, in addition to being able to recognize a threat with a signature database, the security system must also be able to tell if a remote computer is actually a zombie machine. The next generation of proactive security tools is being built with this in mind. These systems are called reputation-based systems.

Firewall Inspection Methods

The level of protection that any firewall is able to provide in securing a private network when connected to the public Internet is directly related to the architecture(s) chosen for the firewall by the respective vendor. Generally speaking, most commercially available firewalls utilize one or more of the following firewall architectures:

- Static packet filter

- Stateful packet filter

- Circuit-level gateway

- Application-level gateway (proxy)

- Intrusion prevention gateway

- Deep packet inspection

- Unified Threat Management (UTM)

Static Packet Filter

Packet filtering firewalls are among the oldest firewall architectures. The static packet filtering firewall operates only at the network layer (layer 3) of the OSI model and does not differentiate between application protocols. This type of firewall decides whether to accept or deny individual packets, based on examining fields in the packet's IP and protocol headers. The static packet filter does not impact performance to any noticeable degree, and its low processing requirements made this an attractive option early on when compared to other firewalls that dragged down responsiveness. However, today's higher-level firewalls deliver excellent performance as well. In addition, faster networks are more capable of handling the greater processing requirements of a firewall that operates at a higher level of the OSI stack.

The packet filtering firewall filters IP packets based on source and destination IP address, and source and destination port. The packet filter may lack logging facilities, which would make it impractical for an organization that has compliance and reporting requirements to which they must adhere. Also, because it examines only the packet headers, attackers can bypass the static packet filter with simple spoofing techniques, since the filter cannot tell the difference between a true and a forged address. Another limitation is that for larger installations, the static packet filter becomes unwieldy because packet-filtering rules are examined in sequential order, and care must be taken when entering rules into the rule base. Another inherent limitation is that the static packet filter does not examine the entire packet, which makes it possible for an attacker to hide malicious commands inside unexamined headers or within the payload itself. Lastly, the static packet filter is not state-aware, so the administrator is required to configure rules for both sides of the conversation. Today, this type of firewall is considered very basic and limited, and may even be included in operating systems as an "extra."

The Stateful Packet Filter

The next step in firewall evolution came with the stateful packet filtering firewall (or the stateful inspection firewall as it is often referred to). This type of firewall has the same limitations as the static packet filtering firewall, with the exception of being state-aware. The stateful packet filter still operates at the network layer of the OSI model, although some may extend into the transport layer (layer 4) to collect state information. Despite the stateful packet filter being application-unaware, it does offer limited advantages over the basic static packet filter.

Like the static packet filter, the stateful packet filter examines each packet's IP and protocol headers to determine whether each packet should be allowed or denied. Also like the static packet filter, it does not examine the packet payload. The fact that it is stateful means that the packet filter is aware of the difference between a new and an established connection, which has some advantages regarding efficiency. Once a connection has been established, it resides in a table in RAM, and subsequent packets are compared to this table. If a packet is part of an existing connection, it is then allowed to pass without further inspection. As a result, it is not necessary to parse the packet filter rule base for every single packet that enters the firewall.

Although there is some performance gain over the static filter, many stateful packet filters operate on a single-threaded process, which cannot take full advantage of symmetrical multiprocessing, and which limits the performance gain possible. Those stateful filters that do support SMP afford up to a 30-percent increase in performance. Nonetheless, the performance advantage gained by packet filtering in general is today negligible, due to the existence of faster processors.

The Circuit-Level Gateway

The circuit-level gateway extends the concept of the packet filter by first performing the same packet filtering operations as the firewalls mentioned earlier, and then adding the extra step of verification of proper handshaking and the legitimacy of the sequence of numbers used in establishing the connection. As such, the circuit-level gateway operates at the Session layer (layer 5). The circuit-level gateway effectively breaks the normal client server model, thereby eliminating a direct connection between the malicious hacker and the protected server and/or SCADA component. The circuit-level gateway examines more data than a standard packet filter. In addition to examining the source and destination address and source and destination port, it examines and validates TCP and user datagram protocol (UDP) sessions before opening a connection. The older packet filter bases its decisions about accepting or denying a packet on the source and destination address and the source port number and destination port number. The circuit-level gateway also adds handshaking and sequence numbers to the equation. It therefore has more data to use in deciding whether to admit any given packet.

The circuit-level gateway has about the same performance metrics as the packet filter, and since it operates at a low level of the OSI model, it does not affect network performance significantly. The disadvantage is that once the connection has been established, any application can run across that connection, because the circuit-level gateway filters packets only at the Session and Network layers—not the Application layer. Nevertheless, the circuit-level gateway still does not examine the data content of the packets being sent.

A hybrid approach for SCADA would be to take advantage of the circuit-level gateway's inherent ability to break the client server model and to then apply signatures to inspect the packet before allowing it to pass to the SCADA system (Figure 2.3).

Figure 2.3 A Hybrid Approach to SCADA

Application-Level Gateway (Proxy)

Operating on the application layer (the highest layer of the OSI model), the application-level gateway, like the other filters mentioned here, intercepts and examines packets that come into, and go out of, the firewall. In addition, it runs proxies, which prevent direct connection between a trusted server or client and an untrusted host. The proxies are application-specific, and they examine the entire packet assembly (unlike packet filtering and circuit-level gateways that do not assemble packet sessions). Because each proxy is application-specific (for example, the HTTP proxy can only copy, forward, and filter HTTP traffic), packets may be unable to access services for which there is no proxy, depending on the security software that you choose. For example, if an application-level gateway only runs FTP and HTTP proxies, only packets generated by these services can pass by the firewall, while all other services are blocked.

This type of firewall therefore has a stronger security infrastructure, because:

1. It eliminates the need for a direct connection between a trusted client or server and an untrusted host.

2. It examines the entire packet assembly, including the assembled payload in context.

3. It facilitates the preferred "deny all unless explicitly allowed" policy by offering deep configuration options over how a protected application can be communicated with.

The proxies are able to filter particular information—on specific individual commands in the application protocols, the proxies are designed to copy, forward, and filter. For example, an FTP gateway could filter multiple commands to allow a high degree of granularity on permission levels for specific users of the protected FTP service.

Because it inspects the complete packet, and because it is application-specific (applications that do not have proxies installed cannot run), the application gateway is one of the most secure firewall architectures available. This type of firewall eliminates many different classes of attacks that could otherwise penetrate firewalls that operate only on lower levels of the OSI model.

Because it breaks the direct connection to the server behind the firewall, the application proxy eliminates the risk of an entire class of covert channel attacks. In addition, the application gateway, when run on a symmetric multiprocessing appliance, consumes only a negligible amount of processing and has little impact on network performance.

Simply described, the path of a packet across a strong application proxy is as follows:

1. The new packet arrives at the external interface. Layer 4 data is tested to validate that the IP source and destination, as well as the service ports, are acceptable to the firewall's security policy.

2. For every "good" packet, a new empty datagram is created on the internal side of the firewall. This eliminates the possibility of an attacker hiding malicious data in an unused protocol header.

3. Protocol anomaly testing is performed on the packet to validate that all protocol headers are within defined protocol specifications.

4. The application proxy applies command-level controls and validates these against the user's permission levels.

5. After the packet has been determined to be protocol-compliant and the application-level commands validated against policy, the permitted content is copied to the new datagram on the internal side of the firewall.

Tools & Traps…

Current Application Proxy Limitations in SCADA Security

While the application proxy clearly raises protocol and application awareness to the highest level possible, its use in SCADA security is today limited due to its lack of SCADA-specific application and protocol support. The use of a circuit-level gateway to break the client server model, along with integrated IPS to compare the traffic against known attack signatures, may currently be a more effective solution.

Intrusion Prevention Gateway

The best modern firewalls go beyond even the capabilities of the application-level proxy firewall with the addition of an integrated intrusion prevention system (IPS). This type of firewall not only examines the data contained in the application payload, but also interprets the intent of that data. Using a combination of pattern matching, heuristics, statistics, behavioral patterns, and reputation analysis, the IPS is able to "sense" malicious activity before it penetrates the network.

Most IPS gateways use a library of signatures, which contain signatures of malicious activity and known vulnerabilities, against which packets are compared as they cross the gateway. The best operation of signature databases will include an automatic frequent update to minimize "zero-hour" attacks that cross the network threshold before the signature has had a chance to make it into the database. However, the alarming frequency of new vulnerabilities and malicious attacks means that there is still a very high likelihood that something will be missed by the IPS. Therefore, an IPS that is strictly based on signatures is limited and exposes the network to an unnecessary risk. The IPS should be used as a complement to, and not a replacement for, an effective Application-layer proxy firewall defense. Furthermore, the IPS should go beyond signature-based defenses to also include predictive and reputation-based technologies that evaluate unknown risks and prevent "zero-hour" attacks.

Deep Packet Inspection

"Deep packet inspection" may sound advanced, but the name is somewhat deceptive. This type of firewall still does little more than inspect packets against outdated signatures, and does nothing to detect and prevent unknown attacks. The signature-based model has merit and it *does* afford a rapid response, but relying exclusively on a signature-based model is dangerous. A simple way to circumvent a deep packet inspection firewall is just to add a little white space in the data before or after a command. White space is usually tolerated by most applications, and the addition of a blank space or two would cause the signature to fail to match the signature database.

With hundreds of new vulnerabilities being detected every week, developing new signatures and adding them to the inspection database is a difficult task.

Tools & Traps...

Deep Packet Inspection Limitations in SCADA Security

With hundreds of new vulnerabilities being detected every week and the recent trend in increased attack obfuscation continuing for vendors, developing new signatures and adding them to the inspection database is a difficult if not increasingly impossible task.

The deep packet inspection firewall, like most stateful inspection firewalls, focuses on finding, and subsequently denying, bad packets. In fact, the most effective approach, as demonstrated in strong application proxy firewalls, is to allow packets that are known to be good, and then deny everything else. Since most protocols on the Internet are standards-based, the best approach is to create an application proxy that is protocol-aware, and use the standards as the basis for deciding whether or not to admit a packet. The opposite approach taken by deep packet inspection leaves the network vulnerable, because it requires frequent updates whenever any new type of attack is unleashed.

Another major limitation of the deep packet inspection is the lack of protocol anomaly detection. These firewalls, unlike a strong application-proxy firewall, often still take the less secure approach of seeking out "bad" packets and dropping them, and then allowing everything else in that has not been identified as "bad."

Unified Threat Management (UTM)

Unified Threat Management is the latest and most innovative development in firewalling. According to IDC, a leading analyst firm, UTM security appliances unify and integrate multiple security features onto a single hardware platform, including network firewall capabilities, network intrusion detection and prevention, and gateway anti-virus. Some UTM offerings go further, incorporating an anti-spam and URL filtering capability on a hardened operating system as well. The UTM segment is the fastest growing segment of the firewall market.

Reasons exist even beyond convenience and practicality for integrating multiple threat protection applications into the same appliance and under the same interface. Many modern attacks today are blended attacks, which do not utilize any one-attack vector exclusively. For example, a blended attack may target multiple protocols, such as e-mail (SMTP) and the Web (HTTP), and it may do this by first sending out an e-mail, (which in itself may not contain any malware) that then tricks the recipient into clicking a Web link. The recipient is then taken to an infected site, where the malware is downloaded onto the computer. Mitigation of this sort of attack can take place either in the e-mail messaging protection (anti-spam) application, which would recognize the nature of the attack, or in the second stage, when the user attempts to go to the infected Web site, it would be blocked by the URL filter.

The addition of URL filtering is an important part of UTM that is often not included by other UTM vendors. URL filtering is often a first line of defense, especially against zero-hour threats. In addition, spam has also grown into a complicated and dangerous threat, and it is imperative to reduce the risk of spam with a best-of-breed anti-spam capability integrated into the UTM appliance.

Summary

SCADA systems evolved out of isolated pneumatic and analog control systems and are simply not equipped to play a part in today's Internet-connected Web 2.0 world. Even traditional network security procedures such as port scanning (to determine the open ports on a network-connected device) can wreak havoc within a SCADA network.

The first step in SCADA risk mitigation is establishing a SCADA network security policy. Second would be bringing all SCADA component software and firmware up to current stable revision levels. Next would be to eliminate the security issue with what has been regarded as the weakest link in SCADA—the interconnection to the corporate network. Significant risk mitigation can be obtained by installing a firewall between the SCADA network and the corporate network. However, care must be taken in the selection of the firewall architecture. Put simply, current popular solutions are not able to mitigate the risk that the SCADA network is exposed to when connected to the corporate network. The most effective firewall architecture at this time is a circuit-Level gateway that first breaks the client server model and then also applies IPS signatures for known attacks.

Solutions Fast Track

Just What Is SCADA?

☑ SCADA systems evolved out of pneumatic and analog control systems. Once using proprietary technologies, SCADA systems now use generally available TCP/IP networking and are exposed to the very same risks as any other enterprise network.

Common SCADA Components

☑ Remote Terminal Units (RTUs)

☑ Programmable Logic Controllers (PLC)

☑ Human Machine Interfaces (HMIs)

☑ Distributed Control Systems (DCSs)

☑ Hybrid controllers

☑ Event loggers

The Architecture Most Common to SCADA Systems

☑ Most SCADA systems are installed in a distributed architecture.

The First Step in Mitigating Risk in a SCADA Environment

☑ The first step In risk mitigation is the development of a SCADA security policy. Once policies are in place, they must be continuously updated and monitored to account for changes in the SCADA network, SCADA component software updates, and (as with any enterprise network) the addition and subtraction of users (operators).

Typical High-Level Weaknesses Found in SCADA Systems

☑ Typical high-level weaknesses found in SCADA systems in use today are that they:

☑ Do not require any authentication

☑ Do not require any authorization

☑ Do not use encryption

☑ Do not properly handle errors and exceptions

The Weakest Link in SCADA Systems

☑ Most agree that the weakest link in SCADA security is the interconnection between the SCADA network and the enterprise network. This interconnection effectively can connect the SCADA system in some ways to the public Internet.

Eliminating Interconnection Risks with a Firewall

☑ A great deal of the associated risk can be mitigated with the selection of the correct firewall. However, firewall architecture is critical to the amount of risk mitigation that will be gained. Simply put, the most popular firewalls in use today cannot afford any meaningful risk mitigation in a SCADA environment.

The Firewall Architecture that Affords the Highest Risk Mitigation in a SCADA Environment

☑ A circuit-level gateway that first breaks the client server model and then also applies IPS signatures for known attacks is the most effective firewall architecture since it provides the highest level of risk mitigation.

Resources

☑ With the increased awareness of the need to secure SCADA in an effort to protect our critical infrastructure, a growing number of SCADA security resources are available on the Internet. The following list offers resources that the author has found useful.

☑ The Center For SCADA Security, www.sandia.gov/scada/home.htm

☑ DigitalBond – Securing Critical Infrastructure, www.digitalbond.com/

☑ The Cyber Security Alliance, www.csialliance.org/issues/scada/

☑ 21 Steps to Improve the Cyber Security of SCADA Networks, www.oe.netl. doe.gov/docs/prepare/21stepsbooklet.pdf

☑ SANS – Security for Critical Infrastructure, www.sans.org/reading_room/ whitepapers/warfare/1644.php

☑ Tennable Security – Nessus Plug-Ins for SCADA, http://blog.tenablesecurity. com/2006/12/nessus_3_scada_.html

☑ IBM – SCADA Security Best Practices, http://www-935.ibm.com/services/ us/index.wss/offering/iss/a1027203

Frequently Asked Questions

Q: Why all the concern about SCADA security today?

A: SCADA has evolved from proprietary pneumatic to proprietary analog systems and now today to digital systems interconnected over TCP/IP. In the shift away from the use of proprietary systems to the use of TCP/IP SCADA has lost a great deal of its historical Security-by-Obscurity. Further; today's SCADA systems when connected to the enterprise network to share data with back-end systems effectively exposes the SCADA to all of the risks associated with the enterprise network and if that enterprise is connected to the public Internet then the SCADA is also then exposed to all of the risks of the public Internet as well.

Q: How many SCADA security incidents are reported annually?

A: The annual reporting to British Columbia Institute of Technology (BCIT) SCADA database for the past year was just over 100 verified incidents. However, security experts believe the actual number of incidents is between 2,000 and, 3000 because like network security–related incidents, they are under-reported.

Q: Why can't I download one of the open source network vulnerability scanners and run it against my SCADA network?

A: SCADA systems more than five years old were known to have been placed in service with incomplete or missing TCP/IP error handling capabilities. A simple port scan could crash the SCADA network. So, it is recommended to configure a lab environment of "like" components and perform scans to determine if the components are vulnerable to error handling issues.

Q: Why can't I just install a popular firewall between the enterprise and my SCADA network to mitigate my SCADA risks?

A: Today's most popular firewalls are, in fact, popular because of their ease of use, and their low cost and low impact on the network—NOT because of the risk mitigation they provide.

Q: What is the problem with connecting my SCADA system to the corporate network so we can use process data in our back-end systems?

A: Connecting the SCADA system to the enterprise network poses nearly the same risks as connecting the SCADA network directly to the public Internet. Worms, viruses, and malware are common within the enterprise network and can be a major issue within a SCADA network. However, when connected to the enterprise network through a properly configured application firewall, these risks are minimized.

Q: What is the first step in reducing my SCADA risks?

A: As with network security, the first step is a security policy to define the ground rules.

Q: There are so many kinds of firewalls, which one affords the maximum risk mitigation in the SCADA environment?

A: Theoretically, an application-level gateway affords maximum risk mitigation. However, they do not currently offer full support for the many proprietary SCADA protocols and applications. Hence, a circuit-level gateway that first breaks the client server model and then also applies IPS signatures for known attacks is most effective.

Q: Deep inspection is a popular firewall methodology. Why do you recommend not using it for SCADA?

A: Deep inspection does not break the client server model. Thus, a malicious hacker would have a direct connection to the protected SCADA component. Deep inspection does not provide for any protocol anomaly detection, and in SCADA, due to historically poor TCP/IP error handling, even a poorly formed packet for a given protocol can wreak havoc in a SCADA network. Lastly, they rely upon a negative security model that can only protect against attacks for which it has a specific signature. Any packet that it cannot identify is simply passed along to the protected server.

Chapter 3

SCADA Security Assessment Methodology

Greg Miles, *(Ph.D., CISSP#24431, CISM#0300338, IAM, IEM) co-author of Security Assessment: Case Studies for implementing the NSA IAM (Syngress Publishing, ISBN 1-932266-96-8), Network Security Evaluation: Using the NSA IEM (Syngress Publishing, ISBN: 1-597490-35-0), and Security Interviews Exposed: Secrets to Landing your Next Information Security Job (Wiley Publishing, ISBN-10: 0471779873) is the President, and Chief Financial Officer of Security Horizon, Inc. Security Horizon is a Global, Veteran-Owned Small Business headquartered in Colorado Springs, Colorado. Security Horizon provides global information security professional services, training, and publishes The Security Journal, a quarterly online publication. Greg is a U.S. Air Force Veteran and has been supporting the technology and security community for the last 22+ years. Greg's background includes work with NSA, NASA, and DISA. Greg has supported efforts covering security assessments, evaluations, policy, penetration testing, incident response, and computer forensics.*

Greg holds a Ph.D. in Engineering Management from Kennedy Western University, a master's degree in Management Administration from Central Michigan University, and a bachelor's degree in Electrical Engineering (with a concentration in Control Systems and Power Systems) from the University of Cincinnati. Greg is a member of the Information System Security Association (ISSA) and the Information System Audit and Control Association (ISACA). He is also Adjunct Faculty for the University of Advancing Technology (www.uat.edu).

Introduction

Supervisory Control and Data Acquisition (SCADA) Systems have evolved over the years. With the growth of technology, the desire to simplify, the desire to remote manage, and the need to reduce labor costs, SCADA has moved to be more in line with traditional TCP/IP networks. With this evolution, the need for effective, comprehensive assessments of SCADA systems has never been greater. Old paradigms must change, organizations need to understand the threats they face, and appropriate protection measures must be incorporated. This chapter will discuss the need for SCADA security assessments and provide a comprehensive approach to conducting SCADA security assessments.

Why Do Assessments on SCADA Systems?

Historically, SCADA systems have been separate non-Internet-connected systems that provide the "command and control" for critical infrastructure. With the advent of technology and the desire to implement this technology to make communications and support easier and faster, SCADA systems have evolved into being very much like your typical office network. One of the challenges though is that the mentality concerning SCADA system security hasn't always been embraced. Some organizations still don't understand that the threat to SCADA systems has dramatically increased over the last several years due to these network-like connections. "Security by obscurity" is no longer an option for SCADA security.

Tools & Traps...

Security by Obscurity

"Security by obscurity" is no longer an option for SCADA security. SCADA systems are a network presence and face significant threats and vulnerabilities. This requires a paradigm change for many personnel working in the critical infrastructure business.

Assessments Are the Right Thing to Do

Protecting the confidentiality, integrity, and availability of critical process, operational, corporate, and customer information should be enough of a motivator for organizations to assure that their SCADA systems are protected. This is the concept of due diligence and is generally referenced by considering whether the security protections compare sufficiently to what would be considered normal and reasonable in the industry. Organizations must want to protect our critical infrastructure from malicious hackers, botnets, Denial-of-Service attacks, viruses, corporate espionage, and human error.

Events such as the 2003 Northeast power outage that affected parts of the United States and Canada, the 2008 Florida power outage that affected large parts of Florida, and the 2007 sponsored hack at the Idaho National Laboratories where a hacker was able to blow up a generator should be a pretty serious wake-up call for the industry. No longer is SCADA separate and not exposed. It is very much out there as a target, with enough serious threats to warrant significant attention to the protection of SCADA and the information that is processed, transmitted, and/or stored.

Assessments Are Required

Homeland Security Presidential Directive (HSPD)-7 talks about the protection of critical infrastructure. SCADA systems are generally serving a command-and-control function within this critical infrastructure and therefore have a direct mandate for protection. Other requirements come from the North American Electric Reliability Council (NERC). Believe it or not, guidance is available on how to implement and protect SCADA.

Information Protection Requirements

United States Federal Government and Department of Defense (DoD) have done a great deal of work on information protection and information assurance. The National Institute of Standards and Technology (NIST) has developed an entire series of special publications with information on things to do to protect systems. The National Security Agency (NSA) has developed and provided two methodologies that you can be certified in for assessing organizations and information systems for vulnerabilities. The NSA INFOSEC Assessment Methodology (IAM) focuses on an organizational view of vulnerabilities, while the NSA INFOSEC Evaluation Methodology (IEM) focuses on finding technical vulnerabilities within the information systems that process, transmit, and/or store critical information.

This author is a firm believer that if you study the various standards out there for any industry, greater than 80 percent of the requirements are the same. These commonsense requirements reflect a best practice approach to protecting critical information. As we discuss the standards and methodologies in this chapter, you will see some of this reflected in the comparisons.

National Institute of Standards and Technology (NIST) Guidance

NIST has defined a layered security model that has 17 control families (Table 3.1), which covers a tremendous amount of security protection mechanisms. This information can be found in NIST Special Publication (SP) 800-53, Recommended Security Controls for Federal Information Systems. SCADA systems are not necessarily Federal Information Systems; however, NIST's work lays an excellent foundation for security within organizations.

Table 3.1 NIST Control Families

Class	Control Family
Management	Risk Assessment
Management	Planning
Management	System and Services Acquisition
Management	Certification, Accreditation, and Security Assessments
Operational	Personnel Security
Operational	Physical and Environmental Protection
Operational	Contingency Planning
Operational	Configuration Management
Operational	Maintenance
Operational	System and Information Integrity
Operational	Media Protection
Operational	Incident Response
Operational	Awareness and Training
Technical	Identification and Authentication
Technical	Access Control
Technical	Audit and Accountability
Technical	System and Communications Protection

North American Electric Reliability Council (NERC) Critical Infrastructure Protection (CIP) Standards

NERC (www.nerc.com) works with the U.S. Department of Energy and the U.S. Department of Homeland Security to coordinate security needs and requirements. This collaboration allowed NERC the opportunity to create a series of Critical Infrastructure Protection Standards. These standards are:

- CIP-001 – Sabotage Reporting
- CIP-002 – Critical Cyber Asset Identification
- CIP-003 – Security Management Controls
- CIP-004 – Personnel and Training
- CIP-005 – Electronic Security Perimeter(s)
- CIP-006 – Physical Security of Critical Cyber Assets
- CIP-007 – Systems Security Management
- CIP-008 – Incident Reporting and Response Planning
- CIP-009 – Recovery Plans for Critical Cyber Assets

Water Infrastructure Security Enhancement (WISE)

The American Water Works Association, the American Society of Civil Engineers, and the Water Environment Federation have taken a grant from the United States Environmental Protection Agency to develop WISE (Water Infrastructure Security Enhancement). WISE provides security guidance for water and wastewater/storm water utilities. These voluntary (so far) standards are heavily dependent upon physical security in the water utilities, but WISE does address an entire process of risk assessment and risk management that can easily be transitioned into supporting information security needs. It is a good start and may lead to greater guidance on the technical security as well. More information on WISE can be found at www.awwa.org/science/wise/.

The Critical Infrastructure Information Act of 2002

The Critical Infrastructure Information Act of 2002 and subsequent procedure clarifications established how Critical Infrastructure Information (CII) is received, validated, handled, stored, marked, and used. SCADA Systems have both direct and indirect involvement with CII. The United States Department of Homeland Security defines CII as information not normally in the public domain (including system, facility, and operation security information) that is associated with the security of critical infrastructure or protected systems.

An Approach to SCADA Information Security Assessments

A methodology for conducting a security assessment is a process that utilizes a well-defined framework to identify the potential security vulnerabilities and determine what corrective measures must be implemented to protect the confidentiality, integrity, and availability of SCADA data. Figure 3.1 represents a logical flow diagram of the security assessment process. The National Security Agency (NSA) INFOSEC Assessment Methodology (IAM) and the INFOSEC Evaluation Methodology (IEM) are the cornerstone of the assessment process discussed in this chapter.

Figure 3.1 Security Assessment Flow Diagram

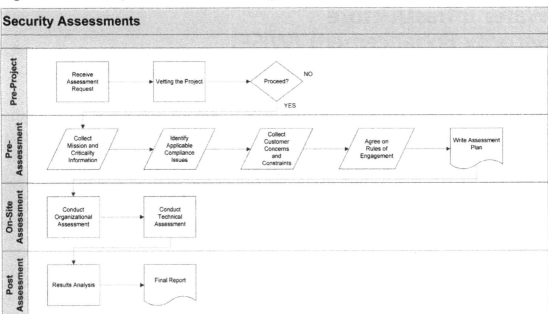

Prior to any project starting, several considerations must be taken into account to assure a complete understanding of the requirements. The pre-project activities will then lead into the three primary phases of the assessment, which are Pre-Assessment, On-Site Assessment, and Post-Assessment. Each phase will be outlined in the following sections. Table 3.2 provides a high-level breakdown of the activities that occur during the full assessment process.

Table 3.2 The Assessment Process

Pre-Project Activities	Pre-Assessment Phase	On-Site Phase	Post-Assessment Phase
Receive the Assessment request.	Refine customer needs.	Explore and confirm the information and conclusions made during the Pre-Assessment Phase.	Finalize analysis.
Vet the assessment with the customer.	Gain an understanding of the customer mission.	Perform data gathering and validation through interviews, documentation, and system demonstrations.	Develop SVCM and OVCM information.
Research the organization.	Gain an understanding of the criticality of the customer's information.	Conduct technical scanning to determine technical vulnerabilities.	Prepare and coordinate a final report.
Research applicable regulatory and policy requirements.	Determine customer impact if confidentiality, integrity, and/or availability is lost.	Provide initial analysis and feedback to the customer.	
Determine if it is a baseline activity or a repeat assessment.	Identify systems, including system boundaries.		
Make a go/no-go decision.	Determine customer concerns and constraints.		
	Coordinate logistics with the customer.		
	Write the Assessment Plan.		

Pre-Project Activities

Pre-project activities include several steps that assist the assessment providers in assuring a basic understanding of the security needs of the customer. Several primary actions in the pre-project area are important to prepare the assessors for conducting the assessment process. These include:

- Vetting the assessment request
- Gaining management and technical buy-in for the assessment
- Researching the organization
- Researching the current regulatory and policy requirements
- Determining whether the action is a baseline activity or a repeated assessment
- Making a go/no-go decision

Vetting the Assessment Request

Vetting, in this case, is simply assuring that the customer is getting both what they expect and what they need from the assessment process. Many times, organizations will catch hold of a buzzword like "penetration testing," "assessment," or "evaluation" without having an understanding of what the terms mean. A good approach to vetting is to spend quality time with the customer discussing the positive and negative aspects of each of the processes and explaining what the customer can expect at the end of the process, including deliverables.

The vetting process is accomplished by a combination of direct interaction with the customer and a small scoping questionnaire. It is then reinforced by educating the customer on the standard best practices for an assessment and any supporting regulations or policies that are applicable. Without the vetting process, you cannot understand or meet customer expectations, which can lead to project failure.

Gaining Buy-In from Management and Technical Personnel

Getting buy-in for the assessment from both the management staff and technical staff is essential to a successful project. Buy-in helps reinforce the importance of the assessment process and brings the organization's attention to the importance and benefits of conducting an assessment within the organization. Without buy-in, official and unofficial roadblocks or constraints may be put on the assessment team, which could lead to project failure. Work hard on the front-end of the project to assure this buy-in, which will assist in a good experience and a smooth-running assessment.

Management Buy-In

Management support for the assessment is absolutely required since management does several things that will drive the success or failure of the project. For instance, it sets the tone of the organization and the necessity to show how important security is to the organization. Management will also enforce the necessity of staff cooperating with, and supporting, the assessment team.

To gain management buy-in, include them in the process. Help them feel ownership of the information, the determinations, and the responsibility to assure security. The use of "Fear-Uncertainty-Doubt" (otherwise known as the FUD factor) as a tool for getting management support should only be used as a last resort. A better way is to help management understand considerations such as:

- Cost Avoidance
- Return on Investment (ROI)
- Regulatory Compliance
- Education
- Information Criticality, System Criticality, and Impact

Technical Staff Buy-In

Can you treat the technical staff the same way you treat management? The answer is, of course, NO! Technical staff will think of things from a different approach than management. Technical staff buy-in is also essential to the success of the project, however, so spend some quality time with the technical staff early in the assessment process. To gain technical staff buy-in, you must:

- Sell the assessment as an educational experience
- Show that you are there to help, not hurt, the organization
- Involve the technical staff in the process
- Demonstrate your knowledge and capabilities without being arrogant
- Develop a rapport with the technical staff

Researching the Organization

Another important step in understanding your customer is to research publicly available information about the organization. This will help display your interest in the customer, plus give you some points of discussion and clarification about the organization. Sources of information for this include:

- **The customer's Web site** Shows how the organization wants to be seen by the public.

- **The competitors of the customer Web sites** Shows the potential areas competitors see as important and may identify some deficiencies, as well as additional questions to ask the organization.

- **Whois** With a "whois" query, you can input a URL and learn what IP address is associated with that URL. In this case, it helps you understand who a customer's Internet service provider (ISP) might be and other possible interconnections within the customer environment.

- **Arin.net (American Registry for Internet Numbers)** Utilizes a special "whois" query of its database through entering an IP range; it will show ownership information of that range of IPs.

- **10Q/10K Reports** These are required quarterly (Q) and annual (K) reports that must be done by public companies to report the status of their business. It includes information like locations, employees, and so on, and may be useful in determining if there are areas of the business that may have been missed for assessment purposes.

- **Business discussion boards** These are Internet locations or blogs which discuss businesses in both a positive and/or negative way. These discussion boards can provide some useful information about the culture of the organization. However, you must be cautious since some of the information is more opinion- or emotion-driven than fact-driven.

- **Internet Search Engines** Any of the Internet search engines can help you find useful information beyond the organization's Web site. You might find articles written about the organization; press releases on products, services, or partnerships; and information about the corporation or leadership of the organization. This will help in better understanding the mission of the organization and its political and leadership structure.

TIP

Learn as much as possible about the customer before starting the project. This will assist in the assessment team's ability to effectively facilitate the assessment process.

Researching Regulatory and Policy Requirements

Most organizations are faced with the reality of falling under some kind of regulatory, legislative, or industry requirements. Especially when dealing with SCADA systems and other systems that affect critical infrastructure. Homeland Security Presidential Directive (HSPD) 7 drives the requirement for protecting critical infrastructure.

The pre-project efforts involve identifying the applicable regulations, legislation, and industry policies. This will vary between different organizations, and this research is essential to assure that you gather the appropriate requirements. You are conducting this research prior to the start of the project so you can talk coherently about the drivers and impacts within the organization. This does not mean you don't have to ask the organization about what they must follow since there may be some unique aspects of their business that must be considered. The following is just a starter list of the different regulatory or legislative requirements the organization may be affected by:

- **HIPAA** Health Information Portability and Accountability Act
- **SOX** Sarbanes-Oxley
- **PCI** Payment Card Industry
- **GLBA** Gramm-Leach-Bliley Act
- **FERPA** Family Educational Rights and Privacy Act
- **NERC** North American Electric Reliability Corporation
- **FERC** Federal Energy Regulatory Commission

Determining if this Is a Baseline Assessment or a Repeat Assessment

You are always hopeful this is not the first assessment that is being conducted on the SCADA system. However, due to the fact that SCADA security has been largely ignored over the years, this may very well be the first security assessment conducted. In that case, it is the baseline assessment. The value of it being a repeat assessment would be the existing information you can pull from to start the process. But if it is a baseline assessment, you need to expect to spend more time on the front-end of the project to document and better understand what is currently in place within the assessed organization.

Making a Go/No-Go Decision

Every project has a go/no-go decision point. In most cases, it will be a "Go"; however, if you cannot get management and technical support, or if there are severe limitations placed on the assessment team, you may have to make the difficult decision of "No-Go."

Pre-Assessment Activities

The Pre-Assessment process is an essential activity that will provide a great deal of information and important mechanisms to assure that the organization gains a level of buy-in from both management and technical staff.

The Pre-Assessment process provides the following important identification activities:

- Organizational mission
- Critical information
- Impact considerations
- Information criticality matrices
- Critical systems
- Defining of security objectives
- Logical and physical boundaries
- Rules of engagement, concerns, and constraints
- Legal authorization
- Writing the Assessment Plan

Determining the Organizational Mission

Understanding the organization mission assists in the remaining activities of the assessment. The mission will provide the final determination of what the security objectives and security requirements are for the organization. It will also drive the critical information considerations, impacts, and will lead to some of the concerns and constraints. To obtain this information, you must talk with the customer and take the information from the research completed in the pre-project activities. An example of a simplified organization mission might be: "Provide reliable electric power to the state of California while operating safely, securely, and within the federal, state, and regulatory guidelines." This will be documented in the Assessment Plan.

Identifying Critical Information

Critical information is simply the information that the organization requires to function. There is a tendency for firms to immediately jump to systems without thinking about what information is important to the organization. One aspect of critical information identification is that it must be done with the customer. In the end, it must be accepted by the organization as their information.

In order to get this critical information, a brainstorm session is typically done with various senior members of the organization in a brainstorming session. You will ask them, "What is the information you must have to make your organization function or to meet your mission?" You will then take that information and roll it up into a manageable set of critical information types. Please understand, this is not an easy process. You will need to spend a day or two with senior members of the organization to sort out this information. Some examples of possible information types might include:

- Power Consumption Information
- Generator Status Information
- Pump Station Information
- Personnel Information
- Scheduling Information
- Customer Information
- Billing Information

The lists will vary by organization and according to the industries in which the organizations function. You cannot do a "cookie cutter" listing of information types even if the organizations are in the same industry. Each organization will have different areas of concern, different customers, and different business processes, all of which will drive different critical information types.

Example: Information Criticality

The Organization for Optimal Power Supply (OOPS) example will be utilized throughout the rest of the chapter—for example, purposes under permission from National Security Agency (NSA) INFOSEC Assurance Training and Rating Program (IATRP). More information on IATRP can be found at www.iatrp.com.

Business Description

The Organization for Optimal Power Supply (OOPS) provides electricity to 1/20th of the United States' citizens. They constantly monitor power consumption and redirect power according to demands. This includes initiating or terminating operations of generator stations.

Historically, OOPS has had a difficult time starting up idle generator stations when they are needed. Therefore, they have decided to place servers in each station to control the generator's output and status. To activate a generator station, the regional office calls into the server and logs onto the machine. After a generator station has been activated, it updates its status and output to the regional server using hourly dial-up connections.

The control of all the OOPS generators is run through a main control center at the corporate headquarters. The control center decides when to activate any generators and which areas are in need of power. All of the regional offices are connected to the main server via frame relay lines, which allow for rapid updates of the current situation. All updates are done automatically by the servers, but can be initiated by authorized users if necessary.

Mission Statement

The Organization for Optimal Power Supply (OOPS) provides electricity to 1/20th of the United States' citizens. OOPS constantly monitors power consumption and redirects power according to demands. This includes initiating or terminating operations of generator stations.

Critical Information for OOPS

Through a brainstorming session and detailed conversations with the OOPS customer, the following critical information types were agreed to between the assessment team and OOPS:

- Power Consumption Information
- Power Forecast Information
- Generator Status Information
- Customer Information
- Corporate Information
- Personnel Information

Please remember, this is not system information, but information that is needed for the OOPS to continue operations. The loss of confidentiality, integrity, and/or availability (CIA) of this critical information may lead to temporary or permanent damage to overall business operations or the business mission.

Identifying Impacts

The next step in the process is to identify the impact to the organization if there is a loss of CIA of the identified critical information. It is important at this point to identify the definitions of CIA.

- **Confidentiality** The information is only viewable by those with a need and an authorization to view it. Others may not view it. Sometimes called "need-to-know."
- **Integrity** The information is unchanged from its original state.
- **Availability** The information is there when needed by those with the authorization to access or view it.

The organization may choose to add additional impact categories based on the business needs. Some of these additional categories may include (but are not limited to):

- Non-repudiation
- Accountability

- Authorization

- Accessibility

Identifying the impacts to an organization is absolutely the hardest part of the assessment methodology. An important aspect of identification of impact definition is that it must be done with the customer since it has to have the customer's stamp of approval when completed. Why is this so difficult? Getting the customer to agree with themselves on what it means to lose CIA of their critical information is very difficult. It requires them to seriously consider their overall business operations, conduct a type of business impact analysis, and actually document and agree to the impacts as a whole based on their mission. The impact definitions are generally defined as High, Medium, and Low Impact.

Example Continued: OOPS Impact

In real-world situations, definitions will typically be between half a page and one page long. For presentation purposes in this chapter, we will keep it simple. However, please understand that this is just an example and more detail is needed to get a full picture of impact. For our purposes, the identified impacts to OOPS for the loss of CIA are the following:

- **High Impact** Competitive market loss greater than 10 percent; rolling blackouts; loss of generator station control greater than one hour.

- **Medium Impact** Competitive market loss greater than 3 percent but less than 10 percent, or a regional blackout; or loss of generator station control greater than 15 minutes but less than one hour.

- **Low Impact** Competitive market loss less than 3 percent or a regional brownout; or loss of generator station control less than 15 minutes.

The Information Criticality Matrix

Taking into consideration the critical information types and the impact attributes, we can now build an information criticality matrix. The top line is simply the impact attributes (CIAs), while the rows are the critical information types identified by the organization. Table 3.3 represents the framework for the Organizational Information Criticality Matrix (OICM).

Table 3.3 OICM Framework

OICM	Confidentiality	Integrity	Availability
Critical Info 1			
Critical Info 2			
Critical Info 3			
Critical Info 4, etc...			

Using the Impact Definitions

The impact definitions previously created are used to fill out the matrix. Be sure to create the impact definitions before trying to complete the matrix. The definitions of High, Medium, and Low will be utilized to determine what the impact is for the loss of any aspect of CIA. Table 3.4 represents what the chart may look like when the values are input into the OICM.

Table 3.4 OICM Sample

OICM	Confidentiality	Integrity	Availability
Critical Info 1	H	H	M
Critical Info 2	H	M	M
Critical Info 3	L	L	M
Critical Info 4, etc...	H	M	L

Organizational Criticality

The last step with the OICM is to take the highest level in each column to summarize the table and indicate the most critical impact areas for the organization. For our sample based on Table 3.5, the Organizational Criticality (sometimes called the "high water mark") would be the following.

Table 3.5 An Organizational Criticality Sample

	Confidentiality	Integrity	Availability
Organizational Criticality	H	H	M

Example Continued: OOPS OICM

Based on the information we obtained from OOPS and through various discussions, we can now create the OICM for OOPS. Remember, we are using the definitions created earlier to fill out the matrix.

To complete this matrix, start with the first information type and ask yourself, "What can happen if I lose the confidentiality of my power consumption information?" Loss of the confidentiality of the power consumption information would result in a 3 percent or less competitive market loss, which is a Low. You then go to the next impact attribute, which is integrity. Again, ask yourself, "What can happen if I lose the integrity of my power consumption information?" In this case, inaccurate power consumption information could result in the generation of too much, or too little power, which could lead to brownouts or blackouts and loss of revenue or competitive advantage and would have a High Impact. The loss of availability of your power consumption information would have the same impact as loss of integrity.

Let us work through the Generator Status Information type. If you lose the confidentiality of the generator status information, you may end up having too much information available to the public, allowing someone with ill intent to attempt to exploit the information to their advantage. For example, if it is known that a particular generator is down for maintenance and the backup generator is in use, someone could target the backup generator as a weak point in the system with no current backup capabilities. Therefore, the loss of confidentiality of the Generator Status Information would be at least a Medium. You do the same analysis with integrity and availability and find they could lead to High Impacts because they could cause brownouts or blackouts and a loss of revenue or competitive advantage. They could also lead to serious damage to the equipment.

Use the same concepts to complete the rest of the matrix, as shown in Table 3.6. Remember, however, that the matrix must be completed with the customer, and ultimately approved by the customer.

Table 3.6 OOPS OICM

OICM	Confidentiality	Integrity	Availability
Power Consumption	L	H	H
Power Forecasts	L	M	M
Generator Status Information	M	H	H
Customer Information	M	M	M
Corporate Information	M	M	M
Personnel Information	M	M	L

Now we determine the organizational criticality based on the highest level in each column and end up with the result displayed in Table 3.7. This shows that integrity and availability have a higher importance than confidentiality in relation to OOPS. This may be a common organizational criticality you might see within the SCADA environment.

Table 3.7 OOPS Organizational Criticality

OOPS Organizational Criticality	Confidentiality	Integrity	Availability
	M	H	H

Identifying Critical Systems/Networks

Critical systems can be defined as those systems that process, transmit, and/or store the critical information that was identified in the information criticality step. For our purposes, a system is not a single box but a group of components that work together to perform a function. You will identify the systems by communicating with the customer, looking at network and system diagrams, and asking many questions.

OOPS Example Continued

Note from Figure 3.2 that there are three (3) primary functional networks: The Main Control Center, the Corporate HQ Network, and the Regional Generator Station

Controller. After the identification of the primary systems/networks, we are going to build a system criticality matrix for each. To do this, we utilize the information from the information criticality matrix and simply identify which critical information types are processed, transmitted, and/or stored on the identified systems/networks.

Figure 3.2 The Logical Network Diagram for OOPS

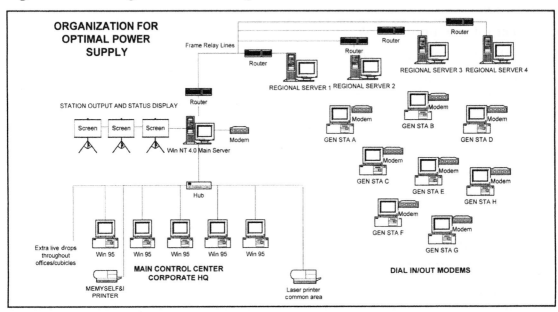

You will want to confirm with the OOPS personnel, but we can make a fairly logical guess that the following information types are processed, transmitted, and/or stored on the following:

- Main Control Center
- Power Consumption
- Power Forecasts
- Generator Status
- Corporate Head Quarters Network
- Customer Information
- Corporate Information

- Personnel Information

- Regional Generator Station Controller

- Generator Status

- Power Consumption

Each system criticality matrix is created by simply cutting and pasting the applicable row from the OICM as demonstrated in the following three (3) tables. For each of the System Criticality Matrices, we can also do an overall "high water mark," which is demonstrated as well.

Table 3.8 Main Control Center System Criticality Matrix

Main Control Center	Confidentiality	Integrity	Availability
Power Consumption	L	H	H
Power Forecasts	L	M	M
Generator Status Information	M	H	H
Overall	M	H	H

Table 3.9 Corporate Network System Criticality Matrix

Corporate Network	Confidentiality	Integrity	Availability
Customer Information	M	M	M
Corporate Information	M	M	M
Personnel Information	M	M	L
Overall	M	M	M

Table 3.10 Regional Generator Station Controllers

Regional Generator Station Controllers	Confidentiality	Integrity	Availability
Power Consumption	L	H	H
Generator Status Information	M	H	H
Overall	M	H	H

Defining Security Objectives

Security Objectives are the targets the customer establishes for their security program. Without security objectives, they do not know what they are trying to accomplish for security and therefore will not reach any goals. Security Objectives are one of those areas requiring the customer's involvement, and so the assessment team cannot make up the information.

Security Objectives come from a combination of inputs, including:

- Customer Mission
- Regulatory Requirements
- Business Objectives
- Best Practices
- Industry Practices

Security Objectives need to be well-defined and made known throughout the organization. Ultimately, the security objectives should be tied to the business objectives of the organization.

TIP

Security Objectives are not where the customer's security posture is today, but where they want it to be in the future. The actual security posture will be determined by the assessment process, and the difference between the Security Objectives and the Security Posture is the Security Gap.

Determining Logical and Physical Boundaries

Understanding the logical and physical boundaries for the assessment plays an important role in managing the scope of the effort and preventing exceeding the bounds of the approved assessment and the scope. Be specific when defining the boundaries to assure a clear understanding.

Physical Boundaries

Physical boundaries are boundaries you can generally reach out and touch. These would include:

- Fences
- Doors
- Locks
- Gate Guards
- Others

Logical Boundaries

Logical boundaries are those you cannot necessarily touch, but that are logical in nature. These include such things as:

- Router ACLs
- Firewall Rule Sets
- Ownership Differences
- Loss of Network Control
- Others

Determining the Rules of Engagement, Customer Concerns, and Customer Constraints

The rules of engagement, customer concerns, and customer constraints play an important role in baselining, scoping, and in better understanding the customer and any existing limitations.

The Rules of Engagement

The rules of engagement establish an understanding between the assessment team and the customer for those actions that will be part of the assessment. By establishing these rules, it allows both the assessment team and the customer to address any special needs. Included in the rules of engagement are:

- Levels of Invasiveness
- Testing Machine Addressing
- Timeframes for Scanning and Interviews
- Notification Procedures
- Scanning Tools and Exclusions

Levels of Invasiveness

The typical technical assessment is not intended to be a penetration test or a red team. However, a customer may want additional activities above and beyond the standard evaluation to address some of their concerns. Some common additions to the standard activities for more invasive testing include:

- Denial of Service testing
- Distributed Denial of Service testing
- War dialing
- Social engineering
- Dumpster diving

Testing Machine Addressing

Arrange with the customer to obtain a static IP address for the scanning machines while conducting on-site activities. If this is not possible, ask the customer to implement an extended DHCP lease for these scanning machines to assure the IP addresses remain unchanged. You desire for the customer to know which scanning is coming from the assessment team. This is a cooperative effort and you don't want someone implementing the Incident Response Plan inadvertently.

For external scanning, assure that the customer is aware of the external IP addresses the scans will be originating from during the testing. Again, you desire the customer to know it is an approved assessment team conducting the scanning and to know when it is an unauthorized entity running scans.

Time Frames for Scanning and Interviews

Every organization varies regarding when they are comfortable having scans run on their systems and networks. Since it is a cooperative effort, the assessment team will need to understand when peak processing times are on the systems and networks, as well as the potential impact to some important clients. In some organizations it is okay to scan at anytime. Others have limitations related to batch processing, or peak access times. These will be taken into account when planning and writing the Assessment Plan.

Conducting assessment interviews will also have an impact on the organization's operations. The interview process should be documented in the Assessment Plan to assure there is an understanding of how the interviews are to be conducted and make certain that facilities are available to hold the interviews themselves.

Notification Procedures

Notification procedures are a necessity to address emergency situations where a system or server may have stopped operating during the testing. It is an objective of the NSA Methodologies to impact customers as little as possible. There also needs to be an understanding that bad things can happen and you must be prepared for any necessary recovery activities. Ask the customer to provide contacts that will be available to cover the time frames the team will be working with on the assessment effort.

Scanning Tools and Exclusions

NSA does not dictate the tools to be used for the technical scanning as part of the IEM process. However, the customer may not want certain tools used in their environment due to either a bad experience or things they may have heard from other organizations. It is important to honor these exclusions but try to understand why they have them.

Customer Concerns

Customer concerns are anything the customer has expressed as something they are particularly interested in or concerned about. This would include concerns about how the assessment might impact the customer's network. They may also express a particular interest in one of the 18 Baseline INFOSEC Classes and Categories, which is introduced later in this chapter. Be sure to document any customer concerns in the

Assessment Plan that were mentioned and be prepared to discuss them in the closing meeting and final report.

Customer Constraints

Customer constraints are simply anything that may limit the execution of the assessment or limit the recommendations that are made as a result of the assessment. Be sure to document any customer constraints in the Assessment Plan that were mentioned and be prepared to discuss these in the closing meeting and final report.

Legal Authorization

Since the assessment work includes a technical component that involves connecting to the customer's networks and systems, there is a definite need to address the legal concerns. NSA recommends the assessment team have a "Letter of Authorization (LOA)" that is signed by the customer, which shows clear approval for the work being done. A copy of the LOA should be in the possession of each assessment team member while performing this work. I am not a lawyer and my lawyer says I cannot give legal advice; therefore, any work on the LOA will need to involve legal counsel from both the assessment team and the customer.

Writing the Assessment Plan

The Assessment Plan will encompass all of the considerations to conduct both an organizational and technical assessment for the organization. This is the scoping document and agreement between the assessment team and the customer to assure the full scope is well defined. Everything we have covered in the Pre-Assessment Process is to be documented in the Assessment Plan. The Assessment Plan will then be signed off on by both sides to assure mutual acceptance.

Components of the Assessment Plan

The following outline for the Assessment Plan takes into consideration the needs for understanding both the organizational and technical information necessary to accomplish the full assessment effort. These would be minimum essential considerations and may require additional business processes built around it to meet your organizational needs. This information is a combination of the Assessment Plan and the Technical Evaluation Plan that is part of the NSA IAM and IEM frameworks.

- Important Evaluation Points-of-Contact POC name, phone number, and e-mail

- Methodology Overview Describe the methodology to be used to conduct the evaluation and identify the specific evaluation tools to be used during the evaluation process.

- Criticality Information A representation of the information criticality for each organizational system determined by discussion with the customer. Should include Organizational Criticality Matrix, System Criticality Matrices, Impact Value Definitions, and System Descriptions.

- Detailed Network Information Include physical boundaries, identified subnets and IP ranges, detailed network diagrams, and contact information for system owners and administrators.

- Customer Concerns Include organizational and technical customer concerns.

- Customer Constraints Include organizational and technical customer constraints.

- Rules of Engagement:

- Network connections and IP addresses, facilities, and so on. Scan windows, relevant IP addresses or subnets to access, and immediate administrator contact information for the customer.

- Internal and External Evaluation Team Requirements.

- Internal and External Customer Requirements.

- Evaluation team's scanning of IP addresses, immediate contact information for assessment team, notification of personnel on assessment activities, CIRT coordination for test purposes.

- Coordination Agreements:

- Level of Detail for Recommendations How detailed does the customer want the recommendations to be? Will the standard low level for the executive summary and the mid-level for technical be ok, or is more detail going to be required?

- List of Deliverables.

- Anything not addressable in the other sections.

- Letter of Authorization Include the approved Letter of Authorization.

- Time-Line of Events A sequence of important events and their associated dates. Some events include the following: the date of the receipt of the request letter, the date of the proposal or contract, customer coordination dates, planned internal and external dates, the report delivery.

On-Site Assessment Activities

The On-Site Assessment is where the majority of the actual vulnerabilities will be identified for the organization and systems. This identification will include both organizational and technical findings. The way vulnerabilities are identified for the organization and the technical areas are different and are discussed next.

Conducting the Organizational Assessment

The organizational vulnerabilities are identified using the following methods:

- Documentation Review

- Interviews

- System Demonstrations

- Observation

The organizational portion of the assessment is focused around understanding the organizational security support concerning a set of control families or classes and categories. NIST identified 17 control families that must be considered as part of the controls put into place for federal government systems. These control families were identified earlier in Table 3.1.

NSA identifies 18 baseline categories to consider as part of any security implementation and are arranged by management, technical, and operational controls. This list of 18 areas is located in Table 3.11.

Table 3.11 NSA 18 Baseline INFOSEC Classes and Categories

Management	Technical	Operational
INFOSEC Documentation	Identification and Authentication	Media Controls
		Labeling
INFOSEC Roles and Responsibilities	Account Management	Physical Environment
	Session Controls	Personnel Security
Contingency Planning	Auditing	Education Training and Awareness
Configuration Management	Malicious Code Protection	
	Maintenance	
	System Assurance	
	Networking/Connectivity	
	Communications Security	

As you can see from the table, these control families and security categories are very comprehensive lists, covering a large volume of security considerations that must be part of a security review.

Documentation Review

Documentation plays a significant role in establishing the foundation for an organization's security program. The organization should use documentation to set the organization's vision and expectations. Documentation serves several purposes, including education, enforcement, and continuity. Lack of documentation within an organization would be a potential security vulnerability; however, it is unlikely it would be your only security finding. Documentation should establish the formal way an organization should be implementing their security program.

Interviews

Interviews are a key way to discover how the organization is actually doing things. Interview techniques are out of scope for this chapter, but understand that there is a psychology to interviews or "discussions." In order to get the information you need from the individuals you are interviewing, you must first gain their trust. Remember you are not an auditor or an inspector—you are there to help the organization (and individuals) improve their security.

System Demonstrations

System demonstrations are an alternative way to get technical information from the organization without being required to run scanning tools or access their systems. It is simply a "Show-Me" activity. If you need clarification or information about something, you can simply say "Show me how you do that."

NOTE

With System Demonstrations, the assessment team does not need to touch the customer network. They are basically shoulder surfing the customer technical person to see how the action is actually conducted.

Observation

The powers of observation are an inherent capability required of the typical security professional. From the very beginning of the assessment, you are watching what the organization does, how they treat employees, how they handle visitors, and the kinds of information that are freely available within the organization. This will lead you to additional questions, system demonstrations, or interviews.

NOTE

Observation is not actually listed as an IAM activity but is an implied part of the IAM.

Conducting the Technical Assessment

The technical portion of the assessment focuses on identifying and understanding the technical vulnerabilities that may exist within the SCADA environment. The technical assessment is referred to as an evaluation by NSA. The primary basis for these activities is defined in the NSA IEM. The IEM utilizes ten baseline activities that are necessary for consideration while conducting the technical portion of the assessment. These ten activities are broken out by enumeration and vulnerability identification areas, as identified in Table 3.12.

Table 3.12 NSA Evaluation Activities

Enumeration	Vulnerability Identification
Port Scanning	Vulnerability Scanning
SNMP Scanning	Host Evaluation
Enumeration and Banner Grabbing	Network Device Analysis
Wireless Enumeration	Password Compliance Testing
	Application-Specific Scanning
	Network Sniffing

Enumeration Activities

Enumeration activities are used to determine what kinds of systems, applications, processes, and devices are on the customer systems. Enumeration activities are basically discovery activities that include:

- **Port Scanning** The act of connecting to potential services or ports on network accessible systems to determine what services and applications may be running on the network.

- **SNMP Scanning** With a known "community string," active SNMP scanning can show information on user accounts, operating systems, services, and shared printers.

- **Enumeration and Banner Grabbing** Enumeration tries to determine information such as users, servers, shared file systems, and other shared resources. Banner grabbing is a process of reaching out to an application and seeing if there is information about the application that can be pulled or "grabbed."

- **Wireless Enumeration** Looks for wireless networks that are part of the organization and how they are configured and secured. Also looks for external wireless networks that may impact the organization and searches for potential rogue wireless networks.

Vulnerability Identification Activities

Vulnerability identification activities are the activities where a majority of the technical vulnerabilities will be discovered. The activities for vulnerability identification include:

- **Vulnerability Scanning** This activity is where the majority of vulnerabilities will be found. Vulnerability scanning runs from the network presence and looks for known vulnerabilities in the tools database.

- **Host Evaluation** Look directly at individual systems to determine if they are configured with secure configurations and settings.

- **Network Device Analysis** Analyze critical network devices to determine secure configuration and to evaluate if the device itself is functioning to provide security.

- **Password Compliance Testing** Test passwords to determine if the password policies are implemented and effective.

- **Application Specific Scanning** Review the security of application functionality and secure programming techniques.

- **Network Sniffing** Analyze network traffic to determine what protocols are being used and if there is clear-text-sensitive information traversing the network.

Are You Owned?

Configuration Issues

The majority of security vulnerabilities found in the technical systems are a result of system configuration issues or lack of up-to-date patching. This is significant because with SCADA systems, integrity and availability are the highest impact attribute concerns. Configuration changes and patching can impact system availability and therefore are often ignored. As an example, a client was having an assessment conducted on their network. The moment a simple port scan started, the network went down and the technical personnel were freaking out. Turns out the organization had an older version of the Cisco IOS on their routers, which had a known flaw of crashing when port scanned. This created only denial of service (an availability issue) but if you remember, availability was rated as High Impact.

Tools

The tools used to conduct the ten IEM baseline activities are determined by the team conducting the assessment work. NSA does not specifically imply or endorse any specific technical security tool or brand of tool. You can use freeware, shareware, or licensed tools. The IEM specifically requires you to run at least one tool to cover each of the ten activities. It is highly recommended you use more than one tool to cover each activity due to the limitations of the tools themselves. The tools are only as good as their underlying databases and the configuration the security consultants give to the tool.

> **WARNING**
>
> One of the most DANGEROUS things you can do while conducting a security assessment is to not understand how your scanning tools work and how the configurations impact the scan results. Creating mass denial of service to a customer because of poor tool configuration is a VERY BAD IDEA and you may never regain the trust of your customer again.

Communication

Communication with the customer is required to assist in managing customer expectations. This involves assuring the proper opening meetings, closing meetings, and update meetings are conducted during the on-site effort. Good communications will reduce the number of potential issues between the customer and the assessment team.

Post Assessment Activities

The Post Assessment process involves taking all the information collected about potential vulnerabilities and determining the real risk to the organization. It is essential that the information gained in the Pre-Assessment process be taken into consideration during the analysis and reporting portion of the assessment.

Conducting Analysis

Detailed analysis not only involves looking at the scan results, it also involves using the skills and talents of the assessment team to determine the impact to the customer if a vulnerability is exploited. The assessment team cannot just "cut and paste" from the scanning tools, they must apply real analysis skills to the process. Effective analysis may involve bringing in additional expertise or conducting additional research to better determine how a particular vulnerability affects a customer.

Final Report Creation

The final report is the record of the activities conducted and the findings discovered during the assessment process. The final report needs to be a clear and concise document that provides a clear picture of the results. The minimum essential components of the final report should include:

- **Executive Summary** A short and concise description of the assessment and the major findings, written so executives can understand the results.

- **Introduction** This section will include a great deal of information from the Assessment Plan since it describes what was done during the assessment, which should be what you agreed to in the Assessment Plan.

- **Analysis** This section identifies what was found during the organization and technical assessment processes. This will include a detailed description of the finding, the analysis of how the finding affects the customer, and recommendations providing options.

- **Conclusion** Answer the question for the organization: "What is my INFOSEC posture?" Recognize good security practices. Provide a recommended priority and roadmap for improving the organization's security posture.

- **Appendices** Include the analysis documents, the Assessment Plan, and a CD or other storage device with the raw scan reports on them.

NOTE

Complete the final report within a reasonable time frame so the process and results are still fresh in the customer's minds. Taking too long to complete the report will make it more difficult for the organization to get started on your recommendations.

Resources

It is always helpful to have recommended resources for your client to get additional information on SCADA security or security assessments. I mention only a few here, but remember that your Web browser is a tremendous research tool. Some Assessment- and SCADA-related sites include:

- **NSA INFOSEC Assurance Training and Rating Program** www.iatrp.com

- **NIST Special Publication 800-82: Guide to Industrial Control System Security** www.nist.gov

- **Digital Bond** www.digitalbond.com

Summary

The evolution of SCADA systems toward standard TCP/IP networking and common applications is driving the need to implement and monitor effective security. Historically, SCADA systems have been considered separate systems that were not interconnected with the corporate network. Now the movement has been toward connecting to the internal intranets and even the Internet. This opens the possibility for the exploitation of holes in the security of these connected components. Implementing effective security and evaluating this security is critical to the continued successful operation of the SCADA environment.

An effective security assessment involves utilizing a solid defined framework that is repeatable. The NSA IAM and IEM provide a framework to work within for purposes of conducting the security assessment process. Four primary activities are discussed as part of the IAM and IEM, which support the security assessment process. These are:

- Pre-Project Activities
- Pre-Assessment
- On-Site Assessment
- Post Assessment

The Pre-Project activities focus on gaining an understanding of what the customer is looking for in their security assessment engagement. Helping the customer get the service that will best benefit them will assist in establishing and managing the customer's expectations. You will also want to address business processes, such as contracting and initiating legal aspects.

The Pre-Assessment process is an essential process for better understanding the customer's needs. A great deal of the Pre-Assessment process involves understanding the customer mission and understanding the business information needed to make the organization run. This is a business focus, not just a security focus. Business risk and security risk are closely associated. An understanding of the impact to the organization if confidentiality, integrity, and/or availability are lost helps the assessment team better recommend improvements to the organization's environment. Following the assessment team's understanding of the mission, critical information, and impact, we go through the process of understanding which systems process, transmit, and/or store this critical information. The remaining portion of the Pre-Assessment process involves finalizing the scope of the assessment, establishing rules of engagement, defining customer concerns and constraints, and establishing timelines to meet and manage customer expectations.

The On-Site Assessment is broken down into two (2) areas: organizational and technical. The organizational assessment focuses on understanding what policies and procedures are in place in the organization and how the organization actually implements the security program. The information for the organizational assessment is collected based on interviews, documentation review, system demonstrations, and observation. The organizational assessment is also conducted based on the NSA IAM 18 Baseline INFOSEC Classes and Categories, or the NIST 17 Control Families. The organizational assessment is flexible enough to pull in the security requirements of any organizational need, including SCADA.

The second part of the On-Site Assessment is the technical assessment (or evaluation). The basis for the technical assessment is the NSA IEM 10 Baseline Activities, which encompass the majority of the technical scanning and analysis needs for a security assessment. The key consideration of using the NSA IEM is that it is not a "cut and paste" from the scanning tools, but a true analysis of the data collected to determine the technical vulnerabilities.

The Post Assessment process involves conducting the final analysis and putting together the final report. This process is important because it outlines the findings from the assessment process and gives the recommendations for improvement of the organization's security posture. A critical aspect of the Post Assessment is to give a well-defined logical roadmap for security posture improvement.

SCADA systems control the majority of our critical infrastructure to include power, water, and sewage. Without the right security implementations and the continuous monitoring and assessment of SCADA system security, there could be a significant loss of confidentiality, integrity, and availability of the critical infrastructure.

Solutions Fast Track

The Evolution of SCADA

- ☑ SCADA systems have historically been treated as isolated entities that are relatively safe from security issues.

- ☑ SCADA has evolved to utilize the same protocols as traditional networks; therefore, additional exposure now exists.

☑ SCADA is now being connected to the business network, exposing it to potential security issues.

☑ SCADA configurations and security must be tightly controlled.

SCADA Assessment Methodologies

☑ Choose a viable repeatable methodology for doing SCADA security assessments.

☑ The NSA IAM and IEM are recognized methodologies to consider.

☑ NIST has created guidance for securing SCADA systems with their NIST SP 800-82.

Pre-Project Activities

☑ Vet the assessment request to assure the customer is getting what they need/want.

☑ Collect and analyze as much publicly available information as possible.

☑ Implement business processes to gain an agreement to proceed.

Pre-Assessment Activities

☑ Collect mission and business critical information, and impact if confidentiality, integrity, and/or availability are lost.

☑ Determine the systems that process, transmit, and/or store the critical information.

☑ Fully scope out the effort with the customer to include concerns, constraints, and rules of engagement.

☑ Write the Assessment Plan based on the Pre-Assessment activities and get a signature from the customer.

On-Site Assessment: Organizational Security

☑ Conduct interviews utilizing the NSA IAM 18 Baseline INFOSEC Classes and Categories as a guide or something similar, such as the NIST 17 Control Families.

☑ Review organizational security and business documentation.

☑ Utilize system demonstrations to verify information or reduce conflict concerning the same.

☑ Use observation to continuously determine how the organization actually implements security.

On-Site Assessment: Technical Security

☑ Conducted based on the NSA IEM 10 Evaluation Activities.

☑ Start by enumerating the network and systems.

☑ Conduct activities to collect actual vulnerability information (for example, scanning).

Post Assessment Activities

☑ Analyze the data to determine the vulnerabilities.

☑ Complete the final report in a timely manner.

☑ Provide the organization with a roadmap to an improved security posture.

Resources

☑ www.iatrp.com

☑ www.nist.gov

☑ www.digitalbond.com

Frequently Asked Questions

Q: I have never needed to worry about SCADA security in the past. Why should I now?

A: SCADA systems have migrated toward common protocols such as TCP/IP instead of previously proprietary protocols. SCADA systems are now being interconnected on the same network as the business network, allowing for greater avenues of attack.

Q: Why are the NSA IAM and IEM recommended as the methodology to use for SCADA assessments?

A: These are extremely flexible methodologies that provide a clear and comprehensive framework for doing any kind of security assessment. The NSA IAM and IEM are not the only methodologies out there and the assessment team can choose which methodology to use. Be sure that, no matter which methodology you use, it covers a similar or better cross-section of information security topics.

Q: Why not just give the potential customer exactly what they ask for?

A: Because what they ask for may not be what they are really looking for. Be sure to conduct the Vetting process to give the customer what they need.

Q: Is understanding critical information and impact important? Don't we just need to know the systems?

A: Understanding critical information and impact is essential to defining appropriate recommendations to improve the security posture. This process answers the question of "Why" security needs to be implemented and how much security is required.

Q: Why is the On-Site Assessment work broken out between organizational and technical?

A: The quick answer is because of the skill set. The skill set required for an individual to conduct the technical assessment is significantly different than those individuals who are conducting the assessment.

Q: Can't I just "cut and paste" the results out of the scanning tools?

A: No. You must conduct an analysis to make it specifically relevant to that particular organization.

Q: Can I get more help when I am conducting an analysis?

A: Absolutely. Don't be afraid to seek assistance either by doing additional research or bringing in additional expertise.

Q: Are the NSA IAM and IEM rigid methodologies?

A: No. The NSA IAM and IEM are very flexible methodologies that are usable across a broad section of organizational types.

Chapter 4

Developing an Effective Security Awareness Program

Sean Lowther is the President and Founder of Stealth Awareness, Inc., www.stealthawareness.com.

Sean is an independent consultant who brings years of experience designing and implementing information security awareness programs at the highest level. He founded Stealth Awareness, Inc. in 2007.

Sean worked at Bank of America for over seven years, managing the enterprise information security awareness program. The program received the highest rating from its regulators and was consistently rated "world class" by industry peer groups.

Sean has worked with BITS, the Financial Services Roundtable Task Force on Privacy, prior to the enactment of the Gramm-Leach-Bliley Act. He produced the video "It's Not If, But When" for the Financial Services Sector Coordinating Council in partnership with the U.S. Treasury Department with the goal to improve critical Infrastructure protection and Homeland Security. Sean was recognized by senior government officials and business executives for his "work to defend our nation's critical infrastructure."

Sean is a sought after speaker for a variety of events and meetings. Most recently he spoke at the Computer Security Institute's annual 2007 conference in Washington, D.C., the Contingency Planning Association of the Carolinas, and the 2008 Charlotte ISSA annual conference.

Sean lives in the Charlotte, North Carolina area.

Introduction

In this chapter, I will talk about how to design and implement an effective information security awareness program. One chapter will not cover all you need to know, but it can serve as the foundation for starting a program and/or making an existing program better.

In today's world, I don't like the looks of data breaches, identity theft, and the apparent inability of people to safeguard sensitive information properly. If the issue is not at pandemic levels, it certainly has reached epidemic proportions. A couple of years ago, corporate America was concerned that the flu pandemic was more than a probability. Disaster recovery experts raced to put in place contingency plans. It was thought that as much as 30 percent of a company's employees would be too sick to work. If the flu hit, many would stay home fearing they might become sick. Fortunately, the pandemic did not happen. I do not suggest the issue of properly safeguarding sensitive information in its electronic and non-electronic forms is an illness that can be cured easily. Like in any epidemic, people become more cautious, keep their hands away from their face, and practice good hygiene. We communicate, communicate, communicate to ensure that people know the risks and what they need to do to avoid becoming infected. So why are we not doing this in a consistent every-company-must-do-it manner when it comes to the proper safeguarding of sensitive information? This chapter is a call to action, because without one, most companies will not implement the resources within their company that ensure all new hires, existing employees, vendors, suppliers, and consultants to their company clearly understand and exhibit the correct information safeguard behaviors. So, let the chapter begin.

There is an old adage that says: *Tell them what you are going to tell them. Tell them, and then tell them what you told them.* In other words, repetition is the aide to memory. Before I tell you what I am going to tell you, I want to raise a major concern. It is not a new concern. It's not a great revelation, and it is no big surprise, but it is probably the greatest risk we are facing in corporate America, as well as government today. It is our inability to safeguard sensitive information properly. Paraphrasing Harold Hill in *The Music Man,* "We've got trouble, right here in your town, and it starts with 'T,' which rhymes with 'P,' which stands for People."

Since 2005, it is conservatively estimated that over 250 million people in America have had their personal sensitive information lost or stolen. The cost to manage this exodus of information is estimated at over $55 billion, give or take a billion. The Ponomen Institute puts the cost at $192.50 for each customer record. These costs, for the most part, are purely administrative and are not related to actual identity theft. That means it is wasted money, and brings nothing to the bottom line other than an unnecessary expense.

If we were working for the CDC (Center for Disease Control), this problem would be way past the epidemic stage. Yet no one is raising the issue to the degree it needs to be heard. Thirty-nine states have enacted legislation requiring companies report compromised customer data. Penalties can be assessed, which is a way for the states to bring in more money, but these laws do not address the real issue. The Federal Trade Commission has entered the arena, threatening the penalty of an "audit" on those companies that fall under their jurisdiction who fail to safeguard sensitive information properly. We have companies, who, on further inspection, were following the latest prescribed security practices when an incident occurred. So, can we find them at fault?

The reality is that no one will ever stay ahead of those who are hacking systems, or those who are using social engineering to get sensitive information from company employees. If we close one hole, the hacker will likely exploit another. Social engineers will survive because they are magicians at extracting information from employees who have been told that providing quality customer service means everything to the company. In a way, company employees are willing to give up sensitive information because they want to help and "do the right thing." Where we are failing (miserably, in my opinion), is in addressing the human side of this epidemic.

What we need is an "antibiotic" to eradicate these ills. Or maybe a chip that, once embedded into each employee, will ensure that he/she will not make stupid mistakes, like leaving sensitive information on the copy machine, or leaving their laptop on the table at the coffee shop when they go to the bathroom—only to find it gone when they return. Unfortunately, that chip has not been developed yet. In a real epidemic, one with viruses, a high temperature, sneezing, and so on, we encourage people to wash their hands, cover their nose when sneezing, and stay home from work when they are sick so they don't infect others. If this was a flu pandemic, that's exactly what we'd be doing. The loss in productivity during a pandemic would probably be higher, in terms of cost, than what is currently experienced with "data breaches," but not by much.

Welcome to the Information Risk Pandemic. It is time to properly educate employees and senior leadership on how to protect their customers, company, and stakeholders from this costly plague by concentrating on the people who design applications, implement programs, and use the technology given to them to perform their function in a safe and secure manner.

When people fail to do the right thing out of ignorance, speed to market, or greed, then the short-term reward is soon lost against the long-term consequences of their actions. A case in point is SCADAs. How one technology has been allowed to be embedded into the fabric of our society with such vulnerabilities to the whole is just unfathomable. Who knew? Today, we know that the unintentional loss of sensitive information is at pandemic proportions throughout corporate America and government. Nevertheless, we continue to not provide adequate information security awareness training to our employees on handling, transmitting, storing, destroying, and transporting sensitive information properly.

For companies that do have information security awareness programs in place, are they designed and implemented to change the overall security behavior of their employees, or are they simply one-time events that make it *look* like the company is taking the issue seriously?

The wake-up call is here and now. Companies need to check their *information security awareness quotient*. In other words, how well do employees know how to properly safeguard sensitive information at your company? Unfortunately, you are the wrong demographic to be preaching this message to. I would suggest you share this chapter with those in your company who are responsible for information security, physical security, privacy, auditing, and compliance. Not providing adequate awareness training to employees on how to safeguard customer, employee, company intellectual property, and other associated risks is simply business suicide in this day and age. I recognize you are not the one to lead the charge, but the more people who are willing to become the messenger brings us one step closer to effectively managing this information risk pandemic.

Why an Information Security Awareness Program Is Important

If the opening to this chapter isn't enough reason to start an information security awareness program at your company, then I'm not sure what is.

How many security conferences have you been to where speaker after speaker brings up the issue of *people* as the major risk to safeguarding sensitive information? I'm sure you have sat in these conferences and listened and agreed, but because the discussion does not affect you personally, it remains in the conference room. "Yeah, it's a big risk, but I'm more interested in securing the Unix platform, or learning what's new in forensics," you say. We seem to be absorbed with chasing the next technology and not so concerned about how we are going to safeguard it. We allow our employees to bring technology into the workplace, such as iPods and USBs, that have enough memory to easily store the company's crown jewels. Information that can easily walk out the door unnoticed. We also give employees equipment to store and access the company's most inner sanctum of sensitive information with little thought or control over their activities. As Deming, a noted quality guru, said in his day, "if you are going to put all your eggs in one basket, then you better watch the basket."

For example, during the 2008 presidential campaign, three candidates had their passport information accessed without a valid need to know. Three separate incidents by contractors who had been given access, but apparently little guidance in their responsibilities. Was it right? No. Was there any intent to steal information? Probably not. It was a stupid mistake that resulted in another example of the government's inability to properly safeguard sensitive information. Unfortunately, this scenario replicates itself in corporations millions of times a day across the world. Even worse, though a disgruntled employee with authorized access may be displaced, his/her access to such information often is not terminated immediately. So, he/she may leave behind a "time bomb," designed to disrupt communications. Or, he/she may decide to steal confidential customer information or intellectual property. This scenario happens every day in government and private enterprise offices around the world. All because an employee's access was not terminated in a timely manner.

We Fail to Recruit Our Employees into the Company's Security Program

Somehow it is expected that everyone will "do the right thing." If I asked a room of 100 people to raise their hands if they thought they would ever be the direct cause of a data breach at their company, guess how many hands would go up? Your're right, none, or at least not yours. But the statistics tell us their answer isn't true. It is pretty safe to say that every company and government agency will lose at least one laptop this year, and it is pretty safe to say that a very high percentage of those laptops will have sensitive information on them. It's also safe to say that a very high percentage of the laptops do not have encryption installed, and that in many cases, the user's ID and password are taped to the bottom of their laptop, thereby making the encryption useless. No one really knows what these statistics are. For sure, not everyone is reporting this type of incident, not to mention the loss of cell phones, iPods, USBs, and other storage devices. We have made information more mobile and far more vulnerable. Because of this, the cost to businesses is skyrocketing. As mentioned earlier, the Ponomen Institute suggests in their most recent study that the loss of one customer record to a company is $192.50. That covers customer notification, customer support, call center resources, and so on. What is the actual cost, and what will that reported cost be as more and more companies and industries come under scrutiny? Just type "data breaches" into your search engine and a wealth of opinions and facts will come pouring forth.

We Need to Take the Issue Seriously

On television is an advertisement where two people are inspecting a dam. They come upon a small leak and look at each other. One person is chewing gum and takes it out of his mouth and sticks it into the leak. They nod in agreement that the problem has been fixed. Of course, we all know what is ultimately going to happen. The dam will burst, questions will be asked, the news media will report the incident, and somewhere along the line the truth will be discovered. Chewing gum is not an effective tool when it comes to maintaining a dam. If the dam collapses due to poor maintenance or undue stress, the potential loss of life, not to mention the possible benefits lost from the power and other factors that could have been gained, could be catastrophic. Of the 79,000 dams in America, the American Society of Civil Engineers considers 10,000 to have a "high-hazard risk of failure." Bridges are another example. According to federal highway statistics, "nearly 50 percent of all rural bridges in America, 20 feet or longer, are structurally or functionally deficient." In some cases, the bridges have simply been closed. In other circumstances, weight restrictions have been posted.

Companies need to look at their infrastructures, and how they were built, and recognize that the information age has moved their most valuable asset, information, outside of the brick-and-mortar establishment and made it easy to access by authorized and unauthorized persons. An information security awareness program will not stop the intentional incidents. In an ideal world, we would have a super-system that would keep everyone honest. If access was attempted by an unauthorized person, or an authorized person was taking information for unauthorized purposes, the super system would identify the action immediately by frying the information. Of course, some of us might dream that such a scenario could be possible, but the legal and ethical ramifications of such a super-system would be beyond our comprehension, and frankly beyond our everyday reality.

How to Design an Effective Information Security Awareness Program

I do not necessarily believe in teams creating your information security awareness program. Consensus can often hinder the design of a program and, in fact, take people down the wrong path. The Aboliene Paradox easily demonstrates my point. The paradox says that a group of people can come together and agree on something that no one wants to do. I am sure that you have been in meetings where this has happened. You walk out of the room thinking the decisions made were nuts, but you agree to follow them anyway. Another problem is when a company takes a Vice President and asks them to wear the *awareness* cap, along with all their other hats. In small companies, you probably do not have much of an alternative. But, if your organization is rather sizable, a full-time employee should be assigned and dedicated to implementing your program.

Creating an information security awareness program is not rocket science. It is marketing. Because of this you should look for someone in your organization that has a flair for marketing. Having a CISSP is not an advantage or disadvantage. When I first introduced the concept of marketing information security awareness back in the '90s, most people in the organization and other companies I talked to thought I was crazy. They used the sledgehammer/fear approach. My CISO happened to be one of the best marketing minds I've ever met, and when I presented my business plan to her, she fell in love with the concept.

Today, based on the many articles I've read, the marketing of information security awareness is universally accepted and applied. Here is what this looks like. If an employee does not value the content of the information you are delivering, then why would they follow it? It is this value proposition that makes a program work.

TIP

Awareness is an individual responsibility, and a team effort!

I don't believe most employees think this way. "It's everyone's responsibility," the slogan says, so if everyone else is doing the right thing, I'm covered and need not worry about it. No matter what expert you read or listen to, they all seem to agree on one thing: "80% of the risks to your company's sensitive information rests on the inside with employees." And yet most companies continue to look over the castle wall, protecting and defending their perimeter. This is why it is so important that management clearly understands the bigger picture, and the bigger risks if an effective information security awareness program is not implemented. It is another reason why a sound business plan is important. It gets everyone in the decision-making process thinking and agreeing along the same lines. This way, as you implement it, there will be no rude awakenings, or at least not with management.

NOTE

Having a slogan or cartoon character or both is a great way to enhance awareness of the messages, materials, and training you use in your program.

Notes from the Underground…

The Awareness Intra-preneur

When I speak to groups about being the "Awareness Intra-preneur," one of the key intra-preneurial behaviors is to never allow an objection to get in the way of the success you wish to achieve. Go around it, over it, or through it, whatever you need to do as long as it's ethical. It's also important to have a win/win attitude in your discussions, to ensure that everyone feels they are a winner when the final decision is made. An "intrapreneur" is someone who uses the skills of an entrepreneur on the inside to move their program forward.

Designing and Planning

Business Plan

Create a business plan that shows your vision for the awareness program. Let's talk about creating a business plan. It says on your performance plan that you will design and implement an information security awareness program this year. Where do you start? What should it include? I'd suggest Everything, including the kitchen sink! Well, that might be going a little too far, but the point here is to create a five-year plan. Not just one about what you are going to do *this* year. Create a vision of what your program will look like and that your program is ongoing. Show how each component supports and ties the program together. It took me 90 days to put together the Information Security Awareness Business Plan. That, in itself was a major accomplishment. Fortunately, my management was supportive. The presentation ended up being over an inch thick. It was spiral bound. It was also very visual. A picture is worth a thousand words, so I wanted my CISO to think in pictures of what the campaign and components of the program would look like. Of course, my CISO also saw the detail I had compiled around the cost to implement. In essence, I wanted my CISO and boss to know that I had done my homework, knew what I was doing, and that I was capable of implementing and managing the program.

The best presentation I ever heard was of a salesperson selling a satellite phone to an Arab sheik back in the 1980s, as I recall. Rather than try and present facts and figures, the salesperson went out and hired a graphic artist. The picture he had drawn was of the sheik in his tent in the desert sitting in his comfortable chair speaking on his phone to someone who was on another continent. The picture also showed the phone communicating with a satellite as well as the price tag for the picture to come to life. I think it all came to 3 million dollars then. The presentation lasted less than one minute, according to the salesman. The sheik looked at the picture. It was clearly what he wanted. He turned the picture over and signed his approval. Deal done! This is exactly how I approached presenting my business plan to my CISO. I painted the picture, showed how it all connected, and what it would cost. It was the plan that would solve her problem. Figuratively speaking, at the end of the presentation, she turned the presentation over and gave me her approval to go forward.

Seven Times, Seven Different Ways

My belief is that an effective plan is one that says the same thing seven times, seven different ways. So this challenges you to look at all the possible products and delivery channels available to you. This is something you need to constantly look for, to constantly seek. For example, I knew that video streaming would ultimately become available at the company. What a great channel for delivering information. We were the first to use the technology at the company simply because we were constantly looking for new channels. I knew it was becoming available, and we were ready to take advantage of the opportunity. In fact, we were the first. You could go to our Web site and view Video Quick Tips on several topics such as SPAM, Encryption, Password Creation, and so on. Not all employees are comfortable with reading guidelines. These Video Quick Tips became very popular and provided "just-in-time" training for the employee. Again, seven different times, seven different ways. Looking for new delivery channels, new ideas allow you to introduce old and new messages through other touch points.

Not everyone will think your ideas are good. I remember making a presentation to use iPods as a delivery channel for some of our messages. My manager at the time was not a proponent of the idea. Listening to your customers is where you will get many of your ideas. Surveying your customers will help determine which delivery channels are preferred, and help you defend the direction you are taking your program, keeping it alive, fresh, and most importantly, in your employees' minds. Today, iPods are being used as a viable delivery channel of awareness messages.

TIP

The other key to creating your business plan is to make sure it gets everyone thinking along the same general lines. As you implement it, you do not want any rude awakenings, especially with management.

I cannot impress upon the reader how important this is to the overall success of your program. If your program is to ever have a chance of success, the vision must be laid out and agreed upon by your CISO. If it is a *stopgap* solution to a particular incident or problem, your program will become exactly (and only) that: "A stopgap solution with no long-term effect." Management is terrific at implementing knee-jerk reaction solutions. An effective awareness program needs to be ongoing and viewed by management and employees as an important company value. "Wow, that's a tall order to achieve?" you might say, but you MUST protect the information assets of your company to reduce exposure to theft. You also MUST reduce the exposure of risk to the integrity of the processes in place or of them being developed to provide the coveted services of your company. The following are what I believe to be the key components of a business plan presentation:

1. What is your objective? An overview of your program.

2. What products and delivery channels are you recommending? (I am a believer, as I mentioned earlier, that if you want to affect change, you must package each message into seven different products, seven different ways. Over time, this reinforces key messages. With management's due diligence, the company's culture will reflect a greater understanding and appreciation about properly safeguarding sensitive information, as exhibited through each employee's attitude, awareness, and behavior.

Warning

An awareness program is not a once-a-year online training program. It is one component of many that should be included if you want to affect behavioral change within your organization. If you limit yourself to this one component, then the mindset becomes one of compliance. Simply checking off a box does not an awareness program make. Just the same, it's better than nothing.

3. What is your schedule to roll out the program? (Here, you want to make sure you have Audit's input on "what" and "how" you are going to accomplish your objective. Build that relationship with Audit. It will make your boss happy that they approved of your plan and efforts.)

4. Budget. What is it going to cost to implement your program? (Always ask for more knowing that you will not get it. I will show you where you can get the money to implement your program if it is not readily available to you.)

> **NOTE**
>
> Getting money to implement a program is a little more difficult. "When the mind is ready, the money is ready." The only reason awareness programs are not supported is because your CISO has decided not to fund it. It's not the CEO.

Show Me the Money!

Can you hear Cuba Gooding, Jr. and Tom Cruise screaming, "Show me the money!" in the movie *Jerry Maguire*? It is one of the key questions asked by those responsible for implementing an information security awareness program. "I can't get the money budgeted!" they exclaim. Would it surprise you that I did not have a budget? Yes, I worked for one of the largest financial institutions in the world, and it would be easy to conclude that there were buckets and buckets of dollars at my disposal, but this wasn't true. Like with anything else, when the mind is ready, the money is ready. This is why a good incident will get the attention of senior leadership or the Audit department. Personally, I never had a large incident that opened the money door for me, but then again I never had a problem getting my program funded either. The following are some suggestions to help you find the money.

1. As discussed earlier, I created a good business plan. A plan that laid out the entire program, including the budget. There were no surprises for management.

2. Ask for the money. If you need additional dollars above and beyond what you requested in your presentation, or that has been allocated to your program, simply ask for it. Present your ideas, why they are important to the overall program, and ask for the money to fund it. Do not worry about whether you receive the funds or not. The following are other resources you can tap:

3. If your company acquires another company, normally transition dollars are available. This is good because those dollars do not come out of your budget, but rather a special fund (bucket) set up by the company. Often, you can kill two birds with one stone by using these additional dollars for the transition as well as other items you want to add to your enterprisewide program.

4. Another source is the supply budget. Budgets are normally lost or lowered if they are not used. The supply budget, especially at the end of the year, is an easy one to pirate.

5. Other people's money. Go back to your alliances, which I will talk about shortly, and see where you can partner with them to share the expense of your program. Online training is an example where information security and privacy can partner and share expense.

6. What budget dollars are available in other departments within your division?

7. Be creative. You are your own best resource. I never took a concept or idea to my manager for approval other than my business plan. I also took what appeared to be a finished product. It was more than "how can I paint the right picture in words." Give it to them in such a way that they can see it, touch it, and even smell it if need be. Sometimes this requires working with alliances you have nurtured.

NOTE

I am a firm believer that an information security awareness program, in order for it to become successful, must come down from the top. Or at least that is the perception that should be made.

To get the CEO's endorsement of your program, simply compose the message you would like to see the CEO make. Contact the CEO's secretary and tell him/her why you are sending the message, why it is important, and that you need the CEO's endorsement. I not only got the message back with a few minor edits, but with his electronic signature, too.

People were amazed that it was that simple, but it was. There isn't a CEO alive who doesn't understand the importance of safeguarding sensitive information properly. He/she trusts that those under him/her are doing the right thing to put in place the processes that will secure the information assets of the company.

The first product I released was a Quick Reference Guide for employees. On the inside flap of the guide was the message from our CEO explaining the importance of safeguarding sensitive information properly at the company, along with his support and request to all employees to follow the information security policy and program.

I never had the question asked again from anyone in the company: "Why do we need to do this?"

Two Important Keys to Implementing an Effective Program

Implementing an information security awareness program can be done without a policy approved by the Board of Directors, but it is a lot easier if you have it. In some industries, a policy is mandated by regulation. Whether it is in your industry or not, it behooves a company in this day and age to have one, if for no other reason than to reduce legal exposure. The key words to look for in the policy are: *All employees are required to follow the Information Security Program . . . failure to do so can lead to discipline up to and including termination.* What Board of Directors would not approve an information security policy and program for their company? It is the right thing to do. You'll notice that the word "Program" is included. This connects all information security guidance and your awareness program to the policy.

Awareness is part of the "Information Security Program." If you do not have an Awareness Standard, compose one. An Awareness Standard says, "Who, what, and when will people comply with the information security awareness program implemented at your company." First, who should receive training? Should it be all employees regardless of whether they have system access or not? I would say yes. This should be required of consultants and vendors, too.

Vendors sometimes challenge this issue. If they are on the premises, I would suggest they take your training, unless their company provides training that is equal to, or greater than, what your company requires. If an employee or vendor, consultant, and so on is a chauffeur, for example, the argument is that they do not have access to company systems, and therefore should not be required to take the training. Company chauffeurs probably have more access to sensitive information than you might think. They can overhear what's being said in car conversations and on cell phone calls, and may even look through important papers left in the car while the senior manager is off at a meeting, if they so choose.

Don't think it can happen? In 1973, I was working for a company in Osaka, Japan. The CEO of the company enjoyed driving to work in his Rolls-Royce. He would pick me up every morning on the way to the office to discuss our marketing plans and status—a good use of commuting time. As time went by, the CEO decided to hire an *Assistant to the President* (AP). Part of his job was to be the CEO's chauffeur and traveling secretary. So, now, the CEO and I were being driven by the AP to the office. To make a long story short, we discovered that the AP was actually employed by one of our competitors, and was a mole in our company. Imagine how upset the boss was, and how it affected some of our marketing plans. Having an employee who does not have system access take your awareness training will not stop this kind of threat, but it does tell someone like the chauffer how important properly safeguarding sensitive information is to the company.

To that end, each employee is a sales representative for your company. If you are out at a party and someone asks, "What does your company do to safeguard sensitive information properly?" What would you say? The final two things you need to consider in your Awareness Standard is the "What" and the "When." "What" are the awareness training requirements you have created (attending new hire orientations, completing an online training program, and so on). And then comes "When." What are the expectations to complete specific awareness training? Should it be done prior to system access, or within 30 days of hire? As I mentioned earlier, write and get your Awareness Standard approved. Don't wait for someone else to write it. You do it. Vet it with your manager and your CISO, and then take it through your company's internal approval process.

You may ask, "Why not have your manager discuss the Awareness Standard (if you do not report directly) to the CISO?" Your CISO needs to know and respect your involvement and responsibility to the program. You are one of the few people in your division, other than those who report directly to the CISO, who is representing your division throughout the enterprise. Having his/her direct ear is an important relationship to develop.

WARNING

What you put in your Awareness Standard is auditable. You may want to mandate certain action, but if you cannot get people to comply, then you have an audit issue.

I certainly know what we would like people to do, but it is not always easy for a company, especially a large one, to ensure that all their employees are complying with your Information Security Awareness Standard in a timely manner. Be sensible with the standard you create to ensure the processes can be followed in a timely manner by all. Otherwise, you could create your own nightmare.

For example: *All employees must complete information security awareness training prior to system access.* I know we would all like to see that, but it's not going to happen, especially in a large organization. Take your proposed Awareness Standard to the Audit department, after it has been viewed with your manager and prior to the CISO's review. This puts you in a better position with your CISO if he/she knows Audit is satisfied with the Standard. The final decision rests with the CISO. You do not want your program to burden the company. You simply want to enhance awareness and validate that all employees are receiving awareness training on a timely basis and that each employee understands and acknowledges their responsibility to safeguard sensitive information properly.

To Print or Not to Print

One of the first products I produced and released was a Quick Reference Guide. Though there is a lot of pressure to utilize the company's intranet to distribute information, I remain a fan of print. There is still nothing like walking into the store and touching the merchandise. So, too, there is nothing like receiving a well-designed brochure or booklet, especially when it has the opportunity to stay around as a reminder. Having said that, there is a lot to be said for an intranet, because it allows you to upload updates on-the-fly and make your materials more current. A printed guide lasted at least one year, and after the initial print to all employees, we only printed enough to support new hire orientations. Of course, in the document was a reference to our Web site and to check for updates.

This Quick Reference Guide should do one very important thing. Tell employees where to find Information Security (through a URL, e-mail, and/or telephone number) when they have a question or concern about securing information properly. For awareness, I had my own extension on our 1-800 number. The following are the key topics you want to cover in this document:

1. What is sensitive information?
2. The importance of a clean desk policy.
3. How to create a good hard-to-crack password.
4. Use of a password-protected screensaver.
5. Remote computing safeguarding procedures.
6. Safeguarding the transmission of sensitive information.
7. The destruction of sensitive information.
8. The risk from social engineers.

9. The risk from insider threats.

10. How to report an actual or suspected incident.

In keeping with "what is sensitive information," a classification of data matrix should be given to every employee so they clearly understand what security levels have been assigned to information in your company. What are the classifications you use to designate sensitivity of information. Examples show each level of sensitive information (see Figure 4.1), how it should be marked, transmitted electronically or non-electronically, stored, and destroyed.

Figure 4.1 Levels of Sensitive Information

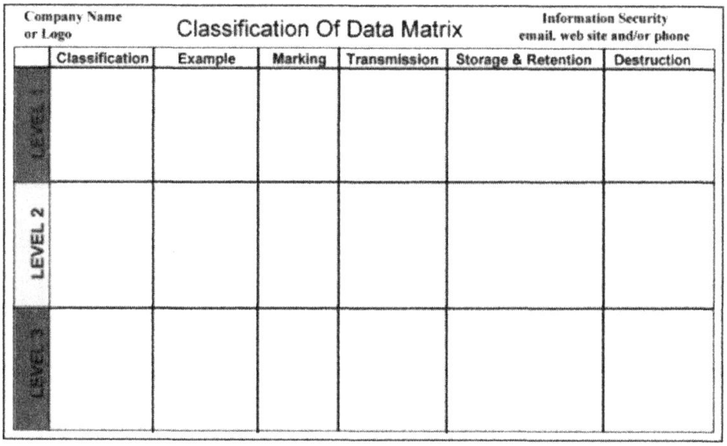

Company Name or Logo	Classification Of Data Matrix				Information Security email, web site and/or phone	
	Classification	Example	Marking	Transmission	Storage & Retention	Destruction
LEVEL 1						
LEVEL 2						
LEVEL 3						

Though all this guidance should be in a standard or other format, putting it in a concise, easy-to-read, and easily accessible resource is important to your overall awareness program. Many employees posted this matrix in their workspace. As you'll notice, it also included a Web site URL and phone number as an easy reminder of how to contact Information Security. Marketing our contact information proved to be a significant benefit to the awareness program. When privacy, through the Gramm-Leach-Bliley Act became an important issue at the company I worked for, the group that was put together to manage that process proceeded to do conduct training. When questions were raised, guess who received the phone calls? Our employees did not know the difference between information security and privacy. This became the impetus of information security and privacy joining forces to implement an online awareness component to our individual programs. Later in the chapter, I'll talk more about how aligning with other departments and divisions within your company can greatly benefit your program.

Online Training Programs

It's better to have something rather than nothing. If all you have for your awareness training program is an annual online training program, then at least you have something. The risk is that you rely on this program as your only touch point and channel to reinforce principles and correct behavior. Some companies have an online orientation program. This should not replace the guide. It should merely supplement the program. Remember, seven different times, seven different ways. If you do have an online training program, it is a good place to get an employee's acknowledgement that they understand their responsibility in properly safeguarding sensitive information at the company. This can soften public opinion if and when a data breach occurs. It is better to hear that "the company has an ongoing awareness program and as grievous as the incident may be, it was not because the company was not paying attention to their responsibility to safeguard customers' sensitive information properly."

Your In-House Web Site

If you have a company intranet, this is a great place to support information security services. If you are a small company, having your policies, standards, procedures, baselines, and other guidance housed on your Information Security Web site so those with a need to know have easy access and know whom to communicate with for the right answers is a good idea.

Figure 4.2 Example of an Information Security Web Site

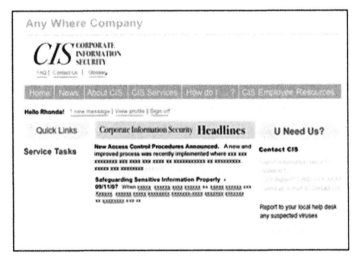

List the "Service Tasks" that information security provides, including your Awareness Program. This is where you can house an archive of articles you have written, as well as other products used in your awareness program, such as your Employee Quick Reference Guide, the Manager's Guide, and even an orientation video. If you make your products easily available (communicate, communicate, communicate!), you'll be amazed at how many within your organization will utilize the materials you've put in place. An example of those materials is shown in Figure 4.3. You should also consider placing "quick links" to other Web sites, such as those regarding privacy and compliance.

Figure 4.3 An Example of Posted Security Awareness Materials

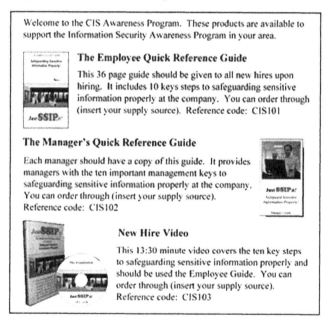

How to Implement an Information Security Awareness Program

Send to every employee in the company a card or sticker that includes the Corporate Information Security name, the intranet URL for your Web site, and a contact number for questions and/or for reporting an incident.

TIP

One of the easiest and best things you can do in support of your program is to ensure that every employee in the company knows how to contact Corporate Information Security (and you) if their question pertains to awareness.

TIP

Search out every other Web site on the company's intranet and have the link to your intranet site appear on those sites as well.

Implementing your information security awareness program is not always as easy as one may think. I know… just put it out there. It's policy and it's what employees need to know. However, it is *how* you implement it that is just as important as *what* you implement. Here's what I mean. You are about to send a document to every employee in the company. How this document will be received is very important, because if employees do not read it, then why send it? Each department within your company has their own priorities, schedules to keep, and day-to-day processes that must be accomplished. If you simply send your document to every employee without advance notice to management that it is coming and why it is important for every employee to read, then you might as well kick back and watch the trash cans fill up. You want management to embrace your program, so communication is really important. You need managers, at all levels, to support your program.

TIP

Identify every employee in other departments responsible for training and new hire orientation. Include them in your mailing list for updates and *touch point communications*. What are touch point communications? This is when, at least once a month, you send an e-mail newsletter out to key individuals in your company, sharing information security safety tips and other thoughts to keep them engaged in your program.

What We Have Here Is a Failure to Communicate

In "Cool Hand Luke," the Captain of Road Prison 36 first used the phrase, "What we have here is a failure to communicate." It is a condition that exists across America's corporate culture and why awareness is so important. Lack of awareness is a failure to communicate. Symptoms of this condition are the appearance of silos, employees not following policy, standards, or other defined process—doing their own thing, rather than the right thing.

Communicate, Communicate, Communicate!

Anyone in a company who works with technology, software applications, and systems can negatively impact the security of the company's information assets. For example: An employee's failure to communicate with information security specialists about an application they are developing can result in the exposure of sensitive information. Even if an application developer is proficient in secure coding, they should include an information security specialist as part of their development team. Undoing months of work, because Information Security was not consulted is no excuse for placing the company in a vulnerable position and incurring additional costs to have the code rewritten. Senior leaders, in my opinion, should mandate this requirement. Conversely, when Information Security releases new applications, processes, and due dates to follow without communicating these changes to the affected lines of business, animosity is generated, which can overtly affect what you are trying to accomplish.

Other Touch Points

If you create a Quick Reference Guide for employees, have it included in the company's post-acceptance package. This is the package you received as a new employee that includes your benefits and other important information that you need to know on your first day at the company. Include the "Classification of Data Matrix" in the centerfold of the guide. This gives the employee an easy way to remove the matrix and post it in their work area. If you are ever going to get an employee to read what is important to the company, it will be during their welcoming process. If your company does not have a post-acceptance package, then the document should be given to the new hire during orientation. If you do not have a formal new hire orientation program, then the manager or their designee should sit down with the new employee and go through the guide. One of the values a new employee is hoping to see when they hire on to a company is that the company is trying to do the right thing. Safeguarding sensitive information properly is just such a worthy value to adopt.

Manager's Quick Reference Guide

Managers, as I have discussed, are a key implementation partner. But how do you get them engaged in the process? Every manager in a company should clearly understand their responsibility ensuring that employees (and themselves) are effectively following the company's information security policy and program. The Manager's Quick Reference Guide should be part of every new hire manager's post acceptance package. This information should be in an Information Security Standard, such as Roles and Responsibilities, or other guidance. The Manager's Quick Reference Guide brings the importance of the manager's responsibilities out of the maze of documented procedures and requirements and gives it the importance it deserves. In this guide, the following topics should be discussed:

1. Information Security is not responsible for safeguarding sensitive information properly. It is a team effort.

2. Application development and working with IT.

3. Know your employees' safeguarding sensitive information properly behaviors.

4. The importance of encryption and the secure transmission of electronic and non-electronic information properly.

5. The downloading of unlicensed software.

6. Being an enabler.

7. Consultant/vendor guidelines.

8. Updating or deleting an employee's system access immediately when they are transferred or terminated.

9. Social engineering risks.

10. The risk of insider threats.

Managers should look to include discussion about information security topics in their staff meetings. When new materials or directions are released from information security, managers should ensure their employees have received the materials or guidance and understand the direction. It can be as simple as pointing out a new poster that is up and why the topic is important, or that a new standard has been released and what it means to both their department and job function. Information security awareness is an ongoing process with which everyone in the company should be engaged. Managers can determine whether employees need to see certain information. As mentioned earlier, imagine that a new standard is released and that employees in your company, who need to know this information, do not receive it!

Let's Talk about Alliances

If you want your program to be successful, then don't do it without input from others in your company. Embrace other divisions within your firm that can assist you in completing your mission. Some of them include the following.

Audit

Yes, Audit personnel are your friends! Any products or programs you create should be approved with Audit's input. This accomplishes a few things. First, it embraces Audit as part of the process, part of the team. So, Audit should be easier to work with along the way. Secondly, your CISO will most likely ask you whether Audit was consulted when you make your presentation, and you don't want to stand there with a stupid look on your face.

Legal

Submitting materials to your Legal department is the right thing to do. Rarely will you ever get a "you can't do this" statement from your legal council. It is managing the perception and protecting your program that counts. Obviously, not everything needs to be sent to Legal, but, say for example, you were creating an online information security awareness program, you would want your legal department's input for obvious reasons, and also to make sure you have not overlooked something, such as co-employment issues.

Privacy

I have mentioned the Privacy division as a good partner previously in this chapter. To me it is a natural fit. If your company is mandated by federal regulation, such as the Gramm-Leach-Bliley Act, to implement an awareness program, then I highly suggest you partner with Privacy. As I mentioned earlier, your employees do not know the difference between Information Security and Privacy. You want to eliminate confusion. It benefits everyone in the company and also provides an additional shared resource to fund your program.

Compliance

Companies are burdened with more and more regulations and requirements than ever before. If you can get your program aligned with the Compliance division, implementing it becomes a lot easier. For example, if you merge your efforts with another division, such as Privacy (suggested earlier), you will find it easier to gain Compliance's support in implementing an annual information security awareness training requirement. Depending on processes at your company, you may find that Compliance is willing to take over and fund the delivery of your annual online training requirement. The greatest benefit to an online training program is its ability to track compliance. This is something you do not want on your plate, if at all possible. Otherwise, your life will become an administrative nightmare, as opposed to allowing you to be creative and move your program forward.

Training and Communications

If your company has a Training and/or Communications division, embrace their services. In some cases, you will have no alternative. For example, your company has a Learning Management System (LMS). To wander away from an established training platform does not make sense. In fact, it could possibly get you in trouble. Additionally, you want to make sure your materials are written in "corporate speak." I don't always agree with this, because it can sometimes stifle creativity, but it is still the right thing to do.

Coordinating your division's internal messages to the enterprise is important, too. You are not the only one in your division communicating to the enterprise. You want to ensure that conflicting messages are not being sent out, that what is being communicated is in "people speak," not "technical speak," unless that *is* your audience.

Personnel

These folks are not critical to your program, but if you have materials that you want sent out to new hires in their post-acceptance package, these are the people to work with. In addition, get to know whom you can rely on to get distribution lists. This helps especially when you are sending out a survey (either print or electronic). They can slice and dice the distribution profile you want to survey. I mean by that the SVPS, VPS, and the corporate officers, by hierarchy, so you have a good representation across the enterprise.

Information Security Consultants

If your company is large enough to have internal consultants working with lines of business, then get to know these people. One of the dangers of implementing an information security awareness program is releasing a product or requirement that is in conflict with another division's calendar. Your internal Information Security consultants can help you with this issue.

> **W**ARNING
>
> You are not a cop! A mistake many make in Information Security is having the attitude of "Gate Keeper." The perception in the enterprise is that you're the cop. This attitude will hamper your program as well as other services Information Security provides.

I think one of the worst things an Information Security Department can do is alienate the other departments in the company from your services and support. Developing the attitude of "enabler" goes a long way toward implementing a successful information security awareness program. There was never a time that I could not find a "Win, Win" solution to an internal customer's need. And that needs to be your attitude to get their willingness to buy in to your program.

Some final thoughts around alliances. Do not forget other direct reports in your division. When building your information security awareness program, ask those who report directly to the CISO to designate someone on their team who you can interact with in the development and/or review of the program you are putting together. Everyone in Information Security should be an advocate of the awareness program. Many of your co-workers support other employees in the company. Make sure everyone knows that information security awareness materials are available, where to find standards and other guidance, and how to contact Information Security for clarification of questions, concerns, or to report an incident. This can be accomplished in staff meetings, brown bag lunches, and e-mail notifications, as well as covering the components and materials in your awareness program.

How Do You Keep Your Program a Successful Component of Your Company's Mindset?

In the beginning of this chapter, I gave you the answer to this question. Repetition is the aid to memory. How many different touch points have you created in your program? I have discussed print, online training, and Web sites. Certainly using posters, Post-It notes, tchotchkes with proper information security behavior reminders, articles, and e-mails can help. And with today's compression and streaming capabilities, video has become a viable delivery channel, too.

IDEA

If you are a university, sponsor a contest for students to create awareness posters or short videos that support the information security messages.

This is a great way to get students on your campus involved and to get these important messages out. If your company has a video production studio, use their resources. What are your creative talents? It might be designing posters. If you have an idea, but not the creative ability, who inside your company can help you create the product? The Awareness Intra-preneur within you is constantly looking for new products, and new channels through which to deliver awareness messages.

WARNING

There is a tendency for management to use those who are responsible for designing and implementing the company's information security awareness program for other projects. This often can become the death knell of the program. That's why it's important to have your business plan in place, working on and implementing the next phase, and measuring your program so you can validate the program's progress and success.

In small companies, this warning is neither true nor prudent, but in larger companies it can create a significant issue in the programs' continuity and emphasis. The need for an Information Security Awareness Specialist is emerging. This is a person who has a good handle on marketing, communications, media, design, project management, and implementation. This individual doesn't necessarily need to be a subject-matter expert, because a lot of what they must know is common sense or outlined in the company's information security policy, standards, and other guidance.

An Information Security Awareness Specialist is also someone who can communicate effectively with all levels in the company. Often he/she will directly support the CISO and other senior leaders in presentation needs supporting the information security awareness messages. I suggest this because I have seen employees who do not have the presence, drive, and maturity to implement and sustain a program. This is not to slight all those who are trying to make a difference. This is to say that the issue is a major one that requires major attention and proven leadership ability. It requires a risk-taker, an intra-preneur, someone who is willing to use entrepreneurial skills on the inside of the company to advance the awareness program.

Now, let's move on to the final portion of this chapter where I describe the most difficult thing you'll need to do: measure an information security awareness program.

How to Measure Your Program

What gets measured gets done. Historically, it is difficult to measure the effectiveness of an information security awareness program. If you can connect your training to specific behaviors and have a way of monitoring those behaviors to see if compliance has improved, then that is what you are looking for. It validates the training. However, I caution that awareness is not training. It is not learning how a widget works. It is understanding and exhibiting the correct safeguarding sensitive information behaviors. So what can you measure to justify the effectiveness of your program?

First, how many employees have received training, whether through an annual class or a new hire orientation? How many employees have received the Quick Reference Guide or other key materials you have distributed? How many "Awareness" calls have you received and what categories are they in? If you do some marketing on creating easy-to-remember yet hard-to-crack passwords, and your password resets go down, this is a good indicator that your program is working. You want to capture this before and after information to show improvement. It is not always easy to find applications or programs that can give you timely and accurate information.

For example, how many sensitive customer documents that include Social Security numbers, account numbers, and so on are not truncated and are being e-mailed outside the company without encryption? If I had a section on encryption in my training, can I document improvement? If you can, great, but in most organizations this is a challenge.

In my experience, I relied heavily on subjective measurements that ultimately validated the effectiveness of our program. It showed steady improvement over time. It also provided critical objectives to the program so that we complied with the Six Sigma quality management process. Here's how I did it.

I created a paper mailer initially, because at that time we did not have an online survey resource. In fact, we didn't really have anyone who knew how to write survey questions. It is a skill. To maximize return of the survey, it was sent out with a way to respond anonymously. I actually had two surveys: one for new hires and one for all employees. The new-hire survey was done on a monthly basis, while the employee survey was done once a year. I needed, on the annual survey, 600 responses to have a statistically valid survey. The easiest way to figure this out was to go on the Internet and search "sample size calculator." I can tell you that when I went from a paper to an online survey, the number of respondents went up. I can also tell you that offering a trinket or other incentive to respond did not make a difference in the number of responses. You want a cross section of your organization, so survey all levels of employees and all hierarchies or divisions. Your personnel department should be able to provide a report that slices and dices this information for you. Obviously, you want the employee's full name, mail code and hierarchy, and position (CEO, SVP VP, Officer). If your survey is being delivered via an online channel, then you would want the employee's e-mail address, too. My response ratio was always high.

I asked questions in six basic categories:

- Passwords
- Viruses
- PC Security
- Information Security Standards
- Data Classification
- Other Threats

I also asked questions that pertained to the level of service our division was providing. I would track all the questions, but for reporting purposes for CTQ (Critical to Quality), we only used ten questions in what we called our "Awareness Quotient," for lack of a better term. It showed over time how the program was working and where there was a need for improvement. Over a five-year period of time, we went from an "Awareness Quotient" of under 50 percent to over 90 percent. The chart in Figure 4.4 reflects one question, but gives you an idea of what improvement looks like over time. Could we define one product or component that made the improvements? I believe it is a cumulative effect of your program over time, as long as it remains consistent, that will show improvement and a cultural difference in your company. I must say that when the company came out of a survey application we could use, the administrative nightmare was over, and surveying became a lot easier.

Figure 4.4 How Improvements in Awareness Can Improve over Time

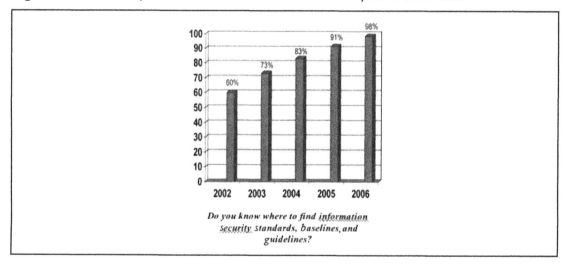

The survey also gave us an indication, by levels in management, of who better understood the behaviors and what areas within the company were complying (for instance, were new hires receiving the Employee Quick Reference Guide?). When our online training program was put into effect, it gave us other collaborating data, such as how many employees within a hierarchy were not taking the annual training. This allowed us to target a hierarchy or division for follow-up and generated discussion on what we could do to ensure compliance was being met. One thing that can help in this arena is support from Compliance and your CEO. The CEO should mandate that all of his/her directly reporting officers ensure at least 93 percent or above compliance to all mandatory training. Historically, that would include regulatory- or industry-required training as well as sexual harassment training, code of ethics or conduct, and privacy and information security awareness training.

The graph in Figure 4.5 is a way of showing over time how your program is doing and, again, where improvement is needed. Post these graphs in your work area. As people visit you, it shows that you have a handle on your program. It also helps if you are working with training specialists and people who design training programs. They are continually trying to find the widget to measure the before-and-after effect of training. Having your own statistics allows you to keep this discussion in a broader perspective.

Figure 4.5 A Graph Displaying Your Program's Progress

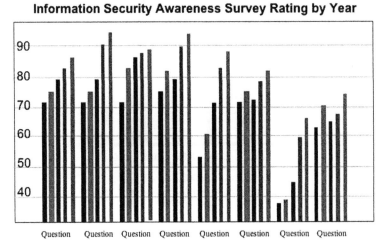

Question Question Question Question Question Question Question Question

Summary

The subject of implementing an effective information security awareness program is something more than what can be included in a single chapter. The Internet affords us access to a lot of good information, and companies that can help you design and implement your program. Nothing, though, will do this better than your own spirit and desire to make such a program "world class."

Specifically in reference to SCADAs, because that is what this book is primarily about, this chapter on awareness would not have been included if the lead author and publisher did not feel it was an appropriate and important topic to discuss. Awareness is communications. Awareness is understanding risks. Awareness is being proactive to those risks with sensible solutions. Each individual can significantly reduce the exposure of sensitive information by following simple behaviors and raising their hand with conviction when they see a potential or real risk. No one has all the answers, but collectively the risk can be addressed and reduced. Each company in America can significantly reduce the loss of sensitive information through an effective employee awareness program. There is no question about that. One lost laptop can be a devastating incident that very well may not have occurred if the employee clearly understood both the risk and their responsibility. The cost to implement an information security awareness program is incalculably far less than what it could cost you later without one.

Today's information risk pandemic should be treated like any other event that requires a disaster recovery plan. Prevention is an important key, and through it we just might bring the level of this risk down from pandemic status to that of a cold.

Solutions Fast Track

Why an Information Security Awareness Program Is Important

- ☑ The failure in security systems often is due to lack of human interest or involvement.

- ☑ Corporations need to treat security seriously, and ensure that employees think and act securely.

- ☑ More investment in security infrastructure is needed.

How to Design an Effective Information Security Awareness Program

☑ Security should have an employee dedicated to creating an implementing a program.

☑ Your program should be treated as a maketing campaign and each employee should be "touched" repeatedly by marketing messages about being secure.

☑ Create a business plan for your program and make sure you have institutional buy-in to ensure its success.

☑ Print a "Quick Reference" gide and eliver the rest of your program online, to make updating information easier.

How to Implement an Effective Information Security Awareness Program

☑ Communication with employees is the most important factor when implementing a security awareness program.

☑ Communicate not only the security policies, but why they are important.

☑ Work with new hires to instill the importance of security in them.

☑ Hold frequent training sessions.

How Do You Keep Your Program a Successful Component of Your Company's Mindset?

☑ Utilize the creative aspects of your company to create videos, web sites, and other forms of presentations to engage your audience.

☑ Create a slogan and produce hand-outs like magnets of desk calendars that reind people of the importance of security.

☑ Repetition of the security message is key.

How to Measure Your Program

☑ Create and administer surveys to measure the effectiveness of your campaign.

☑ Measure how many new employees have received training.

☑ How many employees have "strong" passwords?

Chapter 5

Working with Law Enforcement on SCADA Incidents

Lester J. Johnson Jr. is employed by the SCANA Corporation, a $ 9 Billion, Fortune 500, energy–based holding company, headquartered in Columbia, South Carolina. Mr. Johnson serves in the Corporate Security and Claims Department as a Manager with responsibility for Investigations and Crisis Management. Mr. Johnson leads a staff of professional investigators who conduct investigations of internal corporate compliance issues, criminal violations against the corporation's property and personnel, executive protection, background investigations and risk reduction efforts on behalf of the Corporation. The Crisis Management Department is responsible for the development and continual assessment of security risk management and reduction plans for the critical infrastructure operated by the Corporation. These risk management and reduction plans include the assurance of compliance with the various governmental agencies with oversight responsibilities for the critical infrastructure. Business continuity and emergency procedure planning are also a major component of the crisis management group.

Mr. Johnson is a retired Deputy to the Assistant Director of Investigative Services for the South Carolina Law Enforcement Division. He was responsible for the delivery of all investigative services, which included general investigations, bomb and arson, tactical, computer crimes, special victims, executive protection, behavioral science, public corruption, and insurance fraud.

During his twenty–eight year career Mr. Johnson received numerous awards and commendations, including the Strom Thurmond Award of Excellence in 2004. Mr. Johnson is a graduate of the FBI National Academy and has served as an adjunct instructor for numerous organizations.

Mr. Johnson is married to the former Laura Whelchel of Cordele, Georgia and resides in Lexington, South Carolina with his two children.

Introduction

Law enforcement agencies are receiving increasing requests for the investigation of high technology related criminal activities. The protection of the nation's critical infrastructure is among the highest level priorities for ensured continuity of operation for our nation. At the core of many of these critical infrastructure operations are systems that move data to and from the computerized system that manage and control the operations of the infrastructure. As you can imagine, should these systems come under attack or become compromised and control is assumed by those person(s) intent on creating havoc, a disastrous outcome is imminent. The potential exists for great harm to human life and the national economy if SCADA systems are breached. For this purpose, it is my intent to, in many cases, introduce SCADA systems to law enforcement and discuss potential responses to investigating an attempted or actual breech of these systems. Additionally, you will find several examples of mitigation that law enforcement can pass along in a pro-active attempt to prevent occurrences of system breaches.

The SCADA systems described below are very technical in nature. Law enforcement agencies who lack the personnel with a strong information technology background will find it very difficult to grasp the concepts associated with SCADA systems. Having the knowledge of the system and the associated audit logs are necessary in determining the point of an actual or attempted breach and discovering and preserving the evidence necessary to support criminal charges.

TIP

The concept of law enforcement partnering with subject matter experts from the private sector in the investigation of SCADA breaches is one that should be considered. Caution should be noted if law enforcement is utilizing subject matter experts from the organization whose system may have been breached, as there is always the distinct possibility that an "insider" may be involved. Assistance from Federal Law Enforcement agencies or agencies with experience in the investigation of high technology crime may also be considered.

SCADA System Overview

SCADA stands for Supervisory Control and Data Acquisition. SCADA refers to a system that collects data from various sensors that send data to a central computer, which then manages and controls the systems. There are many parts of a working

SCADA system. These systems usually include signal hardware input and output, controllers, networks, human machine interface (HMI), communications equipment, and software. The term SCADA refers to the entire control system. The control system monitors data from various sensors that may be located in one facility, or they could be geographically distributed across a city, state, or even around the globe.

These SCADA systems are core to much of the nation's critical information technology infrastructure, most of which is owned and operated by private industry. It is vital that both the system owner and law enforcement be proactive in developing partnerships, building collaborative capabilities, and defining processes to facilitate investigations in the event of an attack.

Let's spend just a minute to explain the basic components of a SCADA system and its functions. This will help law enforcement understand the possible attack vectors as we go through the details of each and how to protect them.

One of the key aspects of a SCADA system is its ability to monitor an entire system in real time. To accomplish this, SCADA systems incorporate remote terminal units, or RTU's, and programmable logic controllers, or PLC's. These RTU's and PLCs are the intelligent building blocks of a SCADA system. Usually RTU's or PLC's run a pre-programmed process, such as turning a switch on or off, opening or closing a valve, or sensing temperature changes. Monitoring each of them individually can be difficult, because they often are spread out over the system. The human machine interface HMI is where the information is displayed or monitored by the operator. HMI's are an easy way to standardize the monitoring of multiple RTU's or PLC's. Real-time communications to these units is critical to the health of the system. Because of the possible link to physical outcomes, the requirement for redundant systems is heightened. HMI's often are connected to databases to facilitate providing graphs or trends, logistic information, schematics for a specific sensor or machine, or even troubleshooting guides. SCADA systems are considered closed loop systems and run with relatively little human intervention.

An attacker who wishes to assume control of a SCADA system is faced with three challenges:

1. Gaining access to the control system LAN

2. Through discovery, understanding of the process

3. Gaining control of the process

Unfortunately there are many methods an intruder can use to get this information. Increasingly these systems are well documented on the web and are easily accessible.

Understanding the control systems cyber vulnerabilities is key to understanding the steps needed to protect these systems. The British Columbia Institute of Technology (BCIT) study of 34 incidents shows the SCADA components breached and their origins.

The following charts are divided into two groups, 14 internal events and 25 external. Notice the Virtual Private Networks (VPN); those trusted networks lead to 8 percent of the breaches. Given these statistics, one can begin to get an idea as to where one should prioritize the spending of security money.

Figure 5.1 14 Internal Security Incidents by Entry Point

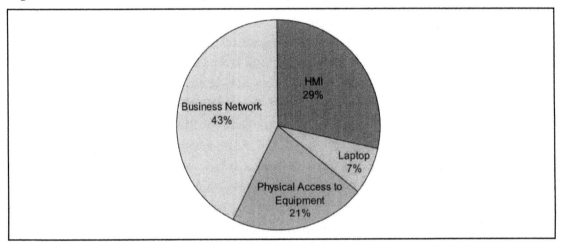

Figure 5.2 25 External Security Incidents by Entry Point

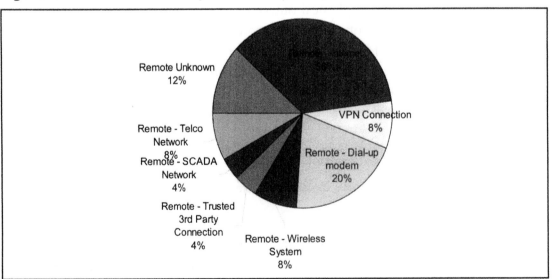

Figure 5.3 BCIT report statistics

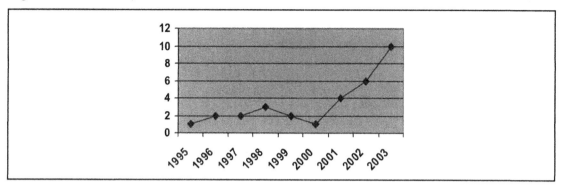

The BCIT's report says 70 percent of attacks reported between 2001 and 2003 came from some external entity. Between 1982 and 2000, just 31 percent of attacks came from the outside. This is an older study, but the trends have continued.

The sharp increase of SCADA intrusions beginning in 2001 indicates a sharp increase in these kinds of attacks, which may or may not be politically motivated.

Secure Network Management
Securing Wide Area Network Perimeter

A well-segregated network is your first step to controlling your systems. The first segregation point is a perimeter security defense using a firewall between the business network and the Internet. Utilize an Intrusion Protection Devise (IPS) as well to monitor and automatically block unwanted traffic entering from the Internet. Do not forget your wireless access points. Treat them the same as an Internet access. Use a firewall to segregate your SCADA control LAN from your business network. Use an IPS to monitor and block unwanted traffic from your business network to your control LAN.

TIP

Segregation at the perimeter is the first segregation that you should consider. Establishing security zones according to data sensitivity should be a standard practice. Develop rules and guidelines for access to and from these zones. A basic rule would allow more secure zones to establish connections to less secure zones, but never from a less secure zone to higher secure zone. For example, a workstation on the SCADA LAN could establish a session with a server on the business LAN, but the reverse would not be allowed. Following this simple principle will go a long way in keeping your environment secure. If during an investigation you discover this, further questioning and log examination may be in order.

Controlling Access

Access control from a physical perspective is obviously important. Secondly and statistically more important is network access control. A human actor using network access can wreak havoc on an unprotected or poorly managed network. Once access is gained, control is just a step away. Using technology such as two-factor authentication is strongly recommended. Tokens, swipe cards, and even biometrics in conjunction with a strong user id / password policy go a long way to controlling access. Once you know with whom you are dealing, then controlling what he or she does is your next challenge.

Performing Network Backup and Recovery

The backup and recovery of a SCADA system has its own unique issues. The all-the-time requirements of SCADA systems means that backups must be done on live systems and recovery times must be very short. The solution is often a mirrored database that can be taken off-line for backup purposes without affecting the production systems. Otherwise business production lines would be shut down, possibly resulting in loss of money and business reputation. Use as much caution as to who and how access is given to these systems as you would the control system itself. The data in these databases can be hacked, giving away enough information to fully understand the processes needed.

WARNING

> These systems use a survivor ability model, not a backup and recovery model. These systems must be investigated while they are online.

Transmitting Legacy Non-Routable Protocol Securely

Many of the SCADA systems have been around long before the advent of the PC or Internet, and many of their communication protocols were developed for closed networks. Transmitting these protocols over a routed network was never envisioned. The Internet protocol Ethernet is designed to get the message there through whatever paths are available and is not a guaranteed delivery protocol. Many of the SCADA systems are very time sensitive and must be delivered on time every time, so using alternate routes that take more or even less time can cause issues.

Figure 5.4 Controlling Access to the SCADA Control System LAN

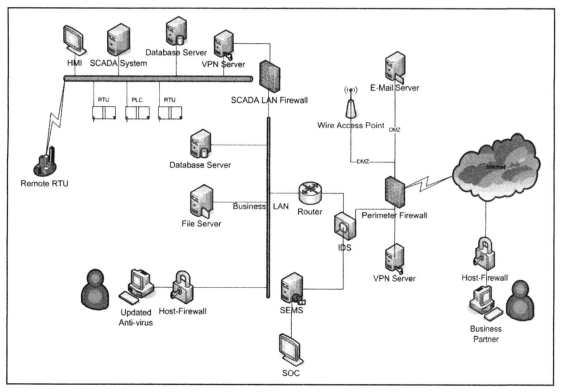

Dial-Up Access to the Remote Terminal Units (RTU)

Modems are often used as backup communications if the primary high-speed lines are down. The attacker will automatically dial every phone number (known as WAR dialing) or every extension in the company looking for modems hung off the corporate phone system. Most Remote Terminal Units (RTUs) identify themselves and the vendor who made them. Most RTUs require no authentication or a password for authentication. It is common to find RTUs with the default passwords still enabled in the field.

> **TIP**
>
> Where possible, configure modems in the call back mode. This helps with the WAR dialing from being successful.

Vendor Support: Dial-Up Modem/VPN Access

Most control systems come with vendor support agreements. There is a need for support during upgrades or when a system is malfunctioning. The most common means of vendor support used to be through a dial-up modem and PCAnywhere. In recent years, this means of support has transitioned to VPN access to the control system LAN. An attacker will attempt to gain access to internal vendor resources or field laptops and piggyback on the connection into the control system LAN. Monitor and manage this access point closely for possible attacks.

IT Controlled Communication Gear

Often the routers and telephone communications are maintained by the business IT staff. A skilled attacker can compromise these devices by gaining access to the field communications.

> **NOTE**
>
> In the BCIT study, 43 percent of the incidents were on the business network, and 36 percent came by way of the Internet. The proprietary systems were

not the most successful targets; it was the support system components that were breached successfully. This could be from the sheer number of systems and their vulnerabilities on the business LAN, the dangerous Internet behavior of the users, or possibly a combination of both.

Corporate VPNs

Virtual Private Networks (VPNs) are often set up for access to the control networks from the business LAN. An often-used attack vector is the end user's workstation utilizing key-loggers and screen scrappers, which piggyback on the legitimate users as they access the control systems through the VPN's. Extra care should be given to every workstation that is allowed to access the control network. Ensure up to date anti-virus software, patch the operating system automatically, and make sure that host-based firewalls are standard on these workstations. Consider whether to allow workstations that access the Internet to connect to the control LAN. Strong cyber security user education training should be required. The business LAN is the most likely access vehicle attackers will attempt to use to access your control systems. The e-mail, web servers, and users browsing the Internet are the most likely entry mechanisms. The latest operating system patches and up-to-date anti-virus software are a must. In 2007 there were, on average, 19 new exploits per day, with an average of a 30-day lead-time between known vulnerability and patch availability. Thus, on any given day, there are possibly 570 ways they can get into your systems that you have no way of stopping. Security in-depth is your only defense.

NOTE

Google conducted an internal research concerning infected websites. The study revealed that 1 out of 10 pages contain malware. That is 450,000 websites are infected with malware files, most of them trying to exploit the user's computer through the Internet Explorer browser. Usually, the malicious files are aiming to install infected files on the user's computers that will allow the attackers to obtain control over the affected system.

Database Links

Databases are often mirrored to the business LAN for disaster recovery or backup purposes. They contain the keys to the entire control systems, and include user id's and passwords, control codes, detailed explanations of how the control systems work, and information about the RTU's and PLS's that control each component of the system. Attackers use specially crafted Sequel Query Language (SQL) statements to take over the database server and extract its contents. Every modern day SQL database allows this type of attack if steps are not taken to block these statements.

TIP

Protect your organization from threats by monitoring and alerting on any hostile and unauthorized activity jeopardizing your critical data. Supply the data and audit trails required for threat identification, policy enforcement, and regulatory compliance so that you can identify and neutralize threats from the perimeter to the core.

Poorly Configured Firewalls

Not providing outbound data rules is the most common configuration problem. This may allow an attacker who can sneak a payload onto a control system machine to call back out of the control system. This is known as phoning home. This is one of the most widely used techniques, often taking advantage of vulnerability in a browser and subsequently pulling down malware from another website without any user interaction.

Business Partner Links

These links have often been thought of as trusted relationships, but what it means is that your systems are only as well protected as your weakest link. The business partners are not automatically that weak link, but it does increase you exposure and make the process much more complicated to secure. Many times, dictating to a vendor how its networks are run can be difficult and verifying that the vendor is following your requirements is even harder.

Managing Security Events

Figure 5.5 A Security Event Management System

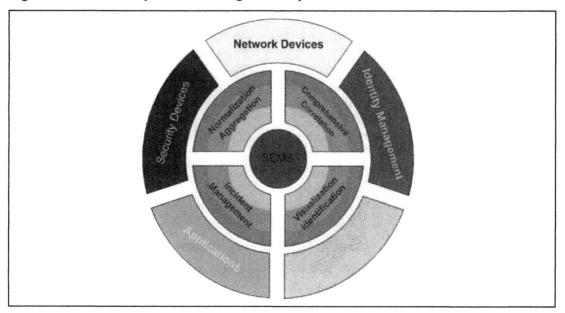

Utilizing a Security Event Management System is the key to effectively managing critical systems in today's Internet-connected world. Without eyes on target giving you situation awareness, you really don't know what is happening on your network. What you don't know can cause you big problems. Most networks use IDS/IPS devices to monitor the front doors and access points to the Internet. There are no more perimeters in today's networks. Devices like PDAs and cell phones with Internet access are inside your building and behind your firewalls. Your partners and vendors are on a virtual private network connected into your network from half a world away. Insider attacks constitute the majority of today's attacks. The SEMS can be used in a post-mortem fashion to assist in lessons learned or during an investigation to determine how the attack was carried out.

TIP

Turn all of your devices into security devices. Devices such as firewalls, intrusion detection systems, virtual private networks, anti-virus software, workstations, active directories, file servers, print servers, modems, and many SCADA control devices could report to the Security Event Management System.

Once your devices are centrally logging, a correlation engine that brings all the events together and visually displays the events in real-time is vital. Filtering through thousands of events daily without this capability would be impossible. The objective is to get out in front and proactively identify attacks before they are successful. Attackers must go through a discovery process or finger printing of your systems prior to penetration. The visibility that you have with a SEMS will afford you the knowledge needed to stop these attacks prior to their gaining a foothold on your network.

Conduct Routine Assessments

A security assessment shows the system's security posture with respect to specific vulnerabilities. The assessment closely examines the network architecture and interprets and compares results against the various business processes to determine whether security controls are in place to appropriately address the vulnerabilities. The assessment testing methodology must be effective at exposing vulnerabilities on complete systems, including networks, applications, operating systems, wireless, security devices, and all supporting systems and their many interconnections. There are many automated tools that can be used during these assessments. Social engineering is also a vital component of an assessment. Remember its people, processes, and technology. Technology is never the complete answer, and often the people and processes are overlooked in these assessments.

Examples of Common Attack Techniques
Man-In-The-Middle Attacks (MITM)

An MITM attack is when the attacker makes independent connections with the victims and relays messages between them, making them believe that they are talking directly to each other when in fact the entire conversation is controlled by the attacker. The attacker must be able to intercept all messages going between the two victims and inject new ones, which is straightforward in many circumstances. For example, the owner of a public wireless access point can in principle conduct MITM attacks on the users.

Key-Logger Software

A key-logger is a type of surveillance software that records every keystroke you make to a log file, usually encrypted. A key-logger can record instant messages, e-mail, and any information you type or that is displayed on your monitor. The log file created by the key-logger then can be sent to a specified receiver. Some key-logger programs will also record any e-mail addresses you use and Web sites you visit.

Summary

Given on average 570 exploits a day, no way to patch the operating systems, and 450,000 infected pages, how can you ever keep your systems protected?

Situational awareness, segregation, security event management, security assessments, and security training are the points that should be stressed.

1. Know what traffic is on your network. Know it well enough that if your traffic goes up or down by 10 percent to 15 percent you know it and you can tell exactly why.

2. Keep your security zones intact. Never access a higher security zone network or device from a lower level security zone or device.

3. Centrally log and correlate all your devices from the core to the perimeter. Correlation between known system vulnerability and attempted exploits against those systems is your actionable data. Actionable data in a sea of otherwise meaningless data is pure gold.

4. Trust but verify with routine assessments of your people, processes, and technology. Scanning or other automated assessments are very beneficial but the people and the processes are where you will either pass or fail on a day-to-day security test. Absolutely do your automated testing of operating systems, virus-patch levels, databases, applications, and network devices and do them often, quarterly or more frequently on the higher value targets. At the very least, yearly review your processes, audit your security training effectiveness, and perform some social engineering audits.

5. Training your IT staff on the possibilities and your users on the impact of their actions can have a very positive affect on your security. Statistically, well-trained people and properly followed processes are the keys to a successful security program, yet we find over and over the lack of training and poorly followed processes.

Solutions Fast Track

SCADA System Overview

☑ SCADA systems are core to much of the nation's critical information technology infrastructure.

☑ It is vital that both the system owner and law enforcement be proactive in developing partnerships.

☑ One of the key aspects of a SCADA system is its ability to monitor an entire system in real time.

☑ Understanding the control systems cyber vulnerabilities is key to understanding the steps needed to protect these systems.

Secure Network Management

☑ A well-segregated network is your first step to controlling your systems.

☑ A human actor using network access can wreak havoc on an unprotected or poorly managed network.

☑ Backups must be done on live systems and recovery times must be very short.

☑ Many of the SCADA systems are very time sensitive and must be delivered on time every time, so using alternate routes that take more or even less time can cause issues.

☑ Where possible, configure modems in the call back mode. This helps with the WAR dialing from being successful.

☑ An attacker will attempt to gain access to internal vendor resources or field laptops and piggyback on the connection into the control system LAN. Monitor and manage this access point closely for possible attacks.

☑ Often the routers and telephone communications are maintained by the business IT staff. A skilled attacker can compromise these devices by gaining access to the field communications.

☑ Extra care should be given to every workstation that is allowed to access the control network.

☑ Your systems are only as well protected as your weakest link.

Managing Security Events

☑ Utilizing a Security Event Management System is the key to effectively managing critical systems in today's Internet-connected world.

☑ Get out in front and proactively identify attacks before they are successful.

☑ A security assessment shows the system's security posture with respect to specific vulnerabilities.

Examples of Common Attack Techniques

☑ An MITM attack is when the attacker makes independent connections with the victims and relays messages between them, making them believe that they are talking directly to each other when in fact the entire conversation is controlled by the attacker.

☑ A key-logger is a type of surveillance software that records every keystroke you make to a log file, usually encrypted.

Frequently Asked Questions

Q: What are some examples of industry using SCADA systems?

A: SCADA systems are used in a variety of plants and processes, from optimizing the most benefit from production lines to supervising and controlling the production of toxic and dangerous chemicals. Some examples are nuclear power generation, electric power generation and distribution, and water purification systems.

Q: What are the key elements to secure a SCADA system?

A: Situational awareness, segregation, security event management, security assessments, and security training.

Q: Between public and private entities, which one is the great user of SCADA systems?

A: The private sector is a greater use of SCADA systems.

Q: What resources are available to law enforcement for assistance in investigating breaches of SCADA systems?

A: Local law enforcement can seek assistance from federal law enforcement, law enforcement agencies that have experienced high technology crime investigative units, or subject matter experts from the private sector.

Chapter 6

Locked but Not Secure: An Overview of Conventional and High Security Locks

Marc Weber Tobias is an investigative attorney and security specialist living in Sioux Falls, South Dakota. As part of his practice, he represents and consults with lock manufacturers, government agencies and corporations in the U.S. and overseas regarding the design and bypass of locks and security systems. He has authored six police textbooks, including Locks, Safes, and Security, (ISBN 978-0398070793), which is recognized as the primary reference for law enforcement and security professionals worldwide. The second edition, a 1400 page two-volume work, is utilized by criminal investigators, crime labs, locksmiths and those responsible for physical security. A fourteen-volume multi-media edition of his book is also available online. His website is security.org.

As a former prosecutor and Chief of the Organized Crime Unit for the Office of Attorney General, state of South Dakota, Marc supervised many major investigations and prosecutions. He continues to work investigations for government and private clients, mainly involving technical fraud issues.

Marc is a member of a number of professional security organizations, including the American Society of Industrial Security (ASIS), Association of Firearms and Tool Marks Examiners (AFTE), American Polygraph Association (APA) and American Association of Police Polygraphists (AAPP).

Marc has lectured extensively in the United States and Europe on physical security and certain aspects of criminal investigations and interrogation techniques. He holds several patents involving the bypass of locks and security systems. Marc contributes a column to engadget.com and has been featured in many publications as well as radio and television stories around the world.

Figure 6.1 A cutaway pin tumbler lock with all six pins aligned at shear line. In this photograph the plug, containing the bottom pins, is free to rotate.

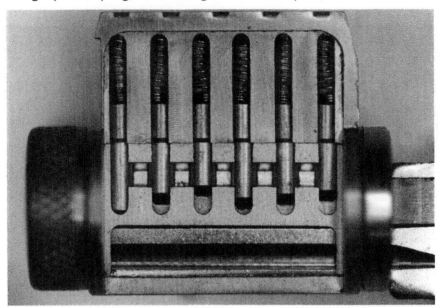

Figure 6.2 A cutaway of a pin tumbler lock in which some of the bottom pins are above and some below the shear line. The plug is not free to turn and the cylinder remains locked. The arrows indicate (1) bottom pins, (2) plug, (3) bitting of the key that raises the individual bottom pins to shear line, and (4) the shell of the lock.

Introduction

In most facilities, mechanical locks are relied upon as the first level of security. They protect doors, safes, and barriers from being opened, and they control the movement of obstacles to entry. The most popular mechanism, at least in the U.S., is the pin tumbler design although in some parts of the world the lever lock is still the first choice. In short, locks are used everywhere, and they are relied upon as the first line of defense.

Security officers, risk managers, information protection specialists, and others who are responsible for the physical security of a facility often base their selection of locks on the representations of the manufacturer in conjunction with security ratings that are established by standards organizations. High security-rated cylinders are most often specified to protect high value targets or critical infrastructure because it is assumed that they have met stringent requirements with regard to anticipated methods of entry during an attack.

Organizations are generally not capable of performing in-house tests to determine the suitability of locks for their specific requirements. They rely on the standards organizations and testing laboratories to promulgate minimum performance benchmarks and then to insure that the locks that are certified to such standards actually meet them. Reliance upon either Underwriters Laboratories or the Builders Hardware Manufacturers Association (BHMA) to insure a certain level of performance or security may not meet either expectation because of significant limitations in how these standards are promulgated and the certification testing that results from this.

The undue reliance upon standards as the primary protection criteria can potentially lead to significant breaches of security by knowledgeable attackers. In some cases, high security rated locks that were thought to be virtually impregnable can be compromised in seconds even by amateurs who are armed with certain information about their design deficiencies.

NOTE

The federal government has defined surreptitious and covert entry with regard to locks and security containers.

- **Surreptitious entry** means a method of entry, such as lock manipulation, which would not be detectable during normal use or during inspection by a qualified person.

■ **Covert entry** is defined as a method of entry which causes physical damage to the door or lock such that the damage can be repaired to the point where it would not be detectable by a user during normal use. The damage would be detectable during inspection by a qualified person.

Understanding the limitations of locks and the standards by which they are rated should create a healthy skepticism about the claims and representations of their manufacturers with regard to resistance against forced entry, covert and surreptitious entry, and the compromise of key control. If you rely upon locks to provide any significant level of protection in terms of complexity to bypass them or time delay for an intruder to reach his or her intended target, then you need to explore further. What you have heretofore been taught with regard to just what protection the locks in your facility are actually providing may surprise you. After reading this chapter you might re-examine the way in which you employ locking hardware and the "real world" vulnerabilities that might be jeopardized by such reliance.

We shall first provide a survey of conventional pin tumbler locks and their attributes so that they can be distinguished from high security cylinders. Within the security community everyone knows that the typical pin tumbler mechanism is not particularly secure; pointing to their high security counterparts as the solution where greater protection against forced and covert entry attacks are required. We shall then review the standards that distinguish conventional from high security locks. Finally, we examine how conventional locks are compromised as a means to compare their attributes to their high security counterpart.

Conventional Pin Tumbler Locks

The generic pin tumbler mechanism comprises perhaps 95 percent of the locks in this country. They are produced in all forms and configurations and can provide any level of security from low to very high. There are billions of them and virtually all of the conventional pin tumbler locks are based upon the original Yale modification of the Egyptian concept. Most high security locks are also based upon a modification of the basic pin tumbler design.

We define conventional pin tumbler locks as those that do not have any special security enhancements. These locks provide the most basic in protection and do not have multiple layers of embedded security as encountered in high security cylinders.

These mechanisms do not carry "high security" ratings and thus are not produced to the same standards as their more expensive and rated counterparts. Conventional cylinders are what you find in hardware stores, Home Depot, Lowes, and the local lock shop.

As we will note there are no real security controls or any legal protection of their mechanical designs or keys. Conventional pin tumbler locks are relatively easy to open and generally offer little resistance against many forms of bypass, including some methods of forced entry, bumping, picking, impressioning, key duplication, and the replication of blanks by impressioning and casting techniques. The tolerances of the internal components may be significantly less than for high security locks, but so is their cost.

Figure 6.3 A conventional pin tumbler lock showing the three basic parts: the plug, the shell, and the keyway slot in the plug.

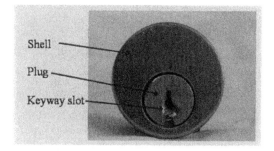

NOTE

A pin tumbler lock is comprised of six primary components: plug, shell, springs, top pins, bottom pins, and retaining mechanism to keep each pin stacked in its respective bore or chamber.

- **Plug:** The plug rotates within the shell and is used to transmit a turning motion through a cam or connecting bar in order to actuate the bolt or latch;

- **Shell:** This is the body of the lock. It contains the springs and top pins;

- **Springs:** The springs exert a downward force against the top and bottom pins to insure that they always block rotation of the plug until they are raised to the correct position;

- **Top pins:** The top pins enter into the plug to stop rotation until they are aligned at shear line;

- **Bottom pins:** The bottom pins make contact with the bitting of the key and are raised to shear line;

- **Spring retainer:** The spring retainer seals each chamber so that the top and bottom pins cannot fall out of the lock.

The Origins of the Modern Pin Tumbler Lock

Figure 6.4 The Egyptian pin tumbler lock was developed 4,000 years ago and relied upon a set of pegs to secure a moving bolt.

The original design of the pin tumbler lock was conceived more than four thousand years ago by the Egyptians. It was soon forgotten and lost in history until the mid-nineteenth century when Linus Yale decided it was time to produce a small, efficient, and secure lock. Yale's invention of the double-detainer locking theory in combination with a shear line offered an alternative to the lever tumbler, which was really the only mechanism that was both practical and secure at the time.

The original Egyptian lock had several pegs (equivalent to pins) that dropped into the plug and were required to be lifted so that the movable portion (equivalent to the bolt) could be withdrawn. Yale decided that the more prudent approach was to incorporate two pegs (split pins) within each bore or chamber so that the key could be made very small and also accommodate many differs or different bitting combinations. This was the beginning of the revolutionary development of the modern pin tumbler lock.

In the Yale lock the two pins and a spring were forced downward to accomplish locking. Several sets of pins (called pin stacks) could be incorporated within one mechanism. Each of the bottom pins had to be lifted to a point called a shear line. Only when all of the bottom pins were elevated to the correct position could the plug be turned by the action of the key. The splitting of pins was the real genius of this invention because it allowed a very slight difference in their position to allow or prevent the key from working. Each bottom pin could have several different depth positions or increments and maintain a relatively high tolerance between the plug and shell.

From its inception, lock manufacturers began improving upon the original Yale design in order to provide for more differs (key combinations) and greater security. There are many variables that can be controlled within the pin tumbler lock to provide for different options and security enhancements.

In a perfect world a lock cannot be opened without the correct key or code. In the real world there are levels of difficulty or resistance levels to forced and covert entry techniques which are dictated by these alterations or modifications to basic designs. These include the type of mechanism, the development of secondary locking systems, and certain embedded security enhancements.

NOTE

The pin tumbler lock is based upon the double-detainer locking theory and is brilliant in its simplicity The lock is comprised of a series of bores or chambers that are drilled through both the fixed body and rotating plug. Each chamber has what is called a pin stack, which is comprised of a spring, top pin, and bottom pin. When the correct key is inserted into the plug, its bitting (cuts) raise each bottom pin so that its top edge is precisely at the same height as the diameter of the plug. Each of the bottom pins must be aligned to this point, called the shear line. If any of the top pins protrude into the bottom chambers, or any of the bottom pins extend into the upper chambers in the shell, then the plug is prevented from turning and the lock cannot be opened.

A Review: The Essentials of Pin Tumbler Lock Design

In its simplest form the modern conventional pin tumbler lock consists of six primary components, as we noted. Many subsystems and attributes determine the security, durability, and option flexibility of the mechanism and include:

- Physical characteristics (strength) of the material that is employed for the shell, plug and pins;

- Manner in which the rotation of the plug is transmitted to the actual locking mechanism (bolt, latch, or other fastener);

- Number of pins, their shape and length, and available depth increments;

- Mechanical and geometric design of the key, including the number of bitting positions and bitting height;

- Design of the keyway with respect to its size and shape and the number, placement, and geometric design of the wards (within the keyway);

- Tolerances between each of the components.

The double-detainer concept of security within the Yale pin tumbler lock is quite elementary and extremely clever. It can be seen that once a pin occupies space in both the shell and plug at the same time the plug is not free to rotate until the bottom pin is lifted to a point where blockage does not occur. That point is called shear line. It is defined as the place where the lower pin is precisely level with the diameter of the plug.

When the lower pin is lifted to shear line there is no longer an obstruction to rotation. This is because the top pin is fully contained within the shell and the lower pin is completely within the plug; no part of either pin is protruding into the other. The upper and lower pins are split at the exact point where a gap occurs between plug and shell. Because of the close tolerances achieved in manufacturing, the tumblers must be precisely leveled at their shear line. If they protrude or are recessed $>\pm.003$", the plug will not turn. The exact tolerance depends upon the quality of the lock.

The keyway was added to the modern pin tumbler lock to limit what can enter the plug, unlike in the original Egyptian design. Once the key clears the wards within the keyway, the bitting can physically raise each of the lower pins to shear line. The bitting replaced the pegs in the Egyptian key.

All of the modern modifications to the Yale lock are but refinements of the simple principle of blocking rotation of the plug with movable detainers (pins, sliders, rotors, or other components). Thus, the rotating tumbler (Medeco®); dimple (Keso®, DOM, and Ikon); magnetic rotating tumbler (EVVA, Chubb); axial pin (Chicago Lock), and other iterations are all based upon the use of the split tumbler to stop rotation of the plug until all pins are lifted to one or more shear lines.

Security Enhancements for Conventional Locks

A conventional cylinder may employ any number of basic security options and convenience features but most do not. Kwikset is an excellent example. They are perhaps the most popular of the cheap locks that are sold in North America; more than twenty million cylinders are produced each year according to the manufacturer. They are everywhere and for the most part offer little to no security against forced or covert entry. Many of the cylinders contain what the author believes to be defective designs from the standpoint of security. Even high quality cylinder manufacturers offer little more in the way of security than does Kwikset. For consumer-level protection the conventional locking mechanisms may be sufficient, especially for residential applications. The security of the locks is minimal at best and they are not recommended for any critical facility.

Anti-Bumping Pins

As a result of the media attention to bumping in 2006, some manufacturers have implemented additional security measures in their cylinders. These steps have been taken to prevent common forms of bypass including bumping. Master Lock now integrates a special pin set in all of its locks to prevent bypass by this technique. Other manufacturers have designed preventative measures, but conventional pin tumbler locks are still inherently insecure. The approach that EVVA (Austria) and Master Lock have taken would appear to virtually eliminate the use of bumping as a bypass technique. Other manufacturers are expected to follow their lead especially because BHMA and UL are likely to add bumping to their testing standards.

NOTE

Security pins can take many forms but they all are designed to perform the same function: to make picking more difficult by creating false indications of a pin that is properly positioned at shear line. We refer to this as being set, which means that the bottom pin is trapped between the plug and shell. Security pins are produced in many different shapes. They are commonly referred to as mushroom, spool, or serrated tumblers. Their geometry causes them to be trapped at the shear line when torque is applied to the plug. When this occurs, the plug may turn slightly and then be prevented from further rotation, requiring a complete reset of its position to clear the trapped pins.

Security Pins

Conventional locks employ security pins to make picking more difficult. The design of these specially shaped tumblers can take many forms, including serrated, mushroom, spool, or a modification of these basic shapes. They do not materially affect the ability to bump open most of these locks, nor will they frustrate certain other forms of bypass. These pins cannot significantly reduce the basic insecurity of conventional locks; they are only a minimally effective enhancement.

Figure 6.5 This pin tumbler cylinder graphically illustrates how the mushroom pin (top pin) is trapped at the shear line. The plug can be only slightly rotated.

Keyways and Related Designs

Other enhancements can include restricted keyways, paracentric keyways, check-pins (such as Schlage Everest®), specially modified check-pins (such as Kaba Peaks®), interactive pins (Mul-T-Lock), changeable key systems (Instakey®, U-Change® and others), and interchangeable cores. The design of paracentric keyways can in some cases frustrate picking to some degree but not all forms of attack. Again, the fundamental problem is that the generic pin tumbler mechanism does not offer significant protection against many forms of bypass. There are only so many enhancements that can be implemented to the basic Yale design; it is still a relatively simple concept.

NOTE

A keyway provides the entry into the internal mechanism for a key that was produced on the correct blank. A number of obstructions, called wards, are set on either side of the opening to form a complex pattern of grooves and ridges that must be mirrored on the correct key in order for it to enter the lock.

The keyway is designed to keep all but the correct keys from accessing the pin tumblers and is the first security barrier that is provided against improper entry. Each manufacturer designs different keyways for its products. This offers added security because a key that does not have the proper set of grooves to match the internal wards is supposed to be incapable of entering the plug. Unfortunately, this is not always the case because of the potential to simulate blanks that will bypass the wards.

A paracentric ward pattern can frustrate picking attempts if the protruding obstructions cross the center line of the keyway. When this occurs, a pick is more difficult to move up and down, which is required in order to manipulate the individual pin tumblers to shear line. Paracentric keyways are required for high security locks.

Bitting Design

The design of the bitting (cuts on the key) can also be modified to enhance the overall security of conventional as well as high security locks. Multiple layers of bitting may be utilized. These are generally referred to as Laser track locks and often employ sliding wafers. Some locks utilize multiple tracks such as the EVVA 3KS, and some are indented or stacked. Certain designs, such as the Mul-T-Lock MT5, employ multiple bitting systems, which use both dimple pin tumbler and a single track for a secondary locking system. Others may use dual bittings (such a BiLock)® or bitting overlays.

Irregular angles such as found with the DOM Diamant® are also popular and can be very difficult to duplicate but not to copy with silicone or other techniques. Interactive components and floating pins (Mul-T-Lock and others) have gained in popularity. Dimples, holes, protrusions, and embedded magnets have also been employed. In fact, perhaps the highest security cylinder in Europe (EVVA MCS) embeds four rare-earth magnets to make the replication of keys virtually impossible.

NOTE

The bitting is the material on the key that comes into contact with the bottom pins and raises them to shear line. Different manufacturers employ variations in bitting thickness and height, but the end result is always the same: to raise or otherwise act upon the bottom pins to set them to the proper alignment at shear line. Some bitting is complex, especially in high security locks. Medeco requires that the bitting of its keys both elevate and rotate or twist each pin to set two independent security layers. The bitting in the Schlage Primus® also performs two functions: to lift a set of pin tumblers to shear line and to act upon a second unique set of finger-pins to both elevate and rotate them in order to align a sidebar. The bitting in conventional pin tumbler locks is generally quite simple and often only performs the single function of lifting the pins to shear line.

Design of the Key

Many security enhancements have been employed in an attempt to make keys and their corresponding internal locking mechanisms more secure. These solutions include side millings to control sliders and other pin sets, protrusions on keys in conjunction with internal sliders (Medeco m3 and Bilevel®), interactive elements (Mul-T-Lock and others), embedded magnets (Miwa, EVVA), notches in keys, rotation of bottom pins (Medeco), special keyways, irregular bitting shapes, single and telescoping dimple pins (Mul-T-Lock), holes in the key, embedded floating bearings, and transponders. The list of modifications to the basic pin tumbler design is endless but at the end of the day nothing can change the fact that it is the same insecure design that can be picked, impressioned, decoded, extrapolated for the top level master key, and bumped.

NOTE

UL 437, contrary to popular belief, is not a high security standard but rather a higher security standard. The only true standard for a high security lock is BHMA/ANSI 156.30, which has three tenets that must be satisfied for a lock to be certified. These relate to forced entry, covert entry, and key control.

Standards for Conventional and High Security Locks

There are three primary standards that address the security of locks in the United States: UL 437, BHMA/ANSI 156.50, and 156.30. It is appropriate that the reader should understand the differences in specifications within these standards in order to clearly differentiate between conventional and high security cylinders.

The UL requirements apply to door locks, locking cylinders, security container key locks, and two-key locks. It does not directly refer to high security locking mechanisms although UL 437 is referenced in BHMA/ANSI 156.30, described later in this chapter. Neither UL 437 nor the BHMA standard addresses what we refers to as "real world testing" issues. Certain UL 437 and BHMA/ANSI rated locks can be bypassed in times much less than these standards provide for forced and covert entry. This issue has come to the forefront since 2006, and the media attention that resulted from reports about lock bumping in Europe and the United States.

Consumers, commercial facilities, and government agencies rely upon these standards because in most cases they do not have the in-house capability to test cylinders for bypass capability. It is incumbent upon UL and BHMA to develop performance ratings and tests to ensure that not only do the criteria contained within the standards reflect real-world techniques that are employed by criminals but also that the locks actually meet such testing criteria.

The process to adopt new standards by both UL and BHMA is based upon a consensus between manufacturers, security experts, insurers, consumers, trade organizations, and other interested groups. The procedure is cumbersome and overly restrictive, and it often results in the lowest common denominator in security because in many instances the lock manufacturers themselves are driving the process. Rather than defining the security of a lock in terms of time and perceived threat, the standards attempt to overly define each technique of attack. If the method that is employed to open a lock by a criminal does not precisely fit this standard, then these organizations deny any responsibility, saying that the standard does not address the issue and would have to be modified to encompass the particular bypass method. This is precisely the problem with bypass techniques for certain high security cylinders; both UL and BHMA have been placed on notice of certain techniques and have chosen not to investigative further.

As a result of research conducted by the author and others in both the United States and Europe, we can demonstrate that in some cases UL and BHMA are certifying locks that may not be secure for the intended purpose. We have advocated that UL and BHMA re-examine their testing protocols to ensure that what the consumers believe they are installing with regard to security is actually the case.

NOTE

A high security lock is produced to more exacting standards and incorporates special enhancements to increase its resistance to specified forms of attack that would be expected when critical or high value facilities are targeted. As we explain in this chapter, Underwriters Laboratories (UL) and BHMA, the Builders Hardware Manufacturers Association, have developed standards that are supposed to offer greater protection against forced, covert, and surreptitious entry; they also ensure key control. We have documented many instances where this premise is not accurate and certified cylinders and associated hardware can be bypassed quickly and easily.

Transforming a Conventional Cylinder to High Security

High security locks are supposed to provide significantly greater resistance against many forms of attack that would be expected and commensurate with high value targets. These locks are more expensive, are produced to more exacting specifications, and have met certain performance criteria that manufacturers tout as their assurance that the locks can be relied upon to effectively stop an attacker for a defined period of time. The problem is that in some cases what the standards protect against may be a myth and can leave a facility vulnerable to forms of attack that may not have been contemplated in the standards when they were drafted.

Both UL and BHMA have made it very clear to the author that if the specific test protocol is not written into the standard then it does not count. Even worse, the manufacturer may not be cognizant of security vulnerabilities in their locks. This was documented through eighteen months of research by the author with regard to the dominant leader in the high security lock market in the United States and is the subject of a new book on the subject that has just been released.[1]

UL 437, BHMA/ANSI 156.50, and 156.30 are the three standards that you need to understand in order to distinguish between conventional and high security locks. The standards clearly distinguish the two categories of mechanisms. An understanding of the basic requirements will provide an insight into the levels of protection these locks are supposed to afford, how some of them can be compromised, and why the ability to do so can be catastrophic.

Notwithstanding the representations of some in the security industry, UL 437 is *not* a high security standard but rather a *higher security* standard. The UL standard primarily relates to pin tumbler locks; the BHMA standard is also directed at pin tumbler designs but does not exclude other locking mechanisms (such as wafer and lever tumblers). Many organizations rely upon UL 437 as the benchmark for security in their locks. However, what they think they are buying may indeed not be the case.

NOTE

The UL standard has been promulgated to define resistance levels against the following actions in conjunction with attacks:

- Jimmying the door
- Picking
- Prying
- Forcing
- Impressioning techniques
- Driving the lock cylinder or assembly
- Sawing the lock cylinder
- Pulling the lock cylinder or plug
- Other methods that involve the use of small hand-tools

Tests to determine physical security against methods of forced attack specify the use of certain tools, timing, and breaking techniques. The standard defines the use of tools to include common hand tools, hand or portable electric drills, saw blades, puller mechanisms, pry bars, and picking tools.

UL 437 establishes minimum resistance times for different kinds of attacks. Net times in minutes are specified for each type of test and the lock upon which the procedure is to be performed. The sequence is not relevant, nor is the number of methods to be applied. One sample may be tested for several techniques or a new specimen may be utilized for each procedure. Door locks must resist picking and impressioning for ten minutes and forced entry attacks for five minutes. Unfortunately the standard does not contemplate that methods of attack that utilize both forced and covert methods can be applied to bypass the security of certain high security cylinders in far less time than is specified.

Deficiencies in the UL 437 Standard

It is submitted that significant deficiencies in the UL 437 standard exist that allow high security locks to be rated under the current protocols but will not actually protect against certain methods of forced and covert entry. UL is quite cognizant of these issues and is concerned about bringing certain standards into line with real world attacks. The organization took the first significant step in September 2007, when it decided that lock bumping might present a significant security issue and formed a bumping task force to examine the issue in detail. We will identify perceived deficiencies in UL 437 and how we believe these issues relate to the security of the locks that you may be using to protect your facility.

NOTE

We think there are many deficiencies in the UL 437 standard with regard to methods of forced and covert entry that are neither contemplated nor covered in the language of the standard the way it is currently written. If you rely solely upon this standard as your assurance of security of a lock, you may find that vulnerabilities exist that may present serious issues that must be evaluated in terms of risk management.

Failure to Specify Real World Testing

The standard fails to allow for the methods that are employed by criminals who may utilize advanced techniques or a combination of methods that may not have been contemplated by those who drafted the test protocols and resistance levels.

By defining specific tests and tools that must be employed, the standard essentially excludes all others. Criminals do not follow the rules that are established in the UL protocols; they just open locks, containers, vaults, and strong rooms.

This point was graphically demonstrated in a recent bank burglary in New York where more than $700,000 was stolen by thieves who compromised a strong room that was rated to require a minimum of thirty minutes to make a small hole in the wall. During their endeavor the thieves started a fire to which the New York Fire Department responded. It took NYFD exactly four minutes to cut a large hole in the strong room wall that UL had certified to resist attack for a substantially longer period of time. That is what we define as a real world attack.

Pick and Impressioning Resistance

Only picking and impressioning techniques are considered in the UL standard. The use of special decoders, picks, electro-mechanical pick guns, borescopes, and many other techniques appear to be ignored although Section 11.2.5 of UL 437 seems to allow for picking tools designed for a specific lock.

The UL standard does not define the term "picking" but states that "any technique can be used to align the detainers." It limits such tools to those commercially available and provides that an ALOA-certified locksmith of five years must conduct the tests. ALOA is the largest professional locksmith association in the United States.

In our view this definition is flawed because it does not contemplate special picking tools that may not be commercially available to locksmiths but may in fact be purchased by government agents and through unauthorized supply channels. Many of the tools that are described in the government version of LSS+ for bypassing high security locks are neither commercially available nor known to the locksmith community, yet the locks are installed to protect those very same government facilities.

This standard appears to apply only to attacks where the intruder may have limited sophistication or access to specialized picking tools. Those performing pick resistance tests may not even be aware of the existence of specialized tools that are available, even those that are sold in the commercial sector. An example is a tool that can be purchased to bypass three different generations of Mul-T-Lock UL rated cylinders. Many locksmiths are not aware of the availability of this pick that allows bypass of UL certified cylinders within a minute or two. If UL knows about this tool then they have chosen to exclude it from testing protocols. If those that are conducting covert entry resistance tests are not aware of its existence, then they are certifying locks that can be bypassed in well under the minimum times specified in the standard. In either event there is a serious problem because the UL 437 certification tacitly represents to insurers, consumer, and the security community that these locks will be essentially impervious or highly resistant to picking for ten minutes. In some cases this is simply not true.

Complex Forms of Picking

It is unclear whether the UL standard addresses advanced and complex forms of picking even though the language states "any method to manipulate the detainers." To pick a Medeco lock, which is one of the most secure in the United States, the attacker must complete certain preliminary steps with regard to the rotation angles of the bottom pins. Whether this mode of picking would be included in UL 437 is unclear because it can be said to involve advanced forms of picking with code setting keys that are specially created for Medeco cylinders. This technique was never contemplated by the language of UL 437 because the Medeco attack requires the use of four special keys. Whether this constitutes a form of picking is an important issue because virtually all Medeco Biaxial and m3 cylinders can be reliably and rapidly picked if the correct procedures are followed, even though they carry a UL 437 rating.

The standard does not address the compromise of Interchangeable Core cylinders, which are utilized in many commercial facilities. They can be bumped and picked to the control shear line and the core removed. If the key code for the control key can be decoded the entire system can be easily compromised or be subject to sabotage.

Forced Entry Resistance

The UL standard specifies the type of tools that can be employed to test for forced entry resistance. We have developed several forms of forced attack that allow access to certain high security cylinders within seconds. These techniques are apparently not covered in UL 437 and can result in the complete bypass of all levels of security of these locks.

Issues Not Addressed by UL 437

The following issues are not addressed by UL 437 and may leave everyone who relies upon their expertise at risk.

Figure 6.6 A conventional bump key can open most of the pin tumbler locks in the United States quickly and easily.

Bump Keys

The industry now recognizes that bump keys are a serious threat both to conventional and high security locks. Any standard must adequately address different expertise levels of attack. A conventional bump key will never open *any* high security cylinder that contains a sidebar or other secondary locking system. If a bumping standard is defined only in terms of traditional bump keys, then it will not address the real issue. Any new standard must speak to advanced methods of bumping to encompass the types of attacks that can open many Medeco, Assa, Mul–T–Lock, and other cylinders within seconds.

NOTE

We introduced the threat from bump keys to America in 2006 when an eleven-year-old girl demonstrated opening a Kwikset pin tumbler lock by striking a special key a few times with a plastic mallet. Bumping is extremely simple to learn, requires essentially no tools or training, and is effective in about 95 percent of the pin tumbler locks in this country. See the report on *http://in.security.org* with regard to technical and legal aspects of bumping.

Decoding Attacks

UL 437 is silent with regard to attacks based upon the decoding of internal components and the development of intelligence from the information that is derived as the result of such techniques. Certain characteristics of a lock can be observed without the necessity of disassembly and the information that results can often be used to circumvent its security. The BHMA/ANSI 156.30 standard *does* address this issue on a very basic level, but does not go far enough. The UL standard is silent with regard to protecting the lock from such attacks.

Key Control

Figure 6.7 Key control is of prime importance in high security locks. In this photograph, a simulated key is shown in a Medeco Biaxial cutaway cylinder. This blank, fashioned from a safe deposit key, can be cut to open all of the latest Medeco cylinders and bypass virtually every keyway, even those that are the most proprietary and restricted.

UL 437 is silent with regard to any issues that relate to key control and for this reason alone it does not constitute a high security standard. The ability to compromise high security locks by copying, replicating, or simulating patent-protected keys is not addressed in UL 437 although it is in BHMA 156.30 to a limited extent. Key control is one of three primary criteria that define a high security lock because the ability to compromise keys can be critical in certain forms of attack, including bumping, picking, and the extrapolation of the top-level master key. An excellent example is the key control provided by the Medeco m3 and some Biaxial high security locks. It has been totally compromised by the author and allows for the simulation of specially coded keys that facilitate bumping and picking even in the most restricted of keyways utilized in government facilities.

NOTE

Key control is extremely important in the context of high security locks. We actually prefer the more encompassing definition of "key security" to denote the physical protection of keys from duplication, replication, and simulation. The most effective method to compromise a security system is through the use of keys. This is especially true in attacks that target the top level master key because that single key can open any lock in the system. For that reason, any lock that is selected to protect a high value target or critical infrastructure must be secure against attacks on its keys. There are very few high security locks that meet this criterion.

Mechanical Bypass of Locking Mechanisms

Neither UL nor BHMA address the problem of mechanical bypass if the attack does not directly involve picking or manipulation of pin tumblers. This is a real problem because there are certain relatively simple techniques that can be employed to circumvent one or more levels of security on Grade 1 (BHMA 156.50) and high security cylinders. The use of wires, shims, magnetic fields, and other techniques should be addressed within the standards.

NOTE

There are many ways to mechanically bypass locks and locking hardware that do not involve traditional methods of forced and covert entry. The most important rule to remember is that "the key never unlocks the lock." Rather, the key actuates the mechanism that controls the bolt or latch. If direct access can be obtained to that mechanism, then you do not need the key. This concept is critical to a broad understanding of bypass techniques because many locks are deficient or defective in their design and will allow one or more techniques to open them quickly. Neither UL nor BHMA/ANSI specifies mechanical forms of bypass in their lock standards.

BHMA/ANSI Standards: 156.50 and 156.30

The Builders Hardware Manufacturers Association (BHMA) in conjunction with the American National Standards Institute (ANSI) has developed two primary standards that relate to locks: 156.50 (for auxiliary locks and cylinders) and 156.30 (for high security locks). Unlike UL, independent laboratories conduct compliance testing for the BHMA/ANSI standards.

BHMA/ANSI 156.50

This standard establishes criteria for auxiliary bored and mortise locks, rim locks, cylinders, and push button mechanisms. The testing protocols provide for operational, finish, dimensional, cylinder requirements, and security testing. BHMA 156.50 establishes three grade levels: 1, 2 and 3; grade 1 is the most secure. Many of the locks that are rated as meeting grade 1 requirements can be rapidly bypassed by both forced and covert methods. 156.50 is not meant as a high security standard, but merely to provide some benchmark of quality of consumer-level cylinders. The reader should never rely on the 156.50 standard for security.

High Security Locks and the BHMA/ANSI Standard

High security locks are designed to provide a greater level of protection against the primary methods of attack that are employed by criminals, saboteurs, and spies – both outside of a protected area and from within by employees, service personnel, or those who may have or gain access to one or more locks. It is expected that a facility that is more likely to be a target will probably specify high security rated hardware.

That is precisely the reason that manufacturers produce locks, deadbolts, access control systems, and other products to defend against more sophisticated forms of compromise.

High security locks are significantly more expensive than conventional cylinders. They are employed where security officers believe there is a higher risk of entry and compromise of infrastructure, assets, systems, and personnel. In many cases, insurers or government regulations demand the installation of this type of hardware because of its perceived resistance to methods of entry that are likely to be employed in an attack.

NOTE

Our 3T2R rule crystallizes the requirements of UL 437 and BHMA/ANSI 156.30 in terms of resistance to different methods of entry. The rule was developed by the author and succinctly summarizes the criteria by which a lock is gauged. We consider the amount of time that is required to open a lock, the simplicity or complexity of needed tools, and the level of expertise to carry out the bypass technique. Bumping is an excellent example. No skill, little training, and almost any hand implement can be used to bump open a lock. Simplicity in attack methodology means higher risk to those that rely upon a specific lock to protect them.

The Concept of Security

The term "security" must always be taken in context when considering mechanical locks and depends for its definition on a number of factors. In order to assess the "level of security" that a lock may provide, several questions must be asked. Specifically, "Secure against whom?" "Secure against what forms of attack?" "Secure for how long a period of time?" "What is the likely expertise of the attacker in terms of skill, training, and tools?" "What is the value of the assets that are to be protected?" "What other security measures are in place (defense in depth)?" and "What is the physical design of the facility?"

This concept of security is embodied in the 3T2R Rule. It is a shortcut that summarizes the requirements of any high security lock standard and relates those standards to five critical issues: Time, Tools, Training, Reliability and Repeatability. This rating expresses the ability to bypass a lock or locking system and is based upon the amount of time that is required, the training of the attacker, and the tools that he or she will employ. In order for the method of attack to be credible, it must be reliable and repeatable.

For example, previous methods of picking Medeco locks were not reliable because they were not completely repeatable. A new procedure has been developed that allows virtually all of the current generation m3 and Biaxial mechanisms to be reliably and rapidly picked open, and in many cases bumped open. Prior to 2007, such a method did not exist and so the criterion that requires that the technique must be both repeatable and reliable would not have been met. Thus the UL and BHMA rating for the Medeco m3 would have been valid and actually representative of the security of the lock prior to 2007.

As defined in BHMA/ANSI 156.30 there are three tenets of high security: protection against forced entry, protection against surreptitious or covert entry, and key control. All three of these criteria must be met in order for a lock to be rated for high security implementation. In contrast, a close examination of UL 437 reveals that only two of these criteria are present; key control is neither addressed nor required. The BHMA/ANSI standard establishes three security levels within its high security classifications (Level C, Level B, and the highest, Level A).

BHMA/ANSI 156.30 High Security Standard

This is the civilian high security lock standard in the United States. Although it references UL 437 for certain surreptitious entry tests, the BHMA definitions establish the criteria for high security lock certification. There are three critical sections that are enumerated within 156.30:

- Section 5, Key control

- Section 6: Destructive testing

- Section 7: Surreptitious entry resistance tests

According to the BHMA, a standard lock must resist the defined forced entry attempts for five minutes and surreptitious attacks for a minimum of ten or fifteen minutes (depending upon security level). Consumers, commercial facilities, and government agencies rely upon these specifications to guarantee a minimum level of security. Unfortunately in certain cases the BHMA requirements, just like UL, do not address what we refer to as real world methods of entry.

They specify the types of tests that will be performed, but fail to address methods and techniques, as with UL, that will allow many high security rated cylinders and systems to be bypassed rapidly. Manufacturers may be unaware of such bypass techniques, may ignore them, may know about them and misrepresent the security ramifications to their customers, or they may be unable to make changes in their mechanical design that will prevent their bypass. If the standard does not address such methods of circumvention, then the public is misled and at risk.

Key Control

Key control relates only to the protection of keys and key blanks from access, duplication, and replication. The protection must encompass mechanical, legal, and tactical considerations. It is a fact of life that almost any mechanical key can be compromised, even those for high security locks. Patent protection will not prevent the illegal duplication or replication of keys, but may restrict the ability of an unauthorized supplier to make such blanks available commercially or otherwise. There are three levels of key control specified in the BHMA standard and they speak to the availability of blanks, legal protection, and factory control of blanks and cut keys. The requirements of 156.30 are intended to prevent or limit the availability of keys or credentials to unauthorized individuals.

The requirements under the BHMA/ANSI high security standard are supposed to protect keys from unauthorized duplication and generation by code. Unfortunately the standard is really directed at casual or non-professional attempts to obtain copies of keys and does not address the real world of determined attacks. We believe this is a serious flaw in the language of 156.30. There are many ways to create or obtain blanks or cut keys in order to circumvent the security of a system.

The requirements of the BHMA standard address only the most obvious aspects of key control and rely upon legal and manufacturer-imposed restrictions to limit access. In many instances this is quite sufficient, but in our view is inadequate when one contemplates attacks on high value or critical targets.

Destructive Testing

Destructive testing for forced entry methods encompass four categories under this standard and define three security levels (A, B, C). A is the highest level. Under these tests, plugs within cylinders are evaluated for their resistance to pulling, impact, torque, and drill resistance. Locks must not yield to these forms of force for a minimum of five minutes. The relevant issue is that some high security locks will not meet these requirements and may be subject to compromise by relatively simple techniques.

Surreptitious Entry Resistance

There are a total of five test criteria and three security levels for surreptitious entry resistance testing in order to receive a high security rating. The individual criteria relate to key changes (tolerance between depth increments), mechanical bitting, allowable differences between two adjacent depths (MACS), and pick and manipulation resistance. The requirements in this portion of the standard also speak to the ability to identify the dimensions of pins by a visual inspection or through the use of probes, shims, or other manual measuring tools.

There are two classifications within this section of the protocol: decoding and pick resistance. Locks must resist picking and decoding attacks for a minimum of ten minutes (as specified in UL 437) for the lower two security levels and fifteen minutes in the highest security level (A).

Pick resistance addresses three critical issues: security pins, paracentric keyways and balanced or graduated drivers (to prevent the use of comb picks). The standard also identifies certain forms of attacks for electronic locks and includes the use of electrostatic discharge, over-voltage, magnetic fields, and conductive liquids.

BHMA 156.30 requires that at least two security pins be placed in the lock to increase resistance to picking. Paracentric keyways must also be employed to make the vertical movement of picks more difficult. Finally, the standard requires that each pin stack length (bottom pin, top pin, and spring) be at least one depth increment longer than the overall length of the chamber. This will prevent comb picking which is a process of lifting all of the bottom pins above shear line to create a new shear line.

Deficiencies in the 156.30 Standard

There are deficiencies in the BHMA/ANSI 156.30 standard relating to key control, forced attacks, and picking that can and have resulted in the certification of cylinders that can be bypassed in far less time than is specified.

- The limitation to "manual manipulation" or picking tools that are commercially available to locksmiths is not sufficient to test high security cylinders against significant threats. The standard certainly would not include the government tools that are produced by John Falle nor would it address any of the bypass techniques that we document with regard to Medeco and other high security mechanisms.

- The standard fails to address the simulation of keys. It only speaks about the physical protection and control of key blanks, but does not address real world attacks. The ability to replicate or simulate restricted keys can be critical to advanced bumping and picking attacks and the copying of keys that are supposed to be secure.

- The standard fails to test for certain methods to mechanically bypass the locking mechanism through the use of force. Most design engineers employed by lock manufacturers fail to understand or remember the first rule in designing a cylinder and related components that we noted earlier: The key never unlocks the lock; it merely actuates the mechanism that controls the bolt, latch, or other device. Many locks and their sophisticated security features can be easily bypassed through mechanical means with or without force.

- The BHMA standard should not be restricted to commercially available picking tools because it fails to consider advanced methods of attack that may be limited to a specific high security cylinder.

The BHMA requirement that ALOA-certified locksmiths must be utilized for those conducting a test does not ensure their familiarity with advanced techniques or competence to bypass certain types of mechanisms. Medeco, Mul-T-Lock, and Assa may perhaps provide the best evidence of this premise. Each of these Assa Abloy companies have vociferously objected and publicly denied that any of their high security rated cylinders could be bumped open, yet all of them can be bypassed in this manner.

Security Vulnerabilities of Conventional Locks: Why High Security Locks Are Supposed to Offer More Protection Against Methods of Entry

We now turn our attention to the limited security that is offered in non-high security locks and their vulnerability to attacks. These attacks have traditionally involved the compromise of the three fundamental criteria that distinguish high security locks from their less secure counterpart. We say "traditional" because there are other means to open locks that do not involve the standard methods of entry and which may be more practical and most often require less time and skill to accomplish. Such bypass techniques are often ignored or not even contemplated by UL or BHMA/ANSI.

There are other forms of bypass that may require advanced techniques: the use of special bump keys, sophisticated decoders, probes, manipulation devices, pin-and-cam systems (that combine picking and decoding), impressioning systems, and other procedures. They are all within the arsenal of the covert entry specialist and some professional burglars.

Most security managers rely upon UL and BHMA to establish the minimum requirements to protect their facilities. Mistakenly they believe that these standards organizations have developed comprehensive requirements that will effectively stop, deter, or resist the three primary methods of entry for a minimum period of time. However, there is a problem: the standards do not address certain forms of bypass and we believe specifically exclude certain tools, methodology, and expertise.

In short, if you rely upon UL or BHMA standards to protect your locks against knowledgeable or determined attackers, our advice would be that you do so at your peril. Their standards could be the model for Catch-22; any divergence from the defined protocols and the lock is not certified to protect against that risk, even though the intent of the specification is violated. To make matters worse, neither UL nor BHMA will even consider a report of the compromise of their rated locks unless such attack is already defined in the standard.

These special locks are employed in the most secure installations: the White House, the Pentagon, nuclear sites, and other critical targets. They are part of the security that protects advanced weapons systems, narcotics, huge amounts of cash, toxins, biological weapons, critical infrastructure, and most importantly, information relating to everything from financial data to top-secret national security issues. Yet some of these locks can be compromised in about thirty seconds when they were specifically designed to be impenetrable for a minimum of fifteen minutes! That precisely is the problem and what this chapter is about.

Conventional Pin Tumbler Locks: Security Vulnerabilities and Their Compromise

Virtually all pin tumbler locking mechanisms can be compromised covertly and by the application of force. At least fifty forms of bypass are indentified in *LSS+* and the list is by no means exhaustive because as locks are examined by different experts, sports picking enthusiasts, and others that have a need to assess security, new methods of compromise are discovered.

NOTE

There is an order of threat level with regard to the compromise of mechanical locks that begins with the simplest and most obvious modes of attack and increase in sophistication. Unfortunately, conventional cylinders are subject to all of these methods of bypass:

- Unauthorized copy of key that fits the lock
- Rights amplification of a key that was not designed to open the target lock
- Mechanical bypass of the lock
- Bumping
- Extrapolation of the top level master key
- Picking using standard techniques, electro-picks, key jiggling, and a combination of decoding and picking with specialized tools

Lock Control Procedures

The concept of lock control is often overlooked, but must be considered in the context of conventional cylinders and their ability to be compromised by removal from the system. Usually the purpose of such activity is to decode the top level master key (TMK). Organizations must define lock control policies to ensure the integrity of all of the cylinders within the system and to immediately account for missing or replaced locks as well as the inventorying or destruction of worn locks or those that are taken out of service. Locks are like hard drives from discarded computers; they can provide a wealth of information about a system and its security if they fall into the wrong hands.

Depending upon the hardware configuration most conventional cylinders can be easily and quickly removed even during normal business hours. This is especially true with regard to mortise cylinders, programmable locks, and some IC systems. If unauthorized access is gained to a cylinder, it can be quickly decoded by shimming or disassembled in order to derive all the possible pin combinations. Even easier is the ability to extrapolate the TMK without the necessity of taking the lock apart. Potentially a greater threat is the derivation of the control key (or, in some cases, the master control key in large systems) for interchangeable cores.

Key Control and Key Security

We have previously noted that UL 437 is silent with regard to key control. In our view a lock cannot be considered for high security installations unless its manufacturer implements certain safeguards with regard to the availability, duplication, and code cutting of keys. In contrast, the BHMA standard *does* address key control, but does not go far enough.

The BHMA/ANSI 156.30 High Security lock standard specifies three different levels of key control within its standard. The standard defines key control in terms of access to blanks and cut keys, but it fails to directly address perhaps the more relevant issue: the ability to replicate keys. Depending upon the security level in 156.30, key control under the BHMA standard attempts to ensure the following protection for the end-user:

- The availability of blanks for specific keyways;
- The duplication of cut keys;
- The legal protection to control the manufacture of blanks;
- Cutting of keys by code.

These three defined levels of key control are meant to prevent someone from having a key duplicated at Home Depot, Lowes, a hardware store, or the local locksmith unless that locksmith is part of a factory program and has the specific keyways assigned to him or her. In the lowest level of key control, designated locksmiths may be provided with certain keyways. Some are commercial and non-restricted, meaning that anyone can come in and have their keys duplicated.

Patent protection of blanks provides the manufacturer with legal remedies for anyone that produces, sells, or duplicates any blank for which a utility patent has been granted. Severe civil penalties are set forth in Title 35 of the United States Code for infringement. Many high security lock manufacturers have aggressively enforced their rights with respect to such infringement. In certain cases such protection may extend to the cutting of keys if the blanks have unique and patented characteristics.

Key Security

We define key security to mean the protection of any key, whether blank or bitted, from replication or simulation which would allow it to be used in an unauthorized manner. The key (and lock) must significantly resist the use of improperly replicated keys as well as altered, simulated, or copied keys. The intent is to prevent someone from obtaining access to one or more locks by using such keys to bypass the security of the internal mechanism. Methods would include picking, bumping, impressioning, simulation of the correct bitting, and other techniques.

The Concept of Key Control As It Applies to Security

The term "key control" may be misleading and identifies only part of the issue that is relevant to high security locks and their keys. Those responsible for ensuring that a facility and its locks are protected may believe their keys cannot be improperly obtained, but such may not be the case. Depending upon the required level of security, we believe that keys should be secure from compromise from casual, semi-skilled, or professional attackers.

The concept of key control usually relates only to the issue of availability of blanks from commercial sources and the implementation of controls for the duplication and generation of keys by code. It does not contemplate the illegal or unauthorized acquisition or production of keys to be used in conjunction with bypass techniques that rely on the use of such keys as a required precursor to a successful opening. In other words, we believe that 156.30 addresses one basic security threat: the acquisition of an original or duplicate key that will open the lock in the intended and normal manner. That is, the standard speaks only to inserting the correctly bitted key into the keyway, properly aligning the pins, and turning the plug. In our view, this is only one aspect of the insecurity of a lock that can be exploited by violating key control and key security.

The Importance of Key Control and Key Security

Why are "key control" and "key security" so important? The answer is quite elementary: the easiest way to compromise a lock is to open it with a key! That may seem obvious and overly simplistic, but it is an accurate statement and precisely why 156.30 addresses the issue of key control as one of its primary tenets. The circumvention of key control (and what should be its inherent key security) can also be used to facilitate several different forms of bypass. The compromise of certain high security locks relies upon the violation of key security to accomplish bumping, picking, master key extrapolation, and some forms of forced entry; it also includes completely compromising and circumventing the protection of restricted blanks (traditional key control of a facility). Medeco provides the classic example of how the simulation of a key can allow multiple levels of attack.

The violation of key security has wider implications and encompasses the compromise of keying systems, the simulation of blanks for restricted keyways, the circumvention of legal protection of keys, and rights amplification of blanks and cut keys. Any discussion of key control and key security should also include the consideration of policies relating to keys that are taken out of service because the bitting codes of associated locks have been changed. The failure to track old keys can provide an attacker with exactly the needed tools to create bump keys, system intelligence, special code setting keys, and the employment of advanced techniques.

Rights Amplification

A key that is subject to rights amplification can result in the compromise of a conventional or even high security cylinder. This term refers to the modification or alteration of a blank or cut key to use it in a manner not intended or to obtain rights to gain access to unauthorized areas. The concept has its roots in computer and software hacking and denotes the manipulation of software to obtain increased access privileges.

Perhaps the greatest threat from rights amplification is the use of a key to extrapolate the top level master key by probing the target lock for the presence of master pins. The tactical use of this technique is discussed in depth by the author in *LSS+*. An equal security threat is the modification of a change key into a bump key.

NOTE

The term "rights amplification" has its roots in the cyber world, but it means the same thing with regard to the manipulation and alteration of keys to obtain unauthorized access to one or more locks. The concept relies upon the ability to modify the physical characteristics of a key to make it do things that it is not supposed to do and that are not authorized. For example, the bitting of an individual office key might be built-up with solder to raise pin tumblers to different positions, which may correspond to the master key code. Any alteration of a key's characteristics to allow it to perform tasks for which it was not designed is a violation of key control and can be extremely serious. It is very important to examine the real key control and security that is offered by the locks that you use in your facility if you are concerned about the protection of valuable assets.

Replication, Duplication, and Simulation of Keys and Key Blanks

The concept of key control and key security necessarily includes protection against the replication, duplication, and simulation of key blanks and cut keys. Conventional pin tumbler locks are especially prone to these forms of attack. There are many techniques for both the replication and duplication of key blanks.

Replication refers to the ability to generate a blank key that precisely copies the warding patterns or approximates them so that the key is able to enter the keyway of a target lock. The concept is distinguishable from duplication of keys, which refers to the capability of copying the bitting pattern on a target key.

The concept of simulation refers to the ability to completely synthesize the requisite critical dimensions of a key blank so that it can be cut or shaped to align the pin tumblers to the shear line. A simulated key will generally be quite thin to allow it to pass through the center line of the wards within the keyway. Simulated keys are very difficult to use in true paracentric keyways because they cannot be properly inserted into the plug in vertical alignment to the base of the tumblers.

Gathering Intelligence About a System from Its Keys

Significant intelligence can be obtained with regard to a lock or system by gaining access to one or more keys. The process can be elementary for keys that fit conventional locks because usually only depth and spacing data is involved once the manufacturer and keyway have been identified. The process can be much more complicated for high security cylinders.

Information can be obtained with regard to the following parameters relating to conventional locks and keys and thus can present a significant threat to security:

- Lock manufacturer;

- Keyway;

- Number of pin tumblers;

- Depth and space information;

- Whether the lock is high security rated;

- Information regarding sub-master keys and bitting values assigned to progressed positions;

- Key codes;

- Whether odd or even progression has been employed in assigning individual codes;

- Whether the system is master keyed and possibly the type of progression scheme;

- Predictability of keying progression;

- The use of secondary locking systems;

- Use of check pins (such as Schlage Everest)

- Limitations on bitting values based upon MACS and the number of available depth increments;

- Other known manufacturer-imposed rules with regard to bitting;

- Whether sectional keyways are employed and their hierarchy;

- Master key system design and hierarchy based upon markings on keys or cylinders;

- Direct-reading codes that are stamped on keys;

- Ability to easily and rapidly decode keys either visually or with handheld instruments or key micrometers;

- Use of commonly available commercial keyways that may be obtained at hardware or DIY stores;

- Ease of photographing or scanning keys and later reproduction.

Covert Entry Techniques: Manipulation of Internal Locking Components

Manipulation of the internal locking components within conventional locks can be quite elementary in comparison to high security cylinders. There are many techniques that are available and they all accomplish the same function: simulating the action of the correct key by moving all the bottom pins (or a combination of master and bottom pins) to shear line. Recognized covert methods of entry include bumping, picking, impressioning, decoding, extrapolation of the top level master key, and mechanical bypass.

Bumping

Virtually all conventional pin tumbler locks can be opened by using traditional bump keys. The technique is easily learned, requires little skill, requires no specialized tools, and can be quite reliable. It is a serious security threat to all non-high security locks. Advanced bumping techniques have been developed to successfully open some cylinders produced by Medeco, Mul-T-Lock, Assa, and others. These procedures require the preparation of modified bump keys and the use of special techniques to circumvent locks with sidebar technology, but are highly effective against certain locks.

Picking

A distinguishing feature of conventional pin tumbler locks is their susceptibility to the manipulation of internal locking components through picking, raking, and key jiggling. The use of mechanical and electro-pick tools, pick-decoders, variable key generation systems, and other simple tools limits the security of these locks and demonstrate the need for higher security cylinders.

Impressioning

Virtually all pin tumbler locks can be impressioned with the result that a key is produced that will open the lock. Although some high security locks can also be impressioned or decoded and opened with this technique, it becomes much more complicated because there are often two or three separate and independent locking systems that must be bypassed. Even if a key is produced, it cannot open Medeco, Assa, or Primus locks without the simultaneous manipulation of the sidebar and its associated pin tumblers or finger pins.

Extrapolation of the TMK

The top level master key for almost all conventional pin tumbler locks can be easily extrapolated by probing the pin stack of each chamber with a change key for any cylinder within a keying system that is associated with the TMK.

Mechanical Bypass

Many conventional cylinders can be bypassed and opened without the use of the correct key because they are not designed to the same security specifications as those with high security ratings. Some UL 437 and BHMA 156.30 locks are not immune to simple methods of mechanical bypass. In *OPEN IN THIRTY SECONDS: Cracking One of the Most Secure Locks in America,* by the author, several techniques to open Medeco deadbolt, rim, and mortise cylinders by mechanically bypassing internal locking components are described. These techniques involve the bypass of multiple security layers that are supposed to prevent such practices.[1]

High Security to High Insecurity: Real World Attacks

In this chapter we have provided a brief analysis of conventional and high security locks and a review of UL 437 and BHMA/ANSI 156.30, the standards that are supposed to assure that certified mechanical locks will provide protection against an attacker. So how does all of this translate to real world threats and potential security vulnerabilities? If your facility employs conventional cylinders, then you have little protection against many forms of bypass, regardless of what any manufacturer represents. Conventional pin tumbler locks are inherently limited in the amount of security that they can provide. Manufacturers will tell you that if greater security against forced and covert methods of entry is required, then high security-rated cylinders must be installed.

That statement is in part true because these locks are manufactured to closer tolerances and generally employ added safeguards against many threats. But is that sufficient? The answer goes back to our discussion of just what constitutes "security" in the context of locks. If the concern is to prevent a knowledgeable attacker from circumventing the security of a lock, then the answer may be no. It is the last five to ten per cent of protection that we are concerned with, where you have to be certain that security cannot be easily compromised in critical areas.

If your facility has installed high security locks, it should be clear that they may still be at risk from threats that were not contemplated or covered in UL 437 or 156.30. The following abbreviated summary offers a view into the world of covert and forced entry and will hopefully cause those responsible for the security of their domains to reassess their locks and associated hardware. Further, if you think you have solved security problems inherent in mechanical locks by implementing an electronic access control system, you might want to consider that most of these systems have a mechanical lock as a backup against the failure of the electronics. The reality is that any such system can be compromised by neutralizing the lock and completely avoiding any smart card, RFID, magnetic stripe, or similar technology.

Virtually all conventional locks and some high security cylinders and their associated systems can be compromised by employing one or more of the following techniques. Caveat emptor!

- Picking;

- Bumping;

- Extrapolation of the top-level master key by probing one cylinder;

- Complete violation of key control and key security by the duplication, replication, and simulation of restricted keys and blanks;

- Rights amplification of cut keys to gain unauthorized access to secure areas by modifying the bitting to other values;

- Creation of bump keys from discarded keys within a system;

- Use of a hybrid attack that involves two or more disciplines (such as forced and covert entry) to bypass deadbolt, mortise, and rim cylinders;

- Employment of simple methods of mechanical bypass to circumvent sophisticated and multiple layers of embedded security within mechanical locks by the use of wires, magnets, vibration, shock, sound, air pressure, and related techniques;

- Determination of the sidebar code of the top-level master key from one key for one lock within a facility;

- Ability to externally view the internal components of a lock and derive significant intelligence that will allow the generation of keys that will open them;

- Ability to decode the control key within an interchangeable core system to allow access to any lock or to create a lockout condition.

Summary

In this chapter we have presented a brief overview of conventional and high security locks. As more and more physical security responsibilities are assigned to information technology managers, it is incumbent upon them to understand "lock basics." This is important in order to accurately assess potential threats against their facilities and infrastructure that may involve the bypass of locks and locking hardware. There is a great deal of marketing hyperbole in the security industry with regard to the resistance of locks against methods of covert and forced entry. Some manufacturers are unaware of certain methods of attack or will seek to minimize or downplay the potential results of such attacks. They often rely upon the UL and BHMA standards as their assurance that their locks have met those requirements and are thus deemed to be secure. If you take away one critical concept from this chapter it is that the standards may not adequately protect against certain threats that you may consider potentially serious.

Solutions Fast Track

Standards for Conventional and High Security Locks

☑ Remember that UL 437 is not a high security rating, but a "higher security" certification for locks.

☑ Require that a lock meets BHMA/ANSI 156.30 for high security installations.

Security Vulnerabilities of Conventional Locks

☑ Be certain that if high security and non-high security cylinders are mixed in the same system that the security of all of the locks is not compromised.

Covert Entry Techniques

☑ Select high security locks that offer significant resistance to forced and covert methods of entry.

☑ Ensure that keys contain at least one element that cannot be easily replicated. Remember that all lock security is about key control.

High Security to High Insecurity

☑ Conduct independent research before selecting high security cylinders to be certain that what they promise is what they actually deliver.

☑ Do not rely solely upon standards when you select a high security solution. Consider specific risks that may be encountered in your facility and consult with covert entry experts that have conducted independent evaluations of the locks you intend to install.

Frequently Asked Questions

Q: Are there any high security locks that you consider secure against real world attacks?

A: There are many cylinders that we would consider suitable for use in high security installations. It all depends on how you define security and what the threat level is perceived to be. Certain locks such as Schlage Primus, Assa Protec, and Medeco m3 will all provide a certain level of protection. If absolute security and key control is required, then we would recommend two locks that are produced by EVVA in Austria: the 3KS and the MCS.

Q: Why are key control and key security so important?

A: The compromise of a key is the quickest and easiest way to circumvent the security of an individual lock or entire system. For this reason, keys for the most secure locks will contain an element that cannot be easily duplicated, replicated, or simulated. The EVVA Magnetic Code System is the best example. It is virtually impossible to replace one of the four rare-earth magnets in these keys, so the system cannot be compromised.

Q: Are there any high security locks that are bump-proof?

A: All high security cylinders can be said to be bump-proof against conventional forms of bumping. However, many of them can be opened with advanced bumping techniques. The answer depends upon your security requirements. Some certified cylinders are essentially impervious to bumping and others can be relatively easy to bump open if certain preconditions are met.

Q: Is there any one common exploit that presents the most threat and that a risk manager should be most concerned about when selecting a particular lock?

A: We would look at mechanical bypass, certain forms of forced entry, and the ease with which keys can be compromised. This was graphically illustrated in the new book about the compromise of Medeco locks (by the author). Two tiny screws provided the entire security of the Medeco deadbolt cylinder for the past twenty years. A very simple exploit was developed to break these screws and open the lock. This is what we would consider a mechanical bypass as well as a forced entry attack.

Q: Can master key systems be made secure?

A: Very few master key systems are truly secure. Most are a compromise between convenience and security and for that reason are not recommended unless they are necessitated by security and safety requirements. Most master key systems can be very easily decoded and the top level master key code extrapolated. Once this occurs, every lock within a facility is at risk. There are certain systems that are more secure than others.

Q: Can certain locks on a master key system be made more secure against attack?

A: There are many techniques for securing individual cylinders within a master key system. These techniques often involve keying certain locks with individual keys but not on the top level master key. Perimeter doors should never be controlled to the TMK, and locks on restrooms and public access doors should likewise not be set up on any master key to ensure that they cannot be reverse engineered in order to decode the TMK by an intruder.

Chapter 7

Bomb Threat Planning: Things Have Changed

James H. Windle is employed as a Police Sergeant in Charlotte, North Carolina, where he serves as a certified bomb technician and is assigned as the Bomb Squad Commander and Arson Supervisor. He is certified as a North Carolina Law Enforcement Instructor and has advanced instructor training in Specialized Police Driving, Firearms and Hazardous Materials. He is an instructor of the United States National Domestic Terrorism Preparedness Program and has delivered terrorism training to numerous governmental agencies, both police and military, as well as to private security.

Jim was a member of the United States Marine Corps, providing training in mines and booby traps domestically and with NATO forces abroad. He graduated from the F.B.I.'s Hazardous Devices School at Redstone Arsenal and the ATF's Advanced Explosives Destruction Techniques, Advanced Post Blast Investigation and Home Land Security Live Agent WMD School. He is also crossed trained as a Hazardous Materials Technician. He has worked site security and threat assessment in conjunction with the U.S. Secret Service and U.S. State Department for domestic and foreign dignitary protection missions. He was sent to Israel to train with Israeli bomb technicians on countermeasures against suicide bombers and vehicle bombs and was recently sent to England to work with London Met Police and Royal Navy EOD squads.

Jim is an active member of the International Association of Bomb Technicians and Investigators (IABTI) and also a member of the High Technology Crime Investigation Association (HTCIA). Both groups are highly-respected international organizations whose primary mission is to share information, train and help in the prevention and prosecution of high technology and terrorist crimes.

Introduction

When I look at the history of attacks in the US involving bombings I see a couple of common denominators: first, most of the attacks were made on "soft" targets, and two, there was no threat plan or threat assessment made prior to the attack. As I write this I want you to know that I am coming to you as a practitioner, not as a theorist. I am the one who has to answer to the customer and the employees as part of any plan. When I give a presentation to people I am standing in front of them, preaching the gospel of protection, and the scripture of change. I am selling a difficult product, which is behavior change.

I look at where bombings are taking place and analyze what works and what fails. Let's look at Israel, let's look at London, Ireland, Columbia.… its clearly a numbers game. In the Iraq theater of operations, every day provides new challenges to our military, but many people don't realize that ATF and FBI have agents on the ground learning new things about the enemy. It has proven to be a valuable avenue of intelligence gathering for bomb technicians. The information also provides great threat assessment for us at home.

Iraq is not only a great source of intelligence for us, but it is also a proving ground for bombers: in September 2004 there were 2,400 bombings in Iraq alone. The US has also seen its share of attacks in recent history. The significant attacks are explosive-laden and have caused much loss of life and billions of dollars in property damage. At the end of each year I receive intelligence reports from my federal law enforcement counterparts, which show plenty of activity in the US involving explosives incidents. For example, the ATF reports that in the US as recently as 2006 there were 3,797 reported bombing incidents, with 135 injured and 14 killed.

Terrorists take on many faces, from Arab–Israeli conflict supporters, to Asian radical fundamentalism such as the Aum Shinrikyo attacks in the Tokyo subway, to the radical Muslim movement involving 9/11, to domestic terrorists like Ted Kaczynski, Timothy McVeigh, and Eric Rudolph. In addition to world-wide extremism, we do a pretty good job of attacking each other here in the US. We know that there are terrorist cells working here in the US, and domestic terrorism is alive and well in organized hate groups.

Bomb threat planning and suspicious package mitigation can be daunting for managers. Balancing security and productivity is a difficult task but can be done if everyone realizes that there is a mutual benefit to business and law enforcement. Bomb threats are felonies in most cases, and there must be some mechanism in place for property owners to assist law enforcement in bomb threat investigations. There also must be the realization that the managers of a business are responsible for the safety of their employees. Most businesses that ask me to assist them on bomb planning are shocked when I criticize their plan (most likely last updated in the 1970's), which in some cases calls for a simple automatic evacuation upon receiving a threat. They remember the days of Irish Republican Army, the Red Brigade, and Symbionese Liberation Army, which kidnapped Patty Hearst. They remember the call that said: in thirty minutes there will be a bomb going off in your building….and in thirty minutes it happened. Today, most terrorists take credit after an event happens. I find that many managers are not well versed in threat assessment and find themselves failing to adequately plan for such events. Taking proactive measures for target hardening is good for the company and good for employees.

NOTE

According to the FBI, bombings account for 85%–95% of all the acts of terrorism. ATF reports that as recent at 2006 there were 3,797 reported incidents involving 135 injured and 14 killed in the US alone.

The Day Our World Changed

It was a beautiful crisp morning. The North Carolina sky was blue, there wasn't a cloud in the sky, and it was a brilliantly clear day, a great day for training with our Advanced Local Emergency Response Team (ALERT). The ALERT team is a 90-member team with members of the Charlotte Fire Department (CFD), FBI, Federal Marshals, Mecklenburg County Sheriff's Department, Emergency Medics, and the Charlotte Mecklenburg Police SWAT and Bomb Squad.

As the Bomb Squad Commander, I split my team into two squads, a Render Safe Procedure (RSP) team and a Recon team, for this training event. We dressed out in Level B, splash protection, with breathing apparatus and headed down range to locate the simulated WMD that had been released into the air, killing several and wounding hundreds. We partnered with our CFD HazMat Techs, for air monitoring. My FBI WMD coordinator partner, Special Agent Dave Martinez and I went over the plans as the buzz of the many troops worked tirelessly setting up tents and preparing triage, all working in concert to complete the mission of scene stabilization, rescue, and rehab. Suddenly Dave received a page on his pager.

He looked surprised and concerned as he read the page. "Is every thing okay?" I asked him. He responded, "That's strange, I just got a page saying that a plane struck the World Trade Center in New York. It's probably a small Piper Cub that got lost in the cloud cover," he said, dismissing it. Minutes later Dave received another page and said, "Jim, we just had a second plane hit the other tower in New York and something is going on. The office is calling me back. I have to go."

An hour later that day the word came down that we were under attack. The training stopped and the realization hit that this would forever change the way we view preparedness. Charlotte is a major banking and medical center, and we are home to some of the largest banks in the country. Because physical protection is paramount for the banking industry and our tallest skyscrapers are bank headquarters, suddenly they are a target. The many days following the attack were met with numerous calls about suspicious individuals and items and vehicles. The calls at the Charlotte Police Department went though the roof, from 10 calls a month to 15 calls a day.

> **W**ARNING
>
> According to the Southern Poverty Law Center, the group that monitors hate groups, stated that the number of hate groups operating in America increased in 2007 to 888, a rise of 48% since 2000. Check your state to see the activity by using this link: (http://www.splcenter.org/)

Insider Information: Where Do These Guys Get This Stuff?

Insider information theft is an integral part of terrorism. Intel theft is at an all-time high with the increase of technological storage devices such as camera phones, iPods, and disguised flash drives. Collecting sensitive information from trash, overheard conversations, stolen laptops, and plain old espionage is clearly one of the first steps in terrorism planning. We call it "recon". Leaked, stolen or improperly shared sensitive information used effectively can motivate criminals to commit crime at the target location. It can allow a peak at the activities of the business or it can allow a criminal to take information and make up half-truths about a target, helping to recruit others to assist in the crime. My investigators have seen bad guys use this type of information early on in crime planning.

TIP

Stolen information, coupled with a lack of physical security, may allow a bomber to focus on a particular area of the target due to its "softness". Some example of softness include staff members sharing electronic pass keys, pass codes that allow access to sensitive areas that are never changed, or company IDs that have no picture on them, allowing anybody to become "Jane in Data Entry". Not denying entry to sensitive areas, not changing pass codes, or using poor housekeeping rules like allowing doors to be propped open are a "bad guy's" dream.

I have worked cases were criminals made access using these strategies and committed a variety of crimes that impacted the business. Free access to any part of your building by anyone is never a good idea. Unrestricted access under buildings with large vehicles is even worse. Clearly, the fact that truck parking without inspection was allowed under a building such as the World Trade Center contributed to the plan to bomb it in 1993. Whether it's theft of sensitive electronic info or building plans, or passive security that allows free roams of your business, every bit of info that the bad guys can use to formulate attack against you should be safeguarded or properly disposed of.

I have investigated thefts of explosives where work crews were storing explosives in an onsite work trailer. The work trailer had a single key hidden under the steps so many of the engineers could have access to the trailer. This was common knowledge to most employees, even at the lowest level. ATF reports that 98,596 pounds of explosives were stolen in the United States from 1998 to 2003 alone. Where did it go? Did half, some, or any of these explosives wind up in criminal hands? Were they smuggled elsewhere for future attacks?

TIP

A bomb threat is a crime. Security officials should ensure that the Bomb Threat Check List is near every phone. *57 should be used immediately at the conclusion of any bomb threat that is received by phone. This electronically flags the last incoming call. It allows law enforcement to identify that call when records are subpoenaed.

A copy of the check list can be found at: http://www.state.tn.us/homelandsecurity/bomb_checklist.pdf

The Terrorist Profile

Domestic terror targets in the US have followings that are usually either far left wing or far right wing extremists. Far right wing extremist entities have deep-rooted beliefs that the government is out of control and that they must help the common man regain his foothold on a free America. These are the Tim McVeigh's or Eric Rudolph's of the world. Common political focus points are gun control, white supremacy, and anti-government/anti-taxation. These types will focus their attention on federal offices, governmental agencies, or businesses that they feel support governmental policies or agendas. Tactics for these groups include property damage, arsons and bombings.

One notable recent example of a right wing extremist is Timothy McVeigh. In 1995, McVeigh and his Army buddy, Terry Nichols, planned and carried out their plan to blow up the Alfred P. Murrah Federal Building in Oklahoma City in military fashion. McVeigh delivered his vehicle bomb filled with thirteen 55-gallon drums of ammonium nitrate and fuel oil causing a catastrophic collapse of that building and damaging an additional 324 surrounding buildings. The blast blew out windows and doors as far away as 50 blocks. The explosion caused the death of 168 people and injured more than 500 others. McVeigh was apprehended less than two hours later. He was tried and convicted of federal murder charges and was executed June 11, 2001. Terry Nichols was convicted of involuntary manslaughter and federal and state bombing charges and is serving a life sentence in a federal prison. He was also ordered to pay the government $14 million for the damage caused to the Murrah Building. Prosecutors said the bombing was an attempt to avenge the deaths of about 80 people in the government siege at the Branch Davidian compound in Waco, Texas exactly two years earlier.

Left wing terrorist groups involve revolutionary socialist doctrinaires trying their hardest to stop capitalism. They believe they are the protectors against imperialism, among other left wing beliefs. Identified under this umbrella are special interest groups such as the Animal Liberation Front (ALF) and environmental groups such as the Environmental Liberation Front (ELF). Other groups may include anti-abortion or abortion-rights groups. These groups target public health facilities, universities, and businesses. Tactics include arson, sabotage, and bombings.

International terror groups are foreign-based and oppose the US and its policies. Foreign terrorists have attacked US citizens and interests overseas, including the bombing of Pan Am flight 103 over Scotland, which killed 189 Americans in 1988, the vehicle bomb outside the Khobar Towers in Dharan, Saudi Aribia, which killed

19 military personnel in 1996, and the bombings of two US embassies in Kenya and Tanzania killing 12 in 1998. No attacks by international terrorists were recorded in the US between 1984 and 1992. All this changed on February 26, 1993 when, for the first time, foreign terrorists bombed the World Trade Center. The FBI has divided these groups into three sections: foreign sponsors of international terrorism, formalized terrorist groups, and loosely affiliated international radical extremists.

The State Department has listed five countries as foreign sponsors of international terrorism: Syria, Iran, Sudan, North Korea, and Cuba. All of these countries have directly supported terrorists and terrorist operations using official state agents. All still support terrorism and some now conceal activities by the use of operatives to conduct certain operations.

Formalized terror groups like Hezbollah, Hamas, and PIJ have their own business infrastructure, financial backing, and training centers. They can plan and operate overseas as well as within the US. They are involved in criminal activity in the US engaging in identity theft, passport fraud, harboring fugitives, and weapons and explosives theft.

Loosely affiliated international radical extremists do not represent a specific nation. Loosely affiliated extremists may pose the most urgent threat to the United States at this time because they remain relatively unknown to law enforcement. They can travel freely, take on a variety of identities, and recruit like-minded sympathizers from numerous countries.

Potential Terror Targets

There are four primary classifications for targets: Statement Targets, Infrastructure Targets, Commercial Targets, and Transportation Targets.

Statement Targets

Statement Targets include certain governmental buildings, like federal court houses, and iconic buildings such as World Trade Center. Local specific targets include sensitive religious sites such as Jewish or Muslim compounds in certain jurisdictions. Depending on the size of these establishments, rescue plans and alternative entrances and exits should be identified. Planning for response and multiple evacuation routes and locations should also be considered. Normally, the workforce in these locations are sensitive to their respective threat levels, but need direction on how to better harden their environment. One clear way is for these organizations to build a relationship with local law enforcement and response entities. Keeping tabs on local threats and fostering two-way communications with local security heads and law enforcement is a good way to head off potential threats.

Infrastructure Targets

Terrorists attack infrastructure targets to cause maximum inconvenience to the general public to ensure that their cause remains in the forefront of public opinion. Targets can include power sub-stations, gas facilities, oil pipelines, water pumping stations, the road and rail system, and airports, among others. It would take a considerable amount of any product to contaminate water sources, although an attack of small proportions could cause a pumping station to fail. A coordinated attack of this nature could leave a region vulnerable when it comes to pumping water for firefighting and decontamination and rescue events. Virtually all major terrorist groups operating in the world today have attacked infrastructure targets at some point.

Another example of a high-value infrastructure target is communications facilities. As an emergency responder, I know the value of a well-balanced and functional communication system and the ability to coordinate efforts. Cellular communication is a viable means of communication, although somewhat fragile in an emergency situation where large groups of people try to call the police or fire department. Thousands of cellular calls made at the same time can collapse a system, making all cell phones in the area useless. This can be catastrophic if the private sector security is relying on communication with arriving response units to coordinate via cell phones. Most private security companies do not have radio communication with local police and fire departments and rely on other means of communication integration. Cellular communication has become a staple of informal communication and a tool for on-scene coordination. Employees that work communication and utility facilities must take ownership of their environment and realize that they are a valuable target and have a workable plan to with local responders.

Another example of a valuable infrastructure target is a utility facility such as power grid switching stations. Many facilities may have few or no employees and instead rely on SCADA systems to run the facility and have become a regular target for domestic terror. Recently, in south Florida, several power grids went down and prevented the use of traffic signals, lights, and alarms throughout several counties. Although this may not have been a criminal event, it shows the value of the target.

Commercial Targets

Targeting of the commercial heart of a state is an effective means of bringing the terrorist message home to one of the places where it hurts the government most – the financial wealth of the country. In Charlotte we are the largest banking center on the east coast south of New York. We have implemented several buffer zone protection strategies throughout the city. Target hardening strategies require increased threat knowledge for the workforce in these facilities, who represent the front line of defense. The minute that the workforce fails to take ownership of a facility and relies solely on its security staff is when it becomes a "soft target".

Transportation Targets

Transportation security efforts have increased substantially since 911, although there is still a lot to be learned. Events like the Madrid Train bombings in 2004, where four stations were attacked and 191 killed, and London bus bombings in 2005, where three train stations and one bus were attacked and 56 killed, still demonstrate the adage that terrorists attack the easiest targets. The terror organization in Madrid was believed to have stolen the explosives from a mine in northern Spain along with a stolen van used to transport the explosives used to commit the bombing. Once again, intel and theft gained the upper hand.

What Should I Be Looking For?

We have talked about groups, motivation, and a little bit about attitude within your business as to security. Now I want to brush you up on recognition. You need to know what to look for. Often, bits and pieces of evidence to a crime go unnoticed because we fail to recognize what we are seeing. Investigators executing a search warrant at a safe house in New York in relation to the 1993 bombing of the World Trade Center came across several papers written in Arabic that were dismissed as religious literature, failing to recognize that this was evidence of the terrorists' intent to start a holy war against the US. It's this kind of reasoning I use to highlight the importance of being able to recognize parts of an IED. Bombers make mistakes and get interrupted by security and sometimes flee, leaving behind parts and pieces. If you know what to look for as a trained eye you may be able to quickly realize the severity of the situation.

Warning

Never handle or touch any item you believe may be an explosive device. Some bombs are victim activated and are designed to explode only when the item is moved. Let the experts determine if it is a real device or not. Call 911 immediately if you feel unsure about a suspicious package.

There are five components that make up an explosive device: The container, power source, switch, initiator and main charge.

The Container

The container can be used to cover a series of obstacles for the bomber. Typically, it is made to blend into its surroundings. It aids in transporting the explosive device in public and may assist in placing it in a populated location. The container may also enhance the effects of the device. The fact that low explosives are contained makes them more lethal, by combining a fragmentation effect and increasing blast pressure.

As a security official, I am often concerned with lower-level VIP missions that simply use metal detectors as a first line of defense. Containers come in every shape and size. There are plenty of non-metallic containers that can house explosive charges. Many devices are plastic in construction, for example, PVC pipe. Security officials should be aware that some missions require a hand search of bags and containers. Other options for searching for devices in secure areas are the use of magnetometers and explosive sniffers.

The Power Source

Power sources are another component in an improvised explosive device. Several device designs use electrical power, from simple batteries like AAA or 9 volts, to watch batteries, mini 12 volts and specialty batteries. Batteries can also be used as a way to initiate the device by decay. There could be enough battery power to get the device to the target, then, due to a collapsing circuit, the device detonates soon thereafter. Since security officials do not know the true count down time on an electrically powered device, time to perform an evacuation becomes critical.

Switches

Switches are probably the most deadly part of a device. A switch can come in several forms. One device may have several firing and/or arming switches. The creative bomber can use an arming switch to allow him or her to reach the target location safely, and then get away once the device is secreted. Arming switches are normally some type of count down timer, such as a clock, watch, 555 timer, etc. To activate a count down timer the bomber may calculate the time to get to the target or may use another switch to activate the timer. Never assume what a switch may or may not do and never touch any switch on a suspected package!

Firing switches could be victim-operated. An example is a mercury switch that activates the device when the victim or unsuspecting individual picks up the device and the liquid mercury closes the circuit. Other victim-operated switches include photo cells, Magnetic reed switches, and pressure/pressure release switches, such as clothes pins. I have seen devices that have a series of firing switches in them, all victim-activated. Cell phones, pagers and cameras all have switches and have been used to construct devices.

Remote control switches are also worth noting, since most law enforcement and security officials use hand held and car two way radios. Any time there is a belief that a remote control switch may be used, stay away from the use of two way radios within 150 feet of the threatened area, for fear of radio frequency interference or RF interference. This is a constant preaching point for me as a trainer of police officers.

> **WARNING**
>
> Never use two way radios in a known threatened area or within 150 feet of a suspicious package. Radio frequency interference could cause the device to function if the bomber used remote control switching.

Initiators

Initiators are what cause the explosive charge to detonate, the most common being a blasting cap. Blasting caps that are commercially made are the most sensitive of all. They are normally a short tube with one end, the business end, closed, and the other end open, allowing you to look inside. They may have protruding leg wires or a plastic straw-like attachment. Blasting caps are the first step in a firing chain to set off high explosives. High explosives require heat and shock to set them off and the blasting cap does just that. They have caused more damage than any one single component and are very lethal if mistreated. They are sensitive to heat and shock and should never be handled, except by trained personnel. Electric blasting caps are easily recognized by the leg wires coming out of one end. The leg wires are normally single strand wire, coated with an insulator and are different colors. This color coding allows commercial blasters to set up chain explosive charges and makes the difference between a series circuit and a parallel circuit clear to the blaster. Leg wires can range in size from one inch to three or four inches if a delay is built into the cap. It's important to realize that bombers may cut leg wires at the target location for last minute assembly of the components. In post-blast investigations leg wires can often be found and colored insulation still intact. These can be traced back to a manufacturer and sometimes narrow down the purchase or theft location of explosives. Blasting caps also come without leg wires and facilitate the use of time fuses. These caps are completely open on one end, which allows the time fuse to be placed in one end and crimped on to the fuse. Initiators can also be home-made, which makes them even more dangerous than commercial caps. Homemade initiators or improvised initiators can be made from small light bulbs, electric matches and squibs.

Main Charge

The main charge can be either high or low explosives. Low explosives are ones that explode or detonate at speeds below 3,300 f.p.s. Examples include black powder, smokeless powder and double base smokeless powder. All of these can be purchased legally at sporting good stores and reloading supply stores. They are a main charge in any pipe bomb. Just because they are designated as "low" explosives does not mean they are less dangerous than high explosives.

High explosives consist of substances that explode or detonate at speeds greater than 3,300 f.p.s. Some military explosives detonate in the 20,000 f.p.s. range. High explosives can take many forms. Examples are cast explosives like TNT, which look like plaster of Paris, or Dynamite, which is really a liquid explosive poured into an inert substance like sawdust and rolled up in waxed paper. They can also take the form of rope. Detonating cord is a high explosive. It is sometimes used as a booster to cause other explosives to detonate when wrapped. We commonly use Det cord to wrap

TNT or Dynamite to safely detonate it. Slurries and ditching charges like ANFO are common high explosives used in road and land development. Slurries typically look like large sausages. They are flexible and have an outer plastic and fabric skin. They are designed to be forced down a drilled hole and detonated to break up rock and earth. ANFO is an acronym for Ammonium Nitrate and Fuel Oil. When those two ingredients are mixed at the right percentages they become explosive. The industry standard for ANFO is a binary explosive with the proper amounts packaged in separate containers. Most manufacturers use a colored fuel oil mixture which is really Nitro Methane. This allows the user to recognize when the container of fertilizer has become mixed with the fuel and is now an explosive.

Military explosives are normally packaged in OD green with yellow makings and letterings. One of the highest military explosives is C4. It is a plastic explosive that is white in color and is designed to be molded into any shape. Another type of military explosive is the training grenade. They either look like the WWII pineapple grenade or the more current version, which resembles a baseball. Both types have fuses on top with handles, called spoons, running down their sides. The main body, called the hull, has a hole on the bottom to allow spent gases and any fragmentation from the cap on the inside to expel out. The primary way to inspect these training grenades is to look first at the color of the fuse on top with the spoon. It should be sky blue. This indicates training. It does not indicate if it has been shot, however. These are easily booby trapped and modified. Law enforcement officers should not handle these without trained officers with them.

One other common high explosive worth noting is Data Sheet or Flex–ex. It's a sheet explosive that comes in a variety of colors, most commonly OD green or pale white. It has many applications for disposal work for bomb squads and is a favorite for letter bombers.

The main charge can also be made from improvised explosives. Peroxide-based explosives are very common in the Middle East. They commonly take the shape from rock candy to sugar, depending on the skill of the maker. They may also have a brown tint to them. They also normally have a strong chemical smell.

When a bomb has all five components it's called an Improvised Explosive Device or IED. It's imperative to know all you can about the recognition of explosives and the parts of an improvised explosive device.

Searching: What Am I Looking For and Where?

Ok, so now we have looked at organizations, motives, and components… now wouldn't it be nice to know where the bad guys are going to hide the device? As bomb technicians, we sometimes feel we are kind of like professional gamblers. We are highly trained and have numerous strategies and techniques to assist us. We also take into consideration the totality of the circumstances surrounding the event. But on that initial approach you're hoping to have the right cards to win. You must treat every threat or package as if it were the real thing. The minute you don't you will lose. We have a saying in bomb disposal: "initial success or total failure". When we look at the history of bombings world wide and in the U.S., we can see that there are some statistics that crop up. The facts are that most bombings occur outside. When we look at significant events in just our own country the major events have occurred outside: Oklahoma, World Trade '93, Atlanta abortion clinics, Olympic Park, Atlanta night club bombing…all happened outside.

The second most likely place where bombs are hidden in the U. S. is in common areas. For businesses, common areas refer to any place the public can go to with out being restricted. Lobbies, stairwells, and bathrooms are all common areas. Bad guys normally want a soft target, and an unattended lobby is perfect for a bomber to place his package and leave. Bathrooms with cabinets that don't lock or are not secure are another great place. You may have gone into your favorite movie rental store or convenience store and noticed that no matter what the clerk is doing, they turn to you and welcome you. That is not necessarily because they are polite. This is a target hardening strategy or a crime deterrent technique. Bad guys don't want to get noticed, and greeting is equivalent to getting caught in some cases.

The other common denominator is the type of devices. In this country, the most popular type of explosive device is the pipe bomb, hands down. Pipe bombs are the easiest type of explosive device to construct and there is little tracking of the components needed to make the device. Ted Kaczynski and Eric Rudolph were both successful pipe bombers. Almost all the pieces for a pipe bomb can be purchased lawfully and over the counter. A pipe bomb can be activated with a variety of switches, from electric time delay to victim-activated to the suspect lighting a time fuse and walking out of the building. So what does that mean to us? Well several things on the onset. One of which is you are now armed with the knowledge of where most common location devices are placed, and the second most likely location. So if your plan calls for an automatic evacuation on a bomb threat, that means you will take people past the common areas and deliver them to the outside, just where the majority of real bombings actually take place.

Recommendations for Target Hardening

So what should you do? I can not talk about response with out mentioning prevention. Hoping you won't be bombed is not an effective plan. This couldn't be more true when it comes to bomb threat mitigation and planning. If most devices are placed outside, then we need to insure a couple of things. First is employee culture. Express to employees that work has to be a safe place and that it is everyone's responsibility to protect the work location. This means training employees to look for things out of place, especially when they are outside their work environment.

Outside

Make sure that outside storage rooms remain locked and that vegetation is kept away from the building. You should be able to look down the length of a building and see a space between the hedges and the building itself. The bases of trees and hedges should be kept clear so as not to provide hiding places for packages in the foliage. Exterior flower boxes are another great place for bombers to conceal a device easily and have good target value. The window is fragile and produces additional fragmentation. Exterior trash cans overflowing with trash are a perfect place to hide a device. Think twice about having them along evacuation routes.

TIP

Trash cans have been used as hiding locations for bombs in the past and can produce additional fragmentation. Trash cans with black plastic liners make it almost impossible to look into. Clear liners are safer.

Vehicles from visitors should not be allowed to park next to the building. It makes sense to have employees with background checks and cars with employee stickers to park next to the building as a layer of added protection. A bomb threat involving a vehicle could take a bomb squad several hours to remotely search it. Extra precautions should be made if your parking is below the building.

Employee Identification

Security should also have a system to recognize employees; a photo ID is always a good thing. Visitors should be escorted, or at least issued temporary badges with the date and time on the badge. This allows anyone to examine a badge and check its authenticity.

Cameras

Cameras that monitor the outside and common areas are a great tool for security. Any camera mounted outside communicates to bad guys that you have taken steps to advance your security efforts. After the World Trade Center bombing in 1993, security installed cameras that only clicked on when movement was detected. This type of system allows security staff to focus on actual activity, and not just constant closed-circuit television viewing. Detectives solve many crimes through the use of recording cameras. These recordings also allow us to broadcast still pictures with on local TV stations, and can be used in criminal trials.

Deliveries

Deliveries are always a concern, and you should not let unexpected deliveries under the building. Once the car bomb is close to or, worse yet, under the building, it's too late. In several sensitive targets in Charlotte you will see trucks blocked from entering below-ground parking by retractable Ballards while being swept by security. In some cases, the business entity will not allow entry of the delivery unless it calls ahead using a code stating that they are coming for a delivery.

Interior

When we look to target hardening the interior I must say that the front line of defense is the person that greets you at the door. Several high rise buildings in my jurisdiction have moved a security desk into the lobby area as a deterrent. Having security officials greeting or screening visitors is a great tool.

Security should insure that hallways remain clear of boxes and open storage containers. Not only is this a security problem but a safety problem for evacuation. The same is true for stairwells. Most jurisdictions prohibit the storage of any containers in stairwells. Remember, stairwells are an evacuation route and should always be sterile—even the void under the ground-floor staircase.

Interior doors that house computer switching stations or phone closets or office supply closets. First, they should never be marked. You don't need to direct the bomber where to find the least visited room in the building. These rooms should always be locked and key control should be required.

Bathrooms with storage closest or storage cabinets under the sink are a great place to hide a bomb. These cabinets often contain half empty boxes of paper or cleaning supplies and can easily hide an explosive device. These rooms also contain chemicals that can cause additional issues if the device malfunctions and only partially detonates and causes a chemical spill.

Mail rooms

Mail rooms or delivery drop off points are considered a sensitive area and restricted access should be the rule. All employees, not just mail clerks, should be trained in package recognition. In the fall of 2001 a series of letters laced with anthrax were mailed to news media and congressional staffers. Five people died and twenty two fell ill from the attack. Explosive devices delivered by mail or currier will always be an easy avenue for a bomber to attack a specific target. Since packages are handled roughly, they are not normally activated by movements, and because the time of delivery is not known, they are normally victim-activated, unless delivered by the bomber. Ted Kaczynski in 1978 started one of the most famous mail bomb campaigns in US history protesting advancements in technology. He eluded the FBI for 18 years until his capture. It can be difficult to determine if a package is suspect or not there are some indicative signs:

- **Postage Stamps**: Excessive postage or pre-posted parcels. The bomber doesn't want to get caught and therefore applies more postage required to insure the package arrives at its destination point.

- **The package is heavy for its size and is uneven in weight**: This may be indicative of a pipe bomb on one side of the package and its trigger mechanism on the other side causing it to be heaver than one would expect and lopsided.

- **Wooden containers or containers in containers.**

- **Rigid envelope**: On a small soft sided package the bomber has put cardboard sides in place to protect the device from rough handling or prevent handlers from feeling the components of the device.

- **Protruding wires or foil**: In the event of a package tear or actual directions on the outside of the package to Open here or pull to open, the victim may see protruding wires. Foil is a conductor of electricity and has also been used for device construction.

- **Oily stains or discoloration**: Many high explosives commercially and home made exude a chemical residue that may absorb into the paper package giving clues as to what may be inside.

- **Restrictive markings**: If the bomber has a specific target in mind they may use "for your eyes only" or Personal and confidential". I have even see just the word "photos" used giving the delivery person or victim the urgency of opening the package.

- **No return address or fictitious address**: One key point worth noting is checking the return address to see if it matches the postage stamp location. If the return address says Florida but the postage stamp reflects Texas for instance, that would be a red flag. The use of an unprofessional or incorrect address such as a poorly handwritten address, as if to disguise the penmanship, is also worth noting.

- **Unexpected package**: Unexpected packages are always worth scrutiny. Large facilities have x-ray devices to screen packages as a defensive tool.

Tools & Traps...

Lessons learned for package profile!

In 1995 in Raleigh North Carolina employees of a business in a large business park were trained on the package profile by their local Police bomb squad. A short time later one employee received an unexpected package, which was delivered to her via the interdepartmental mail clerk. When she received the package she said to others that "this package is just like the profile we learned about in the bomb class. It's lopsided, heavier than normal, and unexpected." With that she opened the package and it exploded! Police located a second package at the same business park that day. The secondary device was a diversionary device to throw officials off by killing or injuring a second individual that had no ties to the first victim and suspect. The suspect simply used a name off a marquis to address the package to. Thankfully it was intercepted.

Having learned the profile for suspect packages is a valuable tool … but only if you use it.

TIP

IF YOU BECOME SUSPICIOUS:

1. STOP! Put the item down quickly and gently.
2. Notify everyone in the area.
3. Evacuate the room. Put two or more walls between you and the item.
4. Notify supervisory personnel.
5. Call 911.

DON'T OPEN ANY PACKAGE THAT HAS MADE YOU SUSPICIOUS:

1. Be cautious about receiving well packaged, but unsolicited items.
2. Be more cautious about packages that are delivered by other-than-recognized services, such as U.S. Mail, UPS, Interoffice Mail, etc.

Evacuation Plans

If you are faced with a bomb threat you have three options: evacuate, stay and search, or a blend of both.

If you decide to evacuate you should have a few elements in place. Evacuation elements include assembly locations, routes, accountability of personnel and employee knowledge. Plans should not differ between fire, weather or bomb evacuation planning. The use of fire wardens is recommended for a clear-cut chain of command. Fire wardens should be located on every floor of a building and they should report to managers, ensuring the plans are carried out in each location. Communication among and accountability for employees is paramount, and with a system using fire wardens, facilitates scene stability. Fire wardens need to be held accountable for their respective physical areas. Evacuating employees also need to understand that accountability is very important to responding rescue and law enforcement officials. One way of promoting this is a three-person buddy system. Evacuees should report to their respective fire warden that their partners are accounted for or missing at the assembly location.

There should be more than one evacuation location. Locations should include protection from the elements and potential blast protection. Evacuation assembly locations should be shared with a neighboring building if possible. Partnering for emergencies allows evacuees to move to another shelter for protection in inclement weather and provides blast protection.

A plan should have the following in place:

- Trained management and employees. Training should include where to search, based on risk assessments set out by management. Employees should be taught how to search and have knowledge about vulnerable locations.

- Sterile and completely and rapidly searchable work areas.

- A trained workforce.

- Secure work areas

Management should lead with security in mind on all levels, including information security, physical security and security awareness.

Summary

My philosophy has always been that the more people that are educated about the recognition of explosive devices and the motivation of criminals, the better we can safeguard our lives and businesses against such attacks. Clearly, my time working in Israel in 2004 was an eye opener. Not only have the Israelis suffered hundreds of attacks, but they have prevented thousands. One strategy they have developed is an 80,000 uniformed volunteer force. This allows the paid national police force to focus on true crime leads and the apprehension of criminals and terrorists, while maintaining a connection with the public and their everyday needs. This volunteer force in some form or fashion patrols the streets every day. This group is trained in recognition of components and IEDs. These volunteers also are members of the local economic workforce. They bring these strategies back to their respective place of employment. Educating the work force on not allowing tailgating on secure doors, or not propping open secure doors, challenging visitors, and keeping the workplace clean and free of debris, especially outside, are simple social engineering changes that can have a huge impact on target hardening. I am not suggesting that you go to your local law enforcement department and head up a volunteer force. What I am suggesting is that we take on the posture of watching for things and people that are obviously out of place or in violation and reporting them immediately. If you are a manager, fostering this type of ideal within the business is paramount to safety and security.

Chapter 8

Biometric Authentication for SCADA Security

Ted Claypoole is a Member of the law firm Womble Carlyle Sandridge and Rice, in Charlotte, North Carolina, in the Intellectual Property Transaction group, and a senior member of its Privacy and Data Management Team. He has long concentrated on the business and legal implications of information security and computer crime, first as in-house corporate counsel for CompuServe, Inc. and as assistant general counsel for Bank of America. He now advises business clients and information security companies on contracting for data protection, allocating risk in digital certificate infrastructures and reacting to electronic threats. He has served on a U.S. Justice Department computer crimes task force and the Information Protection Committee for the Banking Industry Technology Secretariat. He has presented talks at the RSA Security Conferences in 2007 and 2008, including a talk on the ethics of pervasive biometrics.

Introduction

Securing the critical infrastructure in the United States requires authentication of people authorized to access the critical systems. These controls can regulate personal access to the physical sites housing the power stations, water facilities, or gas lines encompassing the critical infrastructure, or they may regulate access to either the remote or centralized systems comprising the SCADA networks. Limiting access to authorized personal has been a cornerstone of infrastructure security since its inception.

Technology now exists to tie the authentication of authorized individuals (and the exclusion of unauthorized people) directly to the physical being of the people seeking access. This is managed through a process called biometric security, which measures some physical aspect of any person seeking access to a sensitive element and reconfirms that physical aspect at the time access is requested. The biometric system may measure a person's fingerprints, finger length and shape, head shape or facial features – any one or more of an infinite number of human body features – to confirm whether that person is the same one who has previously received authorization to enter the sensitive computer system or restricted area.

However, biometric technology is not a panacea for authentication and access issues. Like most security solutions, biometrics are appropriate solutions for some security problems and inappropriate answers to others. In addition, biometric authentication produces technical, business, social, and legal problems. Companies using biometrics must build additional security into their systems to protect the authorization databases and understand that such systems can provide strong authentication, but not infallibility.

> ## Warning
>
> What is your fall-back authentication method? Biometric systems may deny access to authorized technicians. Your company must create a trusted method of confirming identity if the biometric system fails to do so.

This chapter will analyze biometric systems as they relate to critical infrastructure protection and SCADA security and discuss how the functioning and weaknesses of biometric systems affects their use to authenticate access to secure systems and locations. It will review vulnerabilities in biometric authentication and issues in system implementation. Finally, the chapter includes a discussion of the social and legal concerns surrounding the use of biometric identifiers for security purposes.

Understanding Biometric Systems and How They Are Best Used for SCADA Security

Biometric analysis is growing as a protection tool. Distance measurements of faces and voices are regular features of identification and authentication in banks and casinos throughout the United States. Law enforcement has used biometric readings for decades, but their utility as a tool against criminals is growing as the science of body measurement is better understood and the variety of distinct measurements grows.

Footprints to DNA Readings

From the footprint analysis by Scotland Yard more than a century ago to DNA capture and comparison in today's crime labs, biometrics has become increasingly more important to the police. A Japanese company has begun selling a urinal to businesses that measures chemical levels in the liquid deposits so that those businesses can monitor employee drug use. Australia is using biometrics for an e-passport system.

Human Measurements Can Slow Machines

Security architects are finding biometrics useful in identifying and authorizing access to networks, computer terminals, and secure facilities. However, biometric technology is not a panacea for protecting valuable systems, and its shortcomings are especially noticeable when used for SCADA security. Most connections, instructions, and messages within the operational structure of SCADA systems must be made at nearly instantaneous speed, whereas the operational function of biometric comparisons is relatively slow. Use of biometrics to trigger operational responses or to provide answers within a SCADA system would be too slow to be productive.

Biometric comparisons work best for identifying human users of a system, authenticating the access rights and responsibilities of those users, and providing records of access and records for non-repudiation purposes. Therefore, in SCADA systems, biometric tools are best utilized to confirm human authentication to access the central systems and to permit and record human access to physical facilities, whether those facilities hold the central processing capabilities or lie in the most remote outpost of the protected system.

Biometric System Imperfections Are at Odds with Perception

Once biometric systems are installed, they still can be problematic. No system is infallible and biometric systems can fail in many directions. Many of these systems can be tricked at various points in the collection and comparison process. The system itself may be poorly installed or metrics may be chosen badly. The biometric readers may fail or the initial collections could be flawed. Temperature, humidity, precipitation, and dirt may affect the accuracy of readers.

Unfortunately, some commentators have assumed that a system that measures human features will provide the best possible security for facilities and networks. In truth, the complexity at which biometric systems operate can undercut their accuracy and utility for many important locations and functions of SCADA security. Choose and implement carefully if you plan to use biometrics in your SCADA system. Biometric comparisons could be a dream solution to your authentication problems, or they could create a nightmare of additional work and security issues.

TIP

Training and education are vital to successful implementation of a biometric authentication program within your SCADA security system. Employees, contractors, and executives are likely to hold misperceptions about biometric capture and analysis and may resist its implementation. Furthermore, people seeking access must be trained in the effective methods of offering biometric samples and the back-up procedures for when they are unable to be authenticated within the system.

What is Biometric Authentication?

Personal authentication is necessary to establish that the person operating a network or entering a secure facility has authority to do so. Authentication regimes tend to rely on the person seeking authentication to provide a token of proof to establish identity and permission. These tokens are called identity factors, and the more factors that are offered to establish identity, the greater the likelihood that the person claiming authorized access is truly the person he or she claims to be.

Multiple Factor Authentication

Most current security systems require one or more of the following factors. They will require that you demonstrate something you know (like a password), something you hold (like an identity card or an encryption token), or something you are (like a signature or a comparative picture). Other factors can include time of system entry and precise global location. For example, your bank requires two factor identifications for you to remove money from your own account at an automatic teller machine; the machine requires a card that you are holding and a personal identification number that you know. However, inside the bank, you may be required to offer two different factors of identity: a thumbprint along with your government-issues identification card for cashing certain kinds of checks.

What Parts of You Can Be Measured for Security Purposes?

Biometric systems measure "something you are" and compare it against a earlier sample of the same measurement. Your written signature is considered to be a biometric measurement because the way you write is a physical feature that is relatively unique and can be compared and evaluated to past samples. A state driver's license contains an old-school biometric identifier – a picture of your face. Certain biometric samples must be offered voluntarily by the person wishing to gain access into a system. Fingerprints, hand geometry, and retinal or iris scans fall into this category and are the most likely to be used as part of a security system. Some biometric measurements like your face or your voice can be taken from a distance. This type of public biometric is used by law enforcement but is generally not part of biometric authentication systems.

Common Measurements for Current Biometric Authentication

The most common biometric security systems for unlocking computer systems and secure facilities compare fingerprints or other hand measurements. These systems require a person being measured or identified to press his or her finger against the reader. Some of these systems record and measure the veins beneath the skin on fingers and hands, either as a primary biometric measurement or as an affirmation of viability, so that the systems are less likely to be fooled. Similarly, some of the biometric security systems that use eye measurements require a close reading of the eyes, either for retinal vein patterns or for iris patterns. Sanitation of readers can be a significant issue when several people are required to authenticate themselves by pressing against readers.

How Does Biometric Comparison Work?

Biometric authentication tools are complicated systems that require detailed set-up and ongoing monitoring. A biometric check is not a simple "yes or no" answer like some other methods of security analysis. For example, when an automated teller machine requests a personal identification number, you either know the number and enter it correctly or you do not. If not, the security function refuses your entry. By contrast, in biometric analysis, the system first takes a sample of the biometric feature that the system administrator has chosen to measure. For the purposes of this example, we will assume that the system is capturing fingerprints.

Rather than an easily identifiable "yes or no" variable like the personal identification number, the biometric fingerprint reading system either captures a full picture of the fingerprint or it captures points of minutia, which are a number of points of detail on the curves and lines on the print. Nearly all biometric systems will request several initial samples so that a clean sample can be attained and validated. Later, when a person wishes to be authenticated under the biometric regime, he or she provides a fingerprint to the reader, which captures the print and compares it to the samples captured earlier. If the system finds the authentication sample matches the initial sample within acceptable parameters, then the person is authenticated by the system and allowed access to the protected network or facility.

Because biometric regimes operate by comparing samples and those samples often are provided on different capture devices under different conditions, the administrator of a biometric system must choose the parameters of comparison between the original (or "reference") sample and the access sample. The fingerprint match may be considered complete if the authentication sample demonstrates twenty points of similarity with the original sample or maybe only ten points of similarity.

This begs the question of why all biometric systems are not organized and calibrated to establish the greatest functional degree of certainty that the person who is asking to be authenticated is truly the person who offered the initial sample held in the biometric system's memory. The short answer to this question is that the calibration of biometric systems tends to mark a compromise between strong authentication capabilities and practical considerations. The stronger and more difficult the authentication, the more likely that the system will keep appropriately authorized people from accessing secure facilities or equipment, therefore causing difficult and sometimes expensive work-arounds and alternative access procedures.

> **NOTE**
>
> How perfect do you need to be? Biometric capture programs allow a wide range of choices in determining the amount of detail measured and the amount of similarities in comparative samples before the system declares a match.

These parameters are often calibrated to minimize false positive matches, in which case the parameters are tightly defined so fewer matches can occur, or to minimize false negative matches, in which case the parameters allow more leeway in matching samples. Biometric systems that authenticate consumers in financial transactions tend to be loosely calibrated, allowing more variation in the authentication sample to be considered matches of the reference sample. This is because consumers have demonstrated little or no tolerance for false negatives. Consumers will not tolerate seeing their real finger prints rejected when matched to reference samples.

Biometric captures and comparisons are not perfect and can be stymied by variations in the angle that a finger is offered to the capture device, variations in dirt or injury to the finger, or even inherent variations in the capture devices themselves. Consumers will rebel against a system that repeatedly holds up the speed of their transactions. And if consumers will no longer use their biometric authentication, then the company installing the system has lost customers and the significant money it takes to purchase, install, and train workers on a biometric identification regime. Therefore, companies using biometric systems for lower-level financial transactions tend to be willing to allow the risk of more false-positive matches so that they minimize the possibility of false-negatives.

By contrast, SCADA systems and other protections of vital infrastructure and facilities tend to organize their biometric system so that they minimize false positive readings. The risks of allowing intruders are greater in this case than the risks of an authorized person being forced to call in the supervisor or system administrator and achieve authorization in a more personal and time-and-resource-intensive manner.

It would be a mistake to think of biometric authentication regimes as simple toggle systems with no allowance for variation. In fact, these regimes are complicated in their structure and intricate in their application. The SCADA manager choosing such biometric authentication must be prepared to spend resources not only on equipment and software, but also on protecting the connectivity between the various parts of the biometric capture and comparison infrastructures, on training the affected employees and contractors to correctly use the system, and on regular monitoring and calibration to assure the system works efficiently for its chosen purpose.

Where Are Biometrics Used in SCADA Systems?

No matter how advanced our technology, managing security for critical infrastructure always entails human contact. Whether it involves water systems, power grids, pharmaceutical manufacturing, or oil and gas, humans manage, maintain, and repair various parts of the system and control the overall network. Wherever humans must access the system, there lies an opportunity to use biometric authentication.

There are portions of SCADA security that are generally inappropriate for use of biometric readers. For example, any imposition of an additional review or authentication step within the internal readings and operations of SCADA systems would be likely to impede the progress of the automated checking system. Therefore, SCADA systems would not insert biometric readers, or any other human authentication step, into the automated checking process between the centralized control system and outlying objects being measured, monitored, and controlled. Furthermore, equipment or valve monitoring and control, or any other system that reads and reviews outlying and remote portions of the SCADA architecture, is unlikely to benefit from biometric authentication devices.

Instead, the parts of a SCADA system most likely to productively use this technology include any and all access points for human intervention in the SCADA world. This can include access to facilities or computers in the central SCADA control room where the operator of a critical infrastructure must regulate access so that only those people with authority to act as system managers can reach the controls. Similarly, the remote portions of critical infrastructure, whether pipelines, switching stations, or transformers, may have biometric readers placed on them for access control and accurate records. System operators are not only interested in stopping unauthorized parties from reaching the remote ends of critical systems, but also in recording each time someone reaches the system. Biometric readers provide an audit trail that is difficult to refute.

TIP

Your company's auditors can be your best friend in securing funding for implementation of biometric authentication equipment and software. Biometric systems provide a high level of recordation and auditing certainty when your company finds it important to establish who has accessed secure facilities at particular times. Ask the auditors for support in demonstrating the system's advantages to senior management.

Choosing the Best Form of Measurement for Your System

The human body contains thousands of possible measuring points, and many of these are already used by companies for identification and authentication purposes. This portion of the chapter discusses the various available measuring methods and provides a method of analysis to determine the best measurement tool for your system. In the end, commercial considerations may ultimately control your choice, as some methods of physical analysis are available in a more cost effective format than others.

Another principal consideration may be whether the biometric measurement you choose for your system is in use by or familiar to another entity. In other words, industry or the government may reach a consensus that entire hand prints or the geometry of three fingers are the standard measurement for confirming the identities of people in certain situations. At the moment, no such standards exist. However, your decision to use a certain biometric system in your own security architecture may be influenced by the choice of industry standards or by the selection of biometric systems used by your customers, your regulatory agencies, or other portions of your own company.

Biometric Measurements Trigger Recognition

We have always identified each other from physical characteristics. You know your father is on the telephone because you recognize his voice. You hear your boss's distinctive walk from down the hall and quickly try to look busy. You recognize a friend from a distance by the way he stands. A person's whole face is the most common biometric identifier and is the one used for official identification; however, even facial recognition has its limitations. Readings depend on the light and the angle of recording, and changes in features like hair loss or facial hair can sometimes trick facial recognition systems.

Famously, the United States Federal Bureau of Investigation (FBI) used facial recognition software to attempt to identify and catch criminals at the Super Bowl in Tampa, Florida, but were relatively unsuccessful in their attempts. However, they were using the technology in a different manner than your company would be if it attempted face recognition as a biometric identifier. The FBI was comparing the faces captured at certain access points in the Super Bowl to a broad database of tens of thousands of facial records and hoping to find a match.

Your company, by contrast, is likely to have the easier task of comparing a face captured in a controlled environment with a database of only a few authorized individuals to make a positive match. Your company will have the advantage of taking the first face picture in the same light and angle as the comparative sample, making a positive match more reliable and a false negative match unlikely.

Biometric Measurements Useful in SCADA Security Processes

Clearly the most accurate biometric measurement for truly identifying a person would be DNA sampling. However, most of us are queasy about providing this level of intimacy and this type of information to anyone. Once recorded for security purposes, DNA records could be used to investigate health risk and even propensities for alcoholism or other physical traits that relate to behaviors.

In addition, taking an accurate DNA sample can be an onerous process involving bodily fluids, skin scraping, or the removal of live hair follicles. The comparison can be expensive and time consuming, making DNA analysis impractical for most biometric security functions, such as permitting or denying access to secure facilities. Finally, your company is unlikely to need the incredibly high level of personal identification and authentication accuracy provided by DNA testing.

For the standard reasons that biometric authentication is used with SCADA systems, a company will not use a body measurement that is not readily readable when an employee is dressed for work. Therefore, it is likely that your company would use a biometric measurement that is taken from the hand, face, or voice.

Voice analysis generally involves the repetition of certain words and comparing them against the same words recorded earlier by the authorized person. Voice systems are not as accurate as some other measurements; some voice systems can be tricked by a good recording. But voice samples are easy to provide, are non-invasive, and can even allow telephone authentications.

Biometric comparisons have been taken of hand measurements for a century. Fingerprints are the most well-known measuring source because of their unique nature and the fact that they are easy to harvest from the subject. Fingerprint readers are commonly available in consumer situations, and fingerprints are being used by the United States Army in Iraq and by the United States Immigration Service at our borders.

Another easy hand biometric measures the geometry of blood vessels in the proffered finger. These vessels lie just beneath the skin's surface and are unique to an individual. Capturing the measurements of sub-surface blood flow also provides the advantage of viability confirmation.

In other words, a finger severed from its original owner doesn't lose its skin print of swirls and loops, but it does lose its blood flow, so measuring active sub-surface blood vessels of the finger confirms that the person seeking to be authenticated is the live owner of that finger. Another hand measurement currently in commercial use is hand geometry, an analysis of the size of a subject's hand and the relation of fingers and thumb to each other and to the rest of the hand.

Disney theme parks are currently using a hand geometry biometric system to confirm the identity of ticket holders for admission to the parks. From palm lines to knuckle shapes, the hand provides several measurable, unvarying attributes that can be used as a basis for biometric authentication systems.

Similarly, the face offers a number of ready samples of unvarying, measurable features to be used in biometric authentication. One of the most common examples is the iris scan, which analyzes the colored tissue surrounding the pupil in a person's eye and allows for over 200 points of comparison. Like fingerprints, iris patterns are set at birth and will not vary during an individual's life.

Another option is retinal scans, which take photographic measurements of the blood vessel patterns in the back of the subject's eye. Retinal scan technology requires a user to remove glasses, position the eye close to the measuring device, and then focus on a specific point. Retinal images are especially difficult to fake because anyone trying to fool the system would not find it easy to capture the retinal reading of another person. The high cost of proprietary hardware for retinal scans makes this an impractical measuring system for many applications. Other biometrics above the neck include facial geometry and ear shape analysis.

Identify Your System Priorities Before Choosing a Biometric Application

Choosing a biometric reader should be a function of your company's priorities and the reader's function in the SCADA system. Is your company's most significant priority convenience of the biometric capture when a person requests system authorization? Many companies are concerned that the capture of biometric samples will slow access to vital facilities for repair and control functions; they therefore wish to find a system that, once implemented, can quickly and simply pass people through to their authorized destination.

You can imagine that, noting an emergency in the water treatment facility, company management would not want its authorized employees to waste time in accessing the facilities that need immediate repair or analysis. In this case, any biometric reading that forces its subjects to hold still for several seconds would be problematic. Retinal capture is clearly not the best solution.

In this instance, it may be best for your company to capture the biometric reading from a distance. If so, then fingerprints or iris scans would be impossible and you should consider voice recognition or facial geometry software. The biometric sample comparison settings in this type of situation would probably allow significant variation between the original sample and the access sample, so that the system unlikely would render false negative readings.

Conversely, your company's priorities may run toward the highest level of security possible for access to controls in a nuclear facility, leading your company to choose a biometric authentication process that minimizes the possibility of false positive readings. Your business would therefore select a system and sample readers that are least likely to be fooled by a terrorist attempting entry to the secure facility, and you would be willing to trade speed of access for certainty of authorization. In this case, a retinal scanning system may be the best match for access control, while distance face readers would not be.

Always remember that the biometric authentication is used as part of a larger, more complex system. If your company plans to implement an intense security regime, it could always measure different sets of biometrics at different locations. For example, they could use voice recognition to enter the facility, while requiring retinal scans at the door to the control room or fingerprint readers to access the control computers.

Of course, your company's priorities in choosing biometric measurements may be driven by entirely administrative concerns, such as cost, available equipment, ease of implementation, the need for simplicity, or problematic environmental issues. No company can brag of limitless resources.

While many organizations aspire to implement the best possible security solutions, they may have the resources only for the lower-cost solutions. In addition, an enterprise looking to purchase a biometric authorization function for its SCADA security regime can choose only from the solutions available at the time from reputable vendors. Creating new hardware and software is likely to be economically impossible, therefore restricting choices to those available within a company's price range.

Often, tried and true methods like fingerprint analysis may be the best solution. They can provide a high level of security while using equipment that has been tested in other environments.

Biometric technology is often viewed as a cutting edge solution, and people who ride the cutting edge are frequently hurt. They may suffer because the technology is untested and does not work as well as everyone had hoped. They may suffer because the technology is overly complex and does not integrate well into a SCADA security system. They may suffer because the technology is not easy to use and the company employees are constantly denied the access they need. The most valuable and practical decision may involve choosing a system that can demonstrate years of predictable behavior and that is understood by all participants.

The company must also consider where and how the biometric readers will be used in the overall security system. Important considerations for allowing access to SCADA security facility and systems can include how the biometric components work within the system. Where are the readers placed and how are they monitored? Will the person seeking access be likely to be carrying papers or tools and therefore not be able to offer free hands to the system? Then an eye or ear scanner or voice recognition system may be the best choice.

If the reader is installed in an outdoor environment, how will the equipment and the test subject be affected by the weather? An oil industry technician seeking access to a pipeline facility north of the Artic Circle should not be expected to remove his gloves and expose his hands when the temperature may be 50 degrees below zero. A power company technician attempting to reach a switching station during a hurricane should not be expected to hold still long enough for retinal scanners to confirm his identity.

Voices can be muffled and overridden in busy sites or by high winds on the open plains. The human element is not the only vulnerable variable when reading biometric signs outdoors. Biometric readers placed outside and exposed to the elements cannot be expected to continually function unaffected by their environment, whether those elements are excessive heat, cold, moisture, or corrosion.

When selecting the type of biometric measurement that your company will capture, all of the company's priorities must be considered and weighed against the administrative realities of the SCADA system that your company is protecting and the budget that is available to spend. However, whether you decide to measure eyes, ears, faces, hands, or voices, the decision should match the objectives of your security system. Map your companies SCADA security priorities to the strengths and weaknesses of the many biometric capture options. Biometric security capture devices offer several choices to match the human authentication needs of any SCADA infrastructure.

Where are Biometric Authentication Regimes Vulnerable?

Biometric authentication systems have several points of vulnerability. This chapter does not address vulnerabilities common to any SCADA security system, like brute force attacks with a fire ax on the door of a secure facility or attempts to disable a system so that its backup methods can be exploited. While these may be common methods of attacking a SCADA security regime, this chapter will only examine those vulnerabilities unique to or characteristic of SCADA systems with biometric components. These include both physical attacks that attempt to replicate biometric impressions and software attacks that require sophistication in computer and database management.

Tricking the Biometric Capture Device

The most commonly considered access point to compromise a biometric system would be at the end reader. This is the point most easily accessible to any scammer and the closest point to the target. In other words, if the scammer seeking access to a secure facility knew a specific person who was authorized to access the facility (and whose biometric comparative data was stored for authentication purposes), then the scammer could attempt to steal or mimic the biometric reading that would pass comparison. If the scammer knew that the system required fingerprint access, he could try to recreate the fingerprint of the authorized person and offer it for comparison at the capture site.

Using complicated tools and resins to pick up, reverse, and resubmit a person's fingerprint to the biometric reader without the person being present are the science fiction methods of Mission Impossible or CSI. Other methods of tricking the reader could include removing the finger that is needed for authentication or simply bringing the authorized person to the access point under duress and forcing him to proffer his print to be authenticated. A Japanese researcher made headlines when he demonstrated a method of scamming a certain brand of fingerprint reader using gummi bears to capture and offer the authenticating print.

Notes from the Underground...

How Gummi Bears Defeat Fingerprint Scanners

Japanese cryptographer Tsutomu Matsumoto of Yokohama National University published his findings on how fingerprint recognition scanners were fooled eighty percent of the time using a molded finger made of gelatine. Matsumoto removed latent fingerprints from a glass, enhanced the print with fumes from Super Glue, and then photographed the prints with a digital camera. He used Photoshop software to further enhance the contrast of the fingerprint image, and he printed the enhanced photo onto a transparency sheet with an inject printer. To finish the process, Matsumoto used the printed transparency to etch the fingerprint into copper and pressed it into a gelatine finger mold. He was able to achieve the same effect by pressing a live finger into a mold and creating a gelatine finger from the mold.

Security expert Bruce Schneier addressed this revelation in his May 15, 2002, Crypto-Gram Newsletter, stating, " Gummy fingers can even fool sensors being watched by guards. Simply form the clear gelatin finger over your own. This lets you hide it as you press your own finger onto the sensor. After it lets you in, eat the evidence." Schneier also reminds security administrators to be wary of the overblown " unbreakable security" claims of biometric scan manufacturers.

Clearly, biometric readers that include viability confirmation, like eye scanners that shift light ranges and measure for pupil dilation or finger scanners that read for blood flow beneath the skin's surface, are harder to fool by some of these methods. Similarly, certain voice capture systems include various tactics designed to thwart scanners using voice recordings to beat the system. Capture units that read internal measurements, like blood vessel patterns in the eye, hand, or earlobe, are much more difficult to beat, because capturing or even perceiving the biometric reading would take more than just a bold spirit and a few simple tools. Copying it would be nearly impossible.

Electronic Manipulation of the Authentication Process

This leads to the next point of vulnerability in biometric authentication: electronic sample or database manipulation. Up to this point, we have been discussing methods of faking or reproducing biometric samples. However, these security systems are ultimately networked computers that compare an electronic sample against a database.

Biometric authentication systems are based on comparisons of one electronic file (representing an original sample measurement of the person's physical characteristic) with a second electronic file (also representing a measurement of a person's same physical characteristic). A smart criminal with computer experience and access to the system could trick the system into fooling itself by suggesting that the files containing mismatched biometric samples actually match. Thus, rather than attempting to copy or spoof a real biometric measurement, a scammer's best method of tricking the system may be to manipulate the electronics so that the computer perceives an electronic match when none exists.

This effect could be managed by building a loop inside the database so that the system software either compares the authorization sample with an exact duplicate of the same file or conversely compares the initial test sample against an exact duplicate of itself. The system would register an authorized sample whether or not one existed, allowing system or facility access to an unauthorized person.

Another method of tricking the system would be to short circuit the reader so that every file looked like a match. A long time might pass before SCADA systems administrators would recognize that the remote reader at the door of the secure room was never turning away any person who asked for authorization. In most cases, only people who are authorized would request to be confirmed by the biometric capture device, meaning that it would not be out of the ordinary for the system to proceed for days or even weeks without denying access to anyone.

If the system administrator trusted the software, then this hack could allow repeated access to the secure facility without system denial. Similarly, the database of initial biometric samples could become compromised if a criminal found a way to bypass the entire database and send a message of affirmative match every time a person offered a biometric sample to the capture devices.

Similarly, the computer-literate scammer wishing to fool a biometric system could also electronically plant a file in the database that he knew he could match at the biometric scanning device. This method could allow the criminal to insert his own fingerprint file or retinal scan so that he would be granted access when he offered his body for measurement. Once again, unless the system's own internal controls were strong, the system administrator may never know that the database was compromised, and the scammer could come and go as he pleased without being detected.

Finally, data files in the initial sample database could be stolen, examined, and copied, so that the criminals would know exactly what to offer the capture device. This method of trickery is not entirely internal to the biometric system, but it could not be accomplished without compromising data security within the system software.

NOTE

Protecting the internal integrity of your biometric security software and the corresponding databases is a crucial element in assuring system effectiveness. Insist that your biometric capture system vendor demonstrates how integrity is maintained and monitored, and schedule (and document) regular software and data integrity reviews when your biometric system is in use.

None of these methods of defrauding biometric systems would be simple, and most involve highly specialized knowledge and a manner of accessing the internal workings of a biometric system; however, each vulnerability can be exploited unless the biometric system and the security regime as a whole contain internal checks to confirm the continued integrity of the data and of the operational software.

Identity Theft with Biometric Files: Capturing Your Essence

Some exploitations of vulnerabilities within biometric systems are not necessarily aimed at compromising the security of the SCADA security structure. In this world of increasing identity theft, the capture of another person's biometric signature profile may be the ultimate form of identity theft.

Once biometric signatures become more commonly used for identification in financial and governmental transactions, then stealing biometric profiles may become an important crime. As governments increasingly demand biometric proof for trans-border travel and financial services companies require biometric signatures for large transactions, identity thieves will need to consider stealing biometric measurements.

Presumptions of Accuracy

Unfortunately, due to the general assumption that biometric systems are always accurate, it would be very difficult to prove that you did not participate in a transaction if your biometric signature was used to complete the transaction. When faced with the fact that the person receiving a certain loan presented your fingerprint as verification of identity, how do you combat the presumption of your presence? This possibility is not simply theoretical, as we learned when the FBI detained an Oregon man for participating in the Madrid terrorist train bombings based on a similarity of fingerprint evidence, when, in fact, the suspect was thousands of miles away at the time of the bombing.

How Can We Replace That Finger?

In addition, theft of a biometric signature is even more dangerous than any other data theft for both the person it identifies and the company holding and using the biometric file. If other security data is stolen, like a bank-issued personal identification number or the customer-chosen password, then both sets of numbers can be changed. However, when a photograph of a person's right index finger print is stolen and used to fraudulently authenticate identity, that person cannot be issued a new fingerprint. Once the biometric genie leaves the bottle, there may be no chance to force it back.

The consequences are similarly tragic for the company whose biometric database has been compromised. If the company has spent hundreds of thousands of dollars building an authentication system around fingerprint files and those files are completely compromised, then the biometric system may no longer be trustworthy, and fixing the problem is not likely to be easy. The company may have to scrap the entire system because it can no longer be trusted, and it can not be reorganized to accept a different form of biometric reading. Even worse is a loss of trust. Once a biometric system is compromised, then its users may never trust it again, even if the system can be technically rehabilitated.

Tools & Traps...

Avoid the Extensive Database

Building, maintaining, and protecting a database of captured biometric signatures can be expensive and risky. If someone broke into the biometric database, the entire security system would be compromised. To avoid the problems associated with storing and protecting the personal identifiers of thousands of people in one place, some biometric technology allows your company to operate without aggregating all the captured data. These systems capture and maintain an original fingerprint on a portable reader held by the authorized person. When the person reaches a checkpoint, he swipes his finger across the portable reader, which includes a stored copy of his biometric reference sample. The portable devise, no larger than a standard keychain fob, reads his thumbprint, compares files and sends a signal to the system if the samples match.

This method of capture provides two factor authentication: the fingerprint comparison and the portable device itself. It can be an efficient and effective method of implementing biometrics without the aggregation risk. If a device is stolen, then only one personal sample is compromised.

Measuring Minutia Can Be Safer Than Storing a Whole Biometric Photograph

For these reasons, operators of biometric authentication systems must build policies and procedures to ensure the integrity of the data within the network, and must create special barriers to access of the biometric data files. Choosing a system that operates by analyzing various points of minutia from a fingerprint or an iris, rather than a full picture of the biological feature makes it more likely that your company could survive a loss or theft of biometric data with the system intact.

When your company uses minutia, it could change the number and type of data collected to make the compromised data worthless to anyone who might steal it. While shifting the system in this manner would entail taking new readings from all biometric authentication system participants, it would not necessarily involve scrapping the entire system. Whereas, if a full photograph of the biometric attribute was stolen from a security system, the entire system may not be able to be rehabilitated.

Anticipating Legal and Policy Changes That Will Affect Biometrics

When choosing the elements of a SCADA security system, the security executive must consider how the system components work together and what special issues each component brings into the picture. What aspects of the SCADA security create the most significant risks for administration and trust in the system?

Biometric components offer a level of complexity that can be problematic for implementation and operation. Biometric readers are famously more fickle and more sensitive to environmental factors than simpler input devices. Unlike password systems that operate in a clear " match or no match" environment, biometric systems provide a sample comparison that must be calibrated between the need to avoid both false positives and false negatives.

However, unlike nearly all other forms of data entry and verification for authenticating people, biometric security brings a non-technical, social element to your defenses. Whenever people are forced to offer and leave a piece of themselves in the system, they will worry what that system is taking from them.

For the past several years, the California legislature has introduced bills to limit or stop the use of biometrics. Soldiers have sued the U.S. military to stop the use of biometric identification programs, and labor unions have sued companies to stop the forced biometric capture of workers' physical data for security purposes. As personal privacy becomes a recognized right under the laws of the United States, then the potential harm of forcing people to participate in biometric capture and storage gains the attention of privacy advocates.

Currently, United States privacy laws leave a significant loophole related to biometric capture and maintenance of personal data. The Health Insurance Portability and Accessibility Act of 1995 (HIPAA) carved out a sphere of privacy in personal health care information. Doctors and hospitals must now protect all personally identifiable health care data received from their patients.

The data relating to a person's medical condition cannot be used for any purpose beyond its original function for diagnosing or treating the person, unless the patient gives permission to use it in another specific manner. This law applies to other information receivers in the health care universe, such as drug stores, insurance companies, and the administrators of company health plans.

However, the protections apply only to data captured in the process of delivering health care. They do not apply to data captured for the purposes of security authentication. Therefore, if your employer takes a sample of your DNA as part of a diabetes screening sponsored by the company health plan, then that DNA sample is protected from disclosure under HIPAA.

Conversely, if the same company takes a DNA sample from you for the purpose of identification and authentication in a biometric security system, then that DNA sample is not protected under HIPAA or any other current federal law in the United States, and the company may be able to use the data for other purposes or even to sell it to other companies.

This leaves a gaping hole in protections for personal data relating to a person's body, health, or other physical traits, and the hole in data protection can be applied to the most personal and private data about a person. Physical information, especially any sample that allows harvesting of DNA, can reveal an enormous amount of sensitive information, from race and parentage, to likelihood of heart disease or high cholesterol, to behavioral propensities. Personal data about individuals has a value, and a company capturing this data may be tempted to use it in ways never intended by the person who offered it.

At some point, the law is likely to change to protect biometric samples. In the meantime, privacy activists and other people concerned about loss of their personal data could create a hostile environment for use of biometrics in security. In this case, collecting biometric signatures would be more difficult for the security department. In addition, various U.S. states have introduced laws to regulate biometric capture and storage. Your company should include the possibility of regulation in its risk calculations when deciding whether to include biometric components into its SCADA security system.

Summary

Biometric authentication regimes can solve important problems within your company's SCADA security system, but they are not helpful in all situations, and they present the system administrator with unique issues and risks. In a SCADA security network, biometric components are useful only at the edges of the network where people interact with the SCADA security and where secure facilities and equipment need authorized access. The variety of biometric readings, both invasive and remote, demonstrates that biometric security can meet a wide array of priorities within your overall security program.

However, each biometric authentication capture device provides its own set of choices, such as whether it is more important to your company to allow ready access in an emergency or whether it is more important take extreme steps to exclude any unauthorized people from accessing secure facilities. These devices are not foolproof and can be beaten at a number of different points of vulnerability, including tricking the scanners or reworking the system software. Storage and protection of biometric samples can also be hazardous. Finally, biometric systems are not yet so widespread that the law and regulations for biometric capture can be expected to remain constant over the several years of your company's investment in these systems.

Solutions Fast Track

Understand the Strengths and Weaknesses of Biometric Solutions

- ☑ Know that biometrics is appropriate only in limited circumstances in SCADA security.

- ☑ Analyze the number of authentication factors needed.

- ☑ Make realistic choices concerning the physical traits measured for identity.

Choose Biometric Technology That Matches Your Security Priorities

- ☑ Is speed of access or certainty of authentication more important?

- ☑ What current, cost-effective product meets your company's needs?

- ☑ Factor complexity and environmental concerns into your decision.

Learn About Your Biometric System's Vulnerabilities

- ☑ Systems mteasuring physical characteristics external to the body may be fooled by presenting a false sample.

- ☑ Biometric systems may be attacked through their software systems.

- ☑ Data and software integrity is critical and must be monitored and confirmed on a regular basis in biometric scanning and comparison systems.

Prepare for Social and Legal Changes

- ☑ Some people refuse to provide invasive biometric samples for any purpose, including security.

- ☑ Current U.S law contains loopholes relating to storage and use of physical data for security purposes.

- ☑ Expect changes in law and regulation of biometrics that could affect the use of this technology in your SCADA security system.

Frequently Asked Questions

Q: What is biometric security authentication?

A: It is application of the science of measuring living beings, humans in this case, and identifying/authenticating a person using some physical characteristic so that the person may interface with the system in an authorized manner.

Q: Where can biometric authentication be used in SCADA security?

A: Biometric authentication regimes are appropriate anywhere that humans interact with the system, but are most often used in authorizing access to secure facilities and equipment, either central or remote.

Q: What physical characteristic should my company be measuring?

A: This depends on your company's security and administrative priorities. Fingerprint capture is common among vendor systems and is well-accepted by the general public. Voice and face recognition can be taken from a distance. Retinal scanning is difficult to spoof.

Q: Where are biometric authentication systems vulnerable to fraud?

A: Biometric capture systems may be attacked by providing a false but similar sample for authentication. Ultimately, biometric security is based on software comparisons of electronic files, where the files represent a physical characteristic of the measured person. Therefore, the systems are vulnerable to several types of software and database integrity attacks.

Q: How is security measured in biometric authentication systems?

A: A biometric authentication system is considered secure if it does not produce a level of false-positive readings or false-negative readings that are unacceptable to the system manager.

Q: What can a system manager do to minimize the possibility that a biometric database will be compromised with biometric files stolen?

A: The manager could choose a system that stores its biometric files separately and remotely. The manager could also choose a system that only measures certain minutia of a characteristic, so that the loss of that data will not compromise the entire regime.

Q: What United States laws or regulations address the privacy of biometric samples taken for security purposes?

A: At this writing, biometric samples taken for security purposes are not explicitly treated as protected private information by U.S. statutes or regulations.

Appendix

Personal, Workforce, and Family Preparedness

Phil Drake is Communications Manager for the Charlotte Observer in Charlotte, N. C. The Observer is a daily newspaper that serves readers throughout North and South Carolina. In addition to the newspaper, the Charlotte Observer produces specialty magazines, voice information, and Internet services.

Phil is responsible for all aspects of communications at Observer operations in both Carolinas, including telephone and data communications, wireless systems, conventional and trunked two-way radio, and satellite systems. He is also responsible for business continuity and disaster response planning and related budgeting. He is responsible for providing emergency communications facilities for reporters and photographers covering breaking news stories.

His background includes photojournalism, mainframe computer support, network management, telecommunications planning and management, and business continuity planning. Phil is a former chairman of the Contingency Planning Association of the Carolinas and currently serves as a Board Advisor of the organization. He is a Certified Business Continuity Professional with the Disaster Recovery Institute International.

Phil speaks to public and private sector groups and has been interviewed by and written for a number of national publications on a wide range of emergency communication issues, and business/homeland defense planning. He leads business continuity training seminars for both the public and private sectors, and he has provided project management in business continuity. He has advised major national clients in emergency planning, workforce protection, threat assessment, and incident response for a number of large national corporations.

He enjoys backpacking and spending time in the outdoors. He also has taught outdoor living skills to youth group leaders. He was appointed by the North Carolina Secretary of the Department of Environment and Natural Resources as a voting member of the NC Geological Survey Advisory Committee.

Introduction

In this chapter, we'll discuss the need for a personal, workplace, and family emergency plan. We'll cover the basics of creating a plan for you and your family, identifying and obtaining the basic supplies you will need in an emergency, and why being prepared is so vitally important to you, your family, your community, and the nation. We'll also discuss workforce preparedness and the new urgency that applies to this important area in business continuity planning.

Threats

We live in a time and a nation where one can no longer take a "neutral position" regarding preparedness. As individuals, families, and workgroups, we are either an asset or a liability for our communities and nation when disaster strikes. To be an asset, we must be prepared.

You must be able to care for yourself and your family or you must depend on others to take care of you when disaster strikes. For too long, we have abandoned one of the founding principles that has made this nation great: self-reliance. "It's not my job" or "we have people to take care of that" when discussing preparedness is a far too common response.

Being prepared is having the ability to take care of yourself and your family at home, work, or school during an emergency situation. Likewise, business and government agencies must prepare to keep operating and supplying the goods and services that our communities need so as to return to normal life quicker.

NOTE

A family that has a disaster plan, supplies, and know-how in order to comfortably shelter in-place or evacuate during a severe storm, natural disaster, or other emergency will lessen the impact of whatever the emergency might bring.

Since September 11, 2001, our nation and the world have awakened to the very real threat of terrorism. While terrorist acts against the United States were not new, the scale of the coordinated attack of September 11 finally made even the most skeptical citizen realize we are a primary target for politically or religiously motivated acts of criminal violence.

While terrorism demands constant vigilance, so do the other threats that cause a tremendous loss in lives and dollars. Natural disasters, accidents, workplace violence, and crime also require our constant attention and preparedness.

While the average citizen can do little to stop these catastrophic events, they can prepare now to lessen the impact on themselves, their families, and their work environment. The first step in this preparedness process is to accept the fact that "it can happen to me" and "it can happen here."

Since Hurricane Katrina ravaged the Gulf Coast in 2005, FEMA and other government agencies have been clear in warning all who will listen that local state and federal government resources cannot save everyone. They cannot supply all the requested food, water, medical supplies, manpower, and infrastructure repairs requested in a widespread disaster in a matter of a few hours or days. With such things as the Katrina recovery, for example, we need to include months and years in our recovery projections.

For many years, the official recommendation was that you must be able to take care of yourself and your family for a minimum of at least 72 hours. Actually, two weeks is a more realistic estimate nowadays, given that the threat of a worldwide pandemic is a growing concern.

Public health experts are warning us that a major health crisis brewing in Asia will affect the entire world. We are being told that *when* a pandemic hits our nation (not if), it will be a very different disaster from any we have experienced in recent history. A pandemic will not only bring interruptions in key services and supply lines, but in the way we work and live for 12 to 18 months, perhaps longer. How can a business survive if the normally reliable electrical power, phone service, customers, suppliers, and workforce are missing?

How will our lives change when the schools and shopping malls close? In a highly contagious pandemic, few of us would want to find ourselves standing in a line to receive food or other basic supplies.

Our workplaces will change dramatically. The new terms of "social distancing," "lone worker," "virtual office," and "virtual workforce" will become commonplace. Not only must a workforce be prepared for power and communications outages, it must now be prepared to use new tactics, including social distancing, family preparedness, sheltering-in-place, and workforce continuity to reduce the impact of this new threat.

Preparing yourself and your family for emergencies requires more than just good intentions and a willingness to take care of yourself and your loved ones. Being prepared means much more than just having cash in your pocket and a "good" credit card ready to go. Preparedness means having a plan and the resources on hand to be totally self-sufficient during a natural disaster or other major emergency until normalcy is restored.

The Internet has made a wealth of family and workplace preparedness material available. "ready.gov," The American Red Cross, and other "official information" sites now offer information for a variety of age and reading levels. Official government pamphlets and booklets promote family preparedness and many commercial publications discuss this important topic. *Being informed is important, but being ready is absolutely imperative.*

"Workforce continuity" is defined as planning to have employees or contractors support the core business functions regardless of their work location. If the workplace is unreachable due to weather, road conditions, or some other workplace emergency, the employees can work from alternate locations or even from home. If an employee can't work for whatever reason, "workforce continuity" planning means training a backup to be ready to fill in for the missing worker. This may be other company employees or in some cases, outside contractors.

Workforce continuity also entails planning for a dramatic increase of absenteeism rates. If 40 or 50 percent of the workforce cannot or will not report for physical or virtual work, how does the enterprise survive?

It's smart to plan for the unexpected and use the Internet and wireless access to it to continue doing business. Virtual call centers and other technology depend heavily on the Internet and communications networks. What happens if those networks and other infrastructures are unavailable or so overtaxed that they become useless for mission critical use?

After all, what is the total capacity of the Internet? *Internet World Stats* reports that as of late 2006 there were 1,093 billion Internet users in the world. Now let's suppose that the majority of these users are currently working at home to support their employer's operations or are trying to keep abreast of the latest emergency information. At what point does the Internet cease to be a useful transport mechanism due to the demand for bandwidth? Probably long before the last user signs on.

A business that depends primarily on the Internet as a solution to a large-scale disaster or manmade crisis will be disappointed. Virtual office and a mobile workforce are ideal solutions to many of today's environmental and business scheduling problems. However, a solution that depends heavily on public infrastructure for success is doomed from the beginning. The only dependable solution is a reliable workforce willing to be there when needed to keep the business running.

Business leaders must understand that they we now face the very real possibility of not having enough employees to keep the business "in business."

Let's talk for a while about what's really important in your life, and what's really important in your family's life: YOU. Do you have a personal emergency plan? Does your family? Most individuals and families believe they will think about this when the time comes. Unfortunately, when a disaster strikes, there is little warning and the "planning" gets replaced by panic and uncoordinated responses to the event.

Your Personal Preparedness Plan

Let's start with that most valuable asset: "you." You need to have a plan, and you need to make sure your family and co-workers know what that plan is. If they are part of your plan, they surely need to know that now. And yes, just as with any plan, yours needs to be tested routinely.

We'll discuss workplace, home, and family preparedness a bit later in this chapter. It is vitally important to remember that personal, family, workplace, and community emergency preparedness complement each other.

Most of us spend the majority of our lives between home and work. If an emergency is preceded by a warning period (a winter storm or hurricane), you will have time to plan your response. In a winter storm, for instance, you'll probably stay at home or will be instructed to report later than usual by your employer. In the event of a fire, earthquake, or other unexpected emergency, your response must be immediate. You must act quickly to save your life and perhaps the lives of others.

TIP

Your personal goal is to make sure you survive and remain healthy, regardless of what the emergency situation may be. Getting out of a dangerous situation and staying out of the way are paramount. Being prepared will reduce your mental and physical stress levels and increase your ability to assist others.

The first step in your plan must be the protection of your own life. Personal safety experts will tell you to "always be aware of your surroundings." That's excellent advice. Look around; walk around your home and workplace. Where is trouble most likely to occur? Is flooding from a nearby creek or river possible? Are you near any major railroads or highways where transportation accidents may impact you?

Do the same "walkabout" inside, too. Are there dangers you've ignored in the past? Could any of these be used against you and/or your home or workplace? Be aware of unlocked exit doors, trip hazards, and blocked exits.

Wherever you work, know the environment, and if the situation requires, know how to get out quickly. Make sure you know where the emergency exits are, and if the one closest to you is blocked, where the next closest exit is located. How long does it take you to exit your facility? Do these exits have battery-operated escape lights? If not, provide your own with a small flashlight or chemical light sticks.

If you work in a multistory building, are you physically able to walk down the exit stairs? If not, make sure you can. Even if you are in good physical shape, stairs can be a challenge. If you are physically unable to walk down stairs because of medical reasons, find "escape buddies" to help you get down or check with your employer to determine the locations of any identified evacuation safe havens.

If you're shopping, at the movies, spending the night away from home, or conducting personal business in a building you're not familiar with, know how to get out.

WARNING

Wherever you are, always know where the emergency exits are located. They are required by law to be clearly marked. In a hotel, I always find the exits before turning in for the evening.

Having a personal preparedness plan will make you and your loved ones safer. After all, they depend on you. A personal plan should include the following:

- A commitment to be aware of your surroundings and current conditions

- Alternate routes to and from home, work, or school

- An emergency contact card with all family contact information

- Knowing the locations of fire, police, and emergency medical facilities near your work, home, and routes of travel

- If you commute, keep a spare car key hidden on the vehicle in case a building evacuation at work forces you to leave everything behind.

- Everyone needs a few basic resources if circumstances strand you en route to home/work/school. (See the next section on the subject of escape packs.)

- Always know the location of the nearest fire escape in your workplace, school, or hotel if traveling.

- Familiarize yourself with the emergency exits and procedures on commercial buses, trains, and aircraft.

- Remember my *3G rule*: "Get out, Get away, and Get in touch." Regardless of where you may be, always remember to get out of danger, get away from the danger, and let your family, friends, and employers know you are safe.

Don't get caught standing outside your workplace due to an evacuation and wondering "now what"? Your personal response plan must cover not only safely getting out, but safely getting away if necessary. If you drive to work, where are your vehicle keys? Can you get into your vehicle if your keys are in your coat, hanging beside your desk? Hide a key under, around, or near your vehicle. In the case of keyless entry, keep an ignition key hidden inside the vehicle. If you're carpooling, make sure everyone in the group knows how to get in, too.

One of the simplest ways to make sure you have basic items to help you respond in an emergency situation is to pack them now before you need them. This small "escape pack" is designed to help get you out of trouble if an emergency interrupts your normal routine. I'll also explain what these items are since I'm not a big believer in buying (or carrying) a bunch of "stuff" just for the sake of doing so. You can also purchase commercially available kits that provide some of the same items. However, if you assemble this kit yourself, you'll be more familiar with the contents and how to use them.

This is not a "survival kit" in the general context. It will supply your immediate needs in case you find yourself "on the street" unexpectedly due to an emergency in your workplace. All of these items can easily be packed in a small nylon pouch generally sold as "camera case."

The Escape Pack

- Thirty-minute high intensity light sticks (two)
- Compass (basic and small)
- Metropolitan or area map
- Disposable plastic rain poncho
- Emergency contact card

- Small note pad

- Pencil

- Matches (one book)

- Aluminum foil (12×24 inches)

- Important phone numbers

- Large handkerchief or bandana

- Change (quarters for payphone or newspaper racks)

- Extra cash (a $20 bill works nicely)

- Critical medication (one or two doses)

- Large 3×4 gauze pads and small roll of ½-inch adhesive tape

- Four Large adhesive bandages (Band-Aids)

- Small pocketknife

- Energy bar or some hard candy

- Ziplock bags (two)

- Vehicle and/or home key if needed

- Bag to carry the above items

Description of Kit Contents

- **Light sticks** Used for escape illumination in office hallways and stairwells.

- **Map and compass** If you must walk home or to safety, you'll be able to navigate your way. Practice this important skill before you need it.

- **Plastic rain poncho** A inexpensive plastic poncho will keep you dry and help you retain body heat.

- **Emergency contact card** Keep those key emergency phone numbers, family, and out-of-area emergency contact numbers written down and handy. In a stressful situation, don't rely on your memory. Your cell phone or PDA may have been left behind, or might not be functioning.

- **Small note pad and pencil** Important for writing messages, notes, or observations. A pencil will not leak in the summer or stop working in cold or rain.

- **Matches (one book)** Can be used for starting a fire for warmth, or lighting up a cigarette if it will make you feel better.

- **Aluminum foil (12×24 inches)** Has a hundred uses. First aid, signaling, and food preparation are three that come to mind quickly.

- **Large handkerchief or bandana** For first aid, keeping your head warm, and cleaning glasses.

- **Change and extra cash** Quarters for payphones (if working) or newspaper racks. Newspapers provide a host of uses. Extra cash in case ATMs aren't working or merchants cannot use checks or read credit cards.

TIP

Your vehicle is an excellent place to store some emergency supplies, including your "escape pack." These items will be available in case of a workplace evacuation or other emergency away from home.

Workforce Preparedness

While the subject of workforce preparedness can fill an entire book, I want to devote some time to discuss its importance and offer some suggestions to help begin the planning process.

The most valuable asset any enterprise or organization has, regardless of its size, is its workforce. These are men and women who make a company run day-to-day and create ideas and products to serve its customers and communities. Until recently, the majority of business continuity efforts revolved around processes and systems that the company depends on to keep operating. Little attention has been paid to the most critical support process, those employees and their families who make the enterprise successful.

Throughout this section I use the descriptions of workplace, organization, agency, business, employer, and enterprise. These are generic terms of that place you call "work." I realize there are thousands of public and private sector operations and agencies that, while not motivated by profit, do have products, services, and delivery obligations.

The threat dynamics have changed dramatically in the twenty-first century and every aspect of our normal lives is now considered a possible target for terrorism.

Senior managers must realize that interruptions to the normal flow of business may include community evacuations, workplace violence, lengthy supply chain interruptions, mass casualty situations, and direct attacks by individuals or groups using unconventional weapons. Do not assume your workplace is safe from these new threats, or old ones such as fire, natural disasters, or criminal activity.

An organization that only prepares for the occasional power failure, fire, hurricane, winter storm, or work stoppage is no longer exercising due diligence in the protection of the assets of that enterprise. Every organization, large or small, must have a *business defense plan* (business continuity plan) that includes protection and preparedness of the core operational functions, employees, and their families. In a community-wide emergency or disaster, companies and public agencies need their employees to return to work as quickly as possible to limit losses. A company or government agency may provide critical services that will be vitally necessary for the recovery of your community from the event. That company or agency *must* be prepared to continue operations. If an employee must choose between family and workplace, family will win every time. Senior executives, managers, and agency directors can no longer tell their employees that "we expect you to be here when we need you, under any circumstances" and be assured of a successful recovery.

Any organization that seeks to prepare their key processes for unexpected interruptions must maintain a prepared workforce to support those critical functions.

You may have heard the relatively new term *workforce continuity*. It's defined as having an uninterruptible and trained workforce that can continue the critical operations of the organization under any circumstances. Generally, this means planning to use virtual workers when weather or other conditions make travel to the primary work location hazardous. Cross-training employees to fill in for job functions that are not ordinarily their responsibility is another workforce continuity tactic. Having contract employees on retainer is yet another.

TIP

Simply having a contingency plan *in case of trouble* is no longer adequate. For the foreseeable future, we must expect trouble and make sure each of us—as well as our families, workplaces, and communities— are at a higher level of readiness.

A well-developed business continuity plan that prepares the key businesses processes, employees, and employee families is no longer just smart planning. It is now critical to the survival of our economy (along with due diligence).

The most valuable asset your business, agency, organization, or home has is *you*. You, your family, co-workers, and stakeholders keep the enterprise running, and successful. What happens at home and in your personal life outside the workplace has a direct impact on how well you do your job. In an emergency situation, most people think of home and family first. Is everyone safe? If you are at home, will you report to work in a time of crisis? Will you leave your family to help your employer continue operations?

It's vitally important that every enterprise, regardless of whether it's a major corporation, small business, or government agency have plans to guarantee the safety of its employees. In fact, law in many instances requires it. However, don't assume that just because you participate in a "fire drill" that you are safe. Does your workplace have a safety committee? Are building evacuation plans documented? If an event happens in your community or workplace that places you in danger, how are you notified? Does your employer expect personnel to report to work under any conditions? If so, what are they doing to guarantee that?

The workplace that prepares employees and families by sharing preparedness information, plans, training, and support will have a workforce that is ready and willing to get things back to normal quicker than the unprepared. Replacing the fear and uncertainty in an emergency keeps the workforce, stakeholders, and families focused on recovery, not only in the enterprise but in the family unit and community as well.

Steps for Successful Workforce Preparedness

- Draw up a written business (or operations) continuity plan (BCP)
- Share the plan with employees and families as appropriate
- Exercise the BCP plan routinely
- Update building evacuation plans and practice carrying them out routinely
- Monitor local and national current events and share pertinent information with employees
- Conduct personal safety, first-aid, and CPR classes for employees
- Offer personal and family preparedness instruction and information

I've heard—and you probably have, too—the story about occupants in a multitenant building looking out of the windows to see a parking lot full of other building occupants. This usually means that the emergency alarm didn't sound or someone forgot to pass the word. Tragically, it can and does happen in real emergency situations generally related to workplace violence or bomb incidents.

An alerting system that can be used to quickly inform the entire population of a building, or an entire community for that matter, saves lives. This tends to be bells, horns, or sirens. However a building "enunciation" or public address system offers more control of the alerting process and evacuation. Electronic message boards, digital paging, and instant messaging to all LAN users are additional and highly effective ways of alerting and sharing emergency information quickly.

Get Out, Get Away, and Get in Touch

Federal, state, and local laws require that a workplace have an emergency evacuation plan (depending on the number of employees and the building structure) that must include an alerting system and annual exercises. Just getting everyone out, however, is not enough. For everyone's sake, you must prove it. That's not a new federal regulation, it's common sense. After all, would you want to be left behind and not be missed until it's too late?

In any emergency, remember the 3Gs rule of personal protection, which help remind you to get out, get away, and get in touch. Get out of danger—in this example, your workplace during an emergency. Get away—don't stand on the sidewalk in front of a building that may collapse or explode. And finally, get in touch with your supervisor, co-workers and family to let them know that you are accounted for.

First responders arriving on the scene at a fire, explosion, or building collapse will ask "is everyone out?" If you're the senior manager or building owner, you'll save time and precious resources by answering "everyone is accounted out" or be able to direct rescue teams to specific locations where missing workers were last seen.

If you cannot account for everyone, firefighters or search and rescue teams may have to search the building, and that puts lives at stake: those left behind and those searching.

In a large facility, your workplace evacuation plan should include "shelter locations." These assembly points inside the building—usually in fire escapes or other safe havens—offer shelter to injured or physically challenged employees. Such locations should be well marked and include some form of communication to a central emergency control point.

Your local fire department can assist your efforts in identification and planning. Preparing a workplace evacuation plan includes the following.

- Senior management must make it clear to every employee that when told to evacuate, they should do so immediately, without hesitation, and in an orderly fashion.

- Permanent "meeting points" outside the building are identified and assigned by department or work location where a roll call is conducted. The results are communicated back to an evacuation control point by two-way radio or runners.

- A central permanent "evacuation control point" is established to collect and distribute information from the evacuation.

- Each department, section, or floor must have assigned "fire wardens" or "evacuation coordinators" who keep current rosters of all shifts and employees. These rosters are carried to, or stored at, the outdoor meeting points.

- The control point relays the roll call and any injury reports to emergency responders.

- The "all clear" signal to return to the facility (or other such information) can only be issued by the evacuation control point. All information or requests for assistance from the meeting points must go to the control point—no exceptions.

- Routinely exercise the plan.

The meeting points mentioned in the preceding list should be located as far from the building as practical. Just being out of the building does not mean the workforce is out of danger. Most buildings today are constructed with beautiful glass exteriors. An explosion can send glass shards and other debris flying hundreds of yards.

One general concern expressed to me by executives of several corporations is that "fire drills" reduce production time and that's why they are rarely done more than once a year—which, by the way, is not enough. I recently helped a large company redesign their evacuation plan based on the preceding information. Each evacuation coordinator was assigned not only rosters but an inexpensive two-way radio and a bright yellow bag to carry them in to the meeting point. That company now routinely evacuates 800 employees from a multistory building, conducts a roll call, reports results, and returns all employees to the building in 15 minutes during evacuation drills. The executives of that company are proud of this accomplishment and their employees are safer.

In the event of an actual emergency, a final evacuation responsibility that you have to your family is to let them know your condition and plans as soon as possible.

If your workplace does not have an updated building evacuation plan, inquire about starting one. Ask your supervisor, safety committee, or safety director. This would also be a good time to get involved by offering to help make it happen or to make an existing program better with your participation.

Some workplaces have well-documented evacuation plans, and area evacuation coordinators ensure that all employees in their respective areas understand the plan, have "escape buddies" to help them if necessary, and "sweep" their assigned areas in an emergency making sure everyone has left the area. This is excellent safety planning, but these plans must be practiced routinely. Unfortunately, far too many organizations pay too little attention to this vital preparedness planning. If you work in an organization that has not updated its evacuation planning or if you don't fully understand the plans, get involved and make your workplace and yourself safer.

Are first-aid kits distributed for emergency use in your workplace? If so, where are they and are they properly supplied? If they are not adequate, point this out to your safety director or supervisor. Know how to use the supplies in a first-aid kit. If you're unsure, enroll in a basic first-aid course. Such skills make you, your family, and co-workers safer in any circumstance. Your employer will probably be more than happy to arrange onsite classes through the local chapter of the American Red Cross.

Family Preparedness Plan

We create and work plans every day of our lives. We plan our days, what to wear, who to meet, where to go and how to get there, and what to eat. These are for the routine, good things in life. Why then don't we plan for the bad things that can surprise us and threaten our safety?

One of the most chilling memories of the 2005 hurricane season was the CNN coverage of the hundreds of cars running out of gas on streets and highways as Hurricane Wilma approached. These "average Americans" were stranded, hungry and scared. I could not help thinking that a bit of planning would have avoided most of this suffering. These families probably didn't have a family ready kit, a full gas tank, or extra cash on hand. They had not considered the possibility that another hurricane might strike so soon after Katrina. They aren't alone in their denial; most Americans believe that bad things happen to other people.

Every book on family preparedness includes a list describing items that should be kept ready for use in an emergency situation. I've included a list (the Family Ready Kit) later in this chapter, but the kit doesn't work by itself. It's more important for family members to know what to do than to count on a box or bag of "stuff." Family preparedness is a state of mind—it's planning, practicing, and working together as a team to thrive, not just survive, in emergency situations.

The most important point in family preparedness is family communication. Talk about what your family plans to do in the event of a major storm, natural disaster, or terrorist incident. Talking through what you expect, what might happen, and what "we as a family" will do removes a tremendous amount of stress and fear from any situation. Children especially need to know that the family has a plan for emergencies and that they are an important part of the plan.

A good way to begin your preparedness planning is to create a family fire plan.

- Check your smoke alarms for proper operation annually and change the batteries.

- Plan escape routes including those from second stories.

- Establish a family meeting point (more on this in the next subsection).

- Call for help once outside.

- Practice your plan until it works flawlessly.

Spend some time explaining that emergencies can happen anytime, and that if we're all home together, we'll be really lucky. In reality, that's not likely to happen and family members will probably be separated for a number of hours (or even longer) until they can be reunited. Mom and Dad may be at work, or the kids may be at school when a major disaster happens. Discuss, now, how best to get together following a major emergency.

Each family member should have assigned tasks and a procedure to follow in the event of an emergency situation. This emergency planning begins with how to get out of the house in case of a fire or other emergency, and establishing a meeting point afterward for all family members.

The 3Gs rule applies to the home as well as the workplace. If you need to leave due to an emergency in your home, "Get Out, Get Away, and Get in touch."

A key component in your family preparedness plan is to have several meeting points for various emergencies. These are locations the family identifies and where they agree to meet if separated due to a disaster or other emergency.

Possible Meeting Points

Here is a list of possible meeting points for your family following a disaster or emergency:

- A neighbor's home, the family swing set, the mailbox, bus stop, or tree in the yard where the family is to meet in case an emergency requires leaving the home on short notice

- A community shelter, relative's home, or neighborhood business in case a neighborhood requires evacuation

- A relative or friend's home or other location outside the community in case the family is separated in a wide-scale disaster

- A virtual meeting place such as an e-mail address or phone number outside the community so family members can check in if separated

Schools have very specific procedures for early dismissal situations. Releasing children to family members is usually an option, but this must be approved beforehand. Allowing the school system to transport your children home may be faster than you trying to pick them up. Find out what your children's school system policies are and discuss these policies with your children.

If students will be sheltered in-place (kept safe at school) how will they be released? Will students be transported to a community shelter? If so, where is that shelter located?

Community Shelter

Your local emergency management agency has designated certain facilities in your city or county as community shelters. These shelters are generally public high schools or other public buildings that can hold a large number of people for an extended period of time. Typically, the American Red Cross is the agency that manages these shelters and provides food services, cots, first aid, communications, and basic health care for individuals who may need it. Community shelters are a safe place to go when needed. In a dangerous situation—such as a tornado, hurricane, or other general emergency—many people will try to stay at home. If the order is given to evacuate, do not hesitate. Leave immediately and go to a shelter as directed.

It's important for you and your family to understand what to take and not take to a community shelter if you go to one of these facilities. You should bring pillows, blankets, toiletry items, prescription medications, games, snacks, and identification. Ask your local Red Cross or emergency management agency—before an emergency—what can and cannot be brought with you to a local shelter. If you're a pet owner, ask what arrangements will be in place for pet care.

TIP

Assemble a personal "evacuation bag" for each member of the family. This small duffel bag or day-pack can be packed with a change of clothing appropriate for the season, as well as other personal items, in case you are forced to leave home quickly.

The Personal Evacuation Bag

- Jeans or heavy pants/slacks with belt

- Two pairs of heavy socks

- Long sleeved shirt/blouse

- T-shirt and change of underclothing

- One pair of shorts in warm weather

- Work gloves and winter mittens or gloves if appropriate

- Cap or hat with brim

- Sunglasses and sunscreen (regardless of temperature)

- Rain poncho or lightweight rain suit

- Personal hygiene items (comb, tooth brush, toothpaste, soap, razor, and towel)

- Sports/emergency or other lightweight blanket

- Copy of government-issued ID (driver's license)

- Flashlight or headlamp

- Pocketknife, whistle, compass, and matches/lighter

- Other personal items as appropriate

Preparedness Pantry

Every home should maintain a supply of nonperishable food and water for the entire family. When asked "how do I buy and store two weeks worth of food?" My response is that you simply have to fill your pantry. Most of us never do that. Instead, we depend on stopping by the supermarket or carry-out on the way home to pick up dinner. Now is the time to change that behavior and it can be done easily (and affordably) over a period of several weeks.

I've mentioned being prepared for at least 72 hours and more realistically two weeks, earlier in this chapter. Over the next several trips to the supermarket, purchase extra cans or packages of the foods you most often use. Supplement these with additional canned meats, vegetables, and fruits. Plan and stock your "preparedness pantry" to provide a two-week supply of meals. Be realistic: In an emergency situation, you won't be entertaining, and in most cases "meals" will be simple and quick. Purchase additional items that store well and can be used in a wide variety of meal planning—rice, dried beans and pasta are ideal choices.

Simply add a few more items each time you grocery shop and plan to have your "preparedness pantry" completed in three trips. Shop with a list and buy shelf-stable items. Once your supply is purchased, date every item and rotate your supply by incorporating them into your normal menus. Always plan ahead by purchasing replacement items first before using anything from your "preparedness pantry."

Once your pantry is stocked, rotate that stock by using the food purchased first and then re-supplying. I mark each can and package with its purchase date using a permanent marker. It's easy to use the first purchased items and then replace on the next trip to the supermarket. If you don't keep your preparedness pantry supplied with "rotated stock" you may find three-year-old tomato sauce that will add nothing but disappointment to your dinner plans.

I should at this point explain the term "shelf stable." Shelf-stable foods are prepared to be stored without refrigeration or any other special conditions for extended periods of time. Dried fruit and meat was the first "shelf-stable" food civilized man discovered. In fact, this food preservation method was used long before kitchens or shelves were invented.

While shelf-stable food purchased at the supermarket will easily last 12 to 18 months, I recommend a six-month storage/use/replacement routine. By incorporating your "emergency pantry" into your normal menus, you'll always have that two-week supply ready for use in an emergency.

Marking each container with the purchase date will help identify the "emergency pantry" items. Use these long-term storage items in normal weekly menus occasionally. You can purchase a replacement before it's actually used if you plan your menus a week beforehand. If you don't have a replacement before use, simply tear the label off and purchase a replacement on your next shopping trip.

An exception to this is MREs (Meals Ready to Eat) and dehydrated long-term storage foods that have a shelf life of six years and longer (depending on storage conditions). It's a good idea, however, to incorporate some of these occasionally into your regular meal planning, too, so family members know what these meals look and taste like. MREs (regardless of what you may hear) are tasty and nutritious.

"Soft pack canning" or MREs became the military standard in the 1960s. This process involves cooking the food in multilayer plastic envelopes that are impervious to the chemical action of the food or environment. This soft container maintains an airtight and almost indestructible "cocoon" for the fully cooked and "ready to eat food." This stuff stores for years and maintains flavor and nutritional benefits. Do not buy "military surplus" MREs; buy them fresh from local or online dealers.

MREs are a great choice for any organization or business that may need to feed employees and or family members in an emergency situation. They are packaged in complete meal servings. Each meal is unit packed in a plastic envelope that includes the entree, side items, drink, dessert, and accessories pack with salt, pepper, eating utensils, and napkin. All that is needed is a method for warming the food which, in a pinch, can be eaten at room temperature. One envelope contains a complete and balanced nutritious meal. This is especially important when mass feeding a large group without a large dining or food preparation facility.

Canned foods will easily store for 12 to 18 months. Some of the new microwave entrees are use-dated for generally a year. Look closely on your grocery store shelves (not freezer section) and you may be surprised at what you'll find that can be used in your emergency pantry. Along with canned vegetables and meats, you'll discover fully cooked meals ready to be warmed in the microwave, which include chicken, turkey, and beef entrees. You'll also find cooked pasta and rice dishes just waiting to be warmed and eaten.

Canning to preserve food and their flavors has been used for over two hundred years and is still the leading food preservation technology. Home canning remains popular especially when home gardens are producing more than we can use or give away.

> **NOTE**
>
> Napoleon offered a cash prize to anyone who could find a way to keep food from spoiling so he could better feed his army on their long campaigns. In 1795, Nicolas Appert discovered that by placing food in sealed containers and cooking them in boiling water the food lasted for long periods of time. He won the prize and his method of food preservation was declared a military secret. It wasn't long, however, before this new preservation method found its way to England where in 1810 Peter Durrand improved the process by using metal containers or "cans."

Home freezing and frozen foods (TV dinners) became popular in the 1950s. Today, refrigeration and freezing are the most popular forms of food preservation. By the way, if you have a freezer full of frozen food and no power, don't panic—and don't open the freezer door. A full freezer will keep frozen food "frozen" for around 48 hours *if* you avoid the urge to open the door.

Freeze-dried foods are very popular with backpackers. These foods are fully cooked and then flash frozen at temperatures around −125 degrees Fahrenheit. Water from the food is condensed and removed, leaving a dried food product, which is then packaged in an airtight (generally plastic/foil) package. All you need to do is add the water back, and heat the product when you're ready to eat.

Freeze-dried foods are very light and compact, and will store for many years. Complete freeze-dried meals are available in any outdoor supply or camping store. One small drawback is that they are a bit more expensive than hard or soft pack canned food items, you must have an ample supply of water to add to the contents, and they are not as easy to incorporate in a normal family menu for pantry stores rotation.

Irradiated food processing is still fairly new and in very limited distribution in the U.S. at the time of this writing. Irradiation offers some major food safety and preservation benefits. This technology uses a radioactive source to "sterilize" the food without cooking it. So, in theory, meat could be stored in a container without refrigeration for weeks and still be safe and favorable. Fruits and vegetables can be stored for months without loosing color, flavor, or food value. No radioactivity is transferred to the food, so your salad will not mutate into some giant walking green thing that chases you around the kitchen. The Food and Drug Administration reports that food irradiation is allowed in nearly 40 countries and is endorsed by the World Health Organization, the American Medical Association, and many other organizations. However, the percentage of food being irradiated is still very low due to the expense and lack of acceptance of this new process. Stay tuned, this process will be commonplace in a few years.

As you can see, we are blessed with an array of well-proven food preservation methods. You must keep a supply on hand and thus avoid the danger of going out to look for something to eat.

Water

Water is the most important item in your "preparedness pantry." Store one gallon of water for each family member for each day you plan to be self-sufficient. Generally plan on using a half-gallon of water per day for drinking, and a half-gallon per day for sanitation for each family member. Date each container and rotate your stock every six months. Most commercial water containers are dated, saving you from having to do it yourself. Most commercially bottled water is use-dated for at least a year or two.

I recommend several one-, two-, or five-gallon containers of water for cooking and sanitation, and smaller 8- or 12-ounce bottles for drinking and refilling.

What's the difference between distilled water, spring water, and drinking water? Generally, the price. Distilled water is of course distilled or boiled into steam, the steam is condensed back into liquid form and bottled. This process removes all of the minerals and impurities and in fact sterilizes the water. Spring water should come from a spring (no guarantees here) and is probably filtered.

Drinking water is just "tap water" from a municipal water supply that may or may not be filtered and then bottled. Most is filtered, but check the label. Do as you please, but I simply buy the cheapest "store brand" drinking water for less than 60 cents a gallon.

If you have a natural water source near your home (spring, stream, or lake), consider purchasing a water purification filter. These filters generally consist of a small hand pump and a high-efficiency carbon or ceramic element that will purify the most questionable water supply. Several new water purification products are on the market. These include filtering straws and even battery-operated ultra-violet systems. For now, these tend to be expensive and produce limited volume. Having access to a water source and the proper purification equipment will reduce the amount of stored water you may need.

Storing a supply of food and drinking water is not just for personal or family emergency planning. The workplace must be able to support employees who may be stranded or "sheltered" in the workplace. Every business continuity plan must address the likelihood of supporting employees who may be required to stay put in order to keep critical operations running if conditions warrant.

Cooking

Simple one-pot "camping" meals are best in an emergency situation. After all, you'll be concentrating on other important issues. Be extremely careful in how you prepare your meals, especially when operating gas or other open-flame stoves that should be used *outdoors*. Never use charcoal grills or other outdoor cooking "appliances" inside your home. *Use them outside where they belong.* The risk of fire (which is great) is overshadowed by the risk of carbon monoxide poisoning.

For one pot meal suggestions, look no further than your "crock pot" recipe book. Search out recipes that use foods stored in your "preparedness pantry" and simply adjust cooking time from s-l-o-w to shorter times with higher heat.

Other good recipe resources are camping cookbooks and the official Boy Scout Field Book. *The Boy Scouts of America Field Book* is one of the best available manuals, not only for cooking but for general self-sufficiency as well.

Try the recipes that look interesting to you and your family. Tailor the ingredients to meet your specific tastes and portion requirements. The ones voted most enjoyable should be written on recipe cards and kept in your pantry.

I'm a lazy cook who loves to prepare and eat but hates to clean up. So after years of practice, I'm pretty good at whipping up some decent meals with little or no clean-up. Heating (see note that follows) foil packed meats, vegetables, and MREs in their packages in a single pot of boiling water allows you to use the water for hot drinks, rice, pasta, kitchen clean-up, and/or personal care. Cooking rice or pasta in "boiling bags" allows you to avoid more clean-up and requires less water, which may be in short supply. Of course, in an emergency, fuel may also be in short supply.

Tɪᴘ

When heating food envelopes ("soft cans"), always tear a small "vent" opening in the envelope to eliminate any bursting hazard. If the contents start to boil and produce steam, the envelope may explode.

Most people have an outdoor gas grill, camping, or backpacking stove that will handle the cooking requirements just fine, just use them outside.

Wᴀʀɴɪɴɢ

Installed home gas appliances are properly vented and have low oxygen shutdown safety features. Any portable cooking stove brought into your home does not. So keep the disaster—and the portable cooking stoves—*outside* your home.

As with any new recipe or cooking technique, it's best to try these first yourself before serving them to others. And, of course, before a disaster; otherwise, you will very likely lose your cooking privileges!

Testing Your Home Preparedness Plan

Just like a business continuity plan, a family preparedness plan is not complete until it is routinely tested and updated. At work, you and your co-workers must be familiar with your employer's business continuity or emergency plan and understand your role in that plan. Semi-annual plan reviews and exercises are the best method of keeping the plan current and the recovery teams competent in their ability to successfully execute the plan.

This is true for your family preparedness plan, too. Family members (regardless of their age or physical abilities) must actively participate and thoroughly understand the purpose of the plan and the importance of their respective roles in making the plan work successfully.

In the business environment, our continuity or preparedness plans are concerned with the safety of the employees and the welfare of the enterprise. At home, our focus is on our loved ones and the survivability of our home and family.

I strongly suggest you use the same tactics for plan testing or exercising at home that you use (or should be using) at work. Tabletop emergency exercises at work can become a great rainy day "board game" at home. Plan "what if" and "how can our family handle an emergency" discussions, and include everyone's input. Hold a "walkthrough" of your plan to see if parts of it are unrealistic. Of course, scheduled exercises or even a few unannounced drills are the best method of keeping your family preparedness plan the best it can be, and as a result, your family will be safer.

One of the most enjoyable ways to test your preparedness plans is to have a "camp-in." Select a weekend evening and announce that you'll all meet in the living room or den and camp out for the night. Off go the lights and the entire family uses only the supplies on hand to "survive the disaster." Pretend there is no phone or power other than what you can supply with your own resources. Meals should be prepared using your "preparedness pantry" and alternate cooking methods.

We can promise three things if you follow our advice in this chapter. Your family will be better prepared for emergencies, you'll all have some fun, and you and your family will discover that doing something a bit unusual as a team brings you closer together and builds a stronger family bond.

Family Ready Kit

Designating a central point where special supplies and basic equipment will be stored saves valuable time in responding to an emergency. While there are a few "family emergency kits" now being marketed online and in some stores, I suggest you make your own. You probably already have many of the things you'll need, and by building the kit yourself and involving the entire family, everyone becomes familiar with the contents and the location of the kit.

Younger family members in particular feel more confident if mom and dad aren't around by knowing that the family ready kit has basic emergency supplies to help them until other family members arrive.

If the family can stay at home and shelter-in-place, the ready kit is "ready" to help the family stay safe and more comfortable. If the emergency requires evacuation to a safer location, the kit is easily carried with the family. Following are some suggested items; adjust as appropriate for your family. Keep your ready kit in a closed container and be sure everyone in the family understands its purpose and storage location.

While not part of the regular "family ready kit," don't forget pet food and pet medications. Your pets are an important part of the family, too.

Family Ready Kit Contents

- Water (one gallon per person per day)

- Maps (local and state) with compass

- Prescription and OTC medication; personal hygiene items

- Identification for each family member (copies of driver's licenses, other government-issued ID, and Social Security cards)

- Copies of financial records (bank and credit card account numbers, brokerage account numbers)

- Document copies (homeowners and other insurance policies, healthcare ID cards, and other important documents)

- Contact telephone numbers (family, relatives, friends, physicians, schools)

- Pre-paid long-distance calling card

- Photos of home (exterior and interior), photos of family members, and pets

- Inventory of home contents

- Cash (including change) or travelers checks

- Extra automobile and house keys

- Reading and religious materials, Boy Scout fieldbook, other reference literature

- Inoculation records (children and adults, if warranted), other health records as needed

- Notepad and pens/pencils, permanent marker

- Board games, crayons, cards, and card games

- Disposable camera

- Shelf-stable foods: MREs, instant drink mixes, soups, energy bars, fruit, trail mix

- Special dietary supplements and/or infant formulas

- Salt, pepper, sugar, instant creamer/milk, hard candy, and other fun foods

- Camping or other small portable stove, extra fuel, and one-quart pot, matches, or lighter

- Paper plates, cups, and disposable eating utensils; manual can opener

- Sewing kit, nylon rope, repair tape, and wire ties

- Flashlight/battery lantern, chemical light sticks (do not use candles for emergency lighting)

- Extra batteries in plastic bag

- Pocket or other folding knife, whistle, and small mirror

- Rescue blanket for each family member and a group first-aid/medical kit

- Chlorine bleach (unscented, 24 ounce)

- Trash and plastic storage bags

- Plastic sheeting/drop cloth; trash and plastic storage bags

- Liquid soap, shampoo, and several small towels

- Multipurpose tool or pliers; screwdriver

- Plastic storage container or sturdy cardboard box to hold your "ready kit" items

No Lights? No Problem!

Lighting is a source of safety and comfort. Most of the conveniences in our homes and the tools in our workplaces are powered with electricity. When the power goes off, we suddenly find ourselves in an unfamiliar and sometimes scary environment. All the stuff we rely on to make us comfortable, help us do our jobs, and make us safe, stops working.

Let's get this out of the way right now, candles are for birthday cakes, *not emergency lighting*. In an emergency situation, you'll have a tremendous number of things on your mind, stress will be affecting your ability to think clearly, and the fire department will probably be busy, so let's not complicate things by adding to whatever disaster you may be dealing with by burning your house down.

The major difference between candles and other sources of flame-dependent lighting is that candles provide little light, usually are not supplied with fire-resistant containers, and have an open flame. Coleman lanterns and the old reliable kerosene type lamps grandma used at least contain the flame in a fireproof enclosure. This enclosure (glass globe or chimney) generally prevents something from accidentally coming into contact with the flame and starting a fire. Generally, anything with a flame requires great caution when used, and can cause a fire or explosion if employed where natural gas pipes may be leaking.

Start with the safest form of auxiliary lighting, chemical light sticks, and then after making sure there is no danger of explosion (broken gas lines, leaking or damaged containers of gasoline or other volatile liquids) work into flashlights and battery-operated lamps. Pressurized gas camping lanterns are for outdoor use. Kerosene and other oil lamps, even the high-efficiency models, require extreme caution if used indoors. In an emergency, avoid any device that uses a flame for lighting—*especially candles.*

In the well-prepared workplace, emergency lighting and power must be provided so critical operations can continue and provide a safe and comfortable working environment. At home, these same reasons apply.

Power outages can be caused by storms, natural disasters, accidents, human error, equipment failure, and intentional acts. Blackouts and brownouts caused by a lack of generating capacity in some areas of the country are becoming a summer routine. Corporations and individuals are searching for ways to avoid the dangers, stress, and financial loss associated with power failures.

Emergency Lighting

"Where's the flashlight?" is the call of the unprepared when the lights go out. It's so simple, but few people know where it is or routinely check to see if the batteries are producing power and the bulb works. When you buy batteries, date them with a laundry marker, test them every three months, and change them at least once a year. By the way, standardize on the type of light—and for goodness sake, the battery size. Shopping for batteries will be much easier this way.

Since we mentioned chemical light sticks first (sometimes referred to as "snap lights"), it's only fitting to explain this safe light source first. My favorite is the Caylume 30-minute or one-hour high intensity white light stick. These six-inch long plastic tubes contain two *nontoxic* chemical agents that, when mixed, fluoresce with a bright white light. You simply bend the plastic tube at a sharp angle, which breaks (snaps) an inner capsule that starts the chemical process. Shaking the stick a couple of times completes the mixing process, and suddenly you have plenty of light to work with. There is no danger of heat, flame, fire, or explosion. These lights can be used safely in any environment, and they have a shelf life of approximately three years.

Light sticks can be purchased in a variety of colors and sizes. Buy high intensity where possible since these produce enough light to work and read by and will emit usable light for nearly an hour. The sticks will continue to glow for many hours, so they can be used to mark stairways, doors, or other locations. These light sticks have equal value as escape lights in both the workplace and home. They are a great source of comfort for children since they can be safely carried around, or even brought to bed.

Battery-operated lights, flashlights, and lanterns are the most common source of emergency lighting for most families.

While there are many flashlights and battery-operated lanterns on the market today, I want to discuss the four main categories of battery-operated lights.

WARNING

If you have gas appliances in your home, be extremely careful after any event (hurricane, tornado, or earthquake) that causes structural damage. Always check for gas leaks before switching on flashlights or anything else that may cause a spark resulting in an explosion.

Handheld Lights

These include the regular two-cell (three-cell, four-cell, and counting) flashlights. Types and prices run from as cheap as a dollar to several hundred dollars (no kidding). Avoid the cheap ones as they will break easily and the switching mechanism my not work more than a few times. Maglites are at the top of the scale in value. They are manufactured with aircraft aluminum, are water-resistant, come in many colors and battery-cell sizes, and contain a spare bulb. Several companies manufacture top of the line, expensive tactical flashlights designed for a military market that needs high intensity, indestructible combat-proven specialty lights. While these lights are bright, small, and indestructible, they are very expensive ($100.00 plus) and are designed more for target illumination than work area and general illumination.

A new family of flashlights has appeared on the market in the past several years and these lights use no batteries or bulbs. They are marketed as "everlasting" since there's nothing to replace. They produce power when the user shakes the light, which causes a magnet to slide back and forth through a coil of wire (generator), which charges an onboard capacitor, which then powers an LED (light-emitting diode). All of this is wrapped in a sealed water-tight plastic housing. These lights can be stored for many years, and when needed can be "charged" and used. A half minute of shaking will produce approximately 20 minutes of light.

Several models of "dynamo flashlights" are now available. These lights use a small hand-cranked dynamo to charge a battery to power the LEDs. Several models are available, including a camping lantern style.

When you purchase a flashlight, headlamp, battery lamp or spotlight, always buy extra bulbs and batteries (the exception of course being the LED models mentioned earlier, which last forever—almost). Remember to label the batteries with the purchase date. Yes, if you're using rechargeable batteries, you still need to date them since a two-year service life is average. After two years, rechargeable cells of all types become somewhat unreliable. OK, so you've had a set working for four years with no problems. I'm talking average commercial expectancy in critical situations.

NOTE

LED technology is advancing at a rapid rate, and soon filament-type incandescent bulbs will be completely replaced in the majority of low-voltage lighting applications. The major benefit is that less power is needed for an equivalent amount of light output, so fewer batteries and longer operation times result. Since these LEDs are solid-state devices, they aren't susceptible to filament breakage and burnout. Have you noticed that many commercial vehicles now use LEDs for brake and marker lights? Most new traffic lights now use LEDs instead of "bulbs."

Maglite and other manufacturers are marketing conversion kits to replace standard filament bulbs with LED modules. Generally, these aren't cheap. Nevertheless, they're worth the expense in my opinion due to the "lifetime" of service expected and the reduced battery replacement. You'll be impressed with the higher light levels produced by LEDs. In fact, the Maglite LED conversion kit for a two-cell Maglite appears to be brighter than the original standard bulb.

Headlamps

Headlamps (my personal favorite) can be worn on your head, leaving both hands free. The new ultra-light weight headlamps using LEDs are fantastic. They are small, lightweight, and produce good usable work light for any situation. The bonus, of course, is that these allow you to use your hands for something other than shining a light on your work. They work well for hiking, camping, or any other outdoor activity. Many search and rescue teams are converting to these lights. By the way, three AAA batteries will power an LED headlamp for 72 hours of *continuous* use.

A variety of larger headlamps are also available on the market. Some of these resemble miner lights, with various sizes of lamp heads, and many have external battery packs. They are, of course, heavier and tend to be more complicated to wear and maintain.

General Illumination Lamps

Illumination lamps are used to light a room or specific area. Battery-operated florescent lanterns or "pop-up" flashlights are the most popular. Many styles exist and some florescent lanterns are rechargeable. These offer good illumination for a room and usually have an option switch to choose between a "bright" setting (both florescent tubes on) for reading and critical work, and a "normal" position (one tube on) for navigating around the room and conserving battery power.

"Pop-up" flashlights are a terrific blending of a hand-carried flashlight (usually with a lanyard) and a general light source or "tent light" with frosted window that distributes light in a 360-degree manner. To convert from flashlight to "tent" or table light, simply pull on the front reflector, which exposes the frosted window. The front reflector serves as a base that stabilizes the light. These will illuminate a small room or your home office with enough light that you can move around safely. They generally use four AA batteries and produce between five to seven hours of light.

A useful hybrid light is the "Syclone" made by Streamlight Inc. This small hand light has a tilting head and flat base that provides a good stable work light that can sit on a desk or work surface. The light has a dual position switch that selects either a regular tungsten bulb or an LED. The four AA batteries will power the LED continuously for 72 hours. This light has a high-impact plastic case, a rubber handgrip, and belt clip, and is supplied with a helmet bracket for fire/rescue or construction use. A bonus feature is that this light is rated for use in explosive atmospheres (this is important when around gasoline, natural gas leaks, or other hazardous environments).

Coleman-type camping lanterns (pressurized gasoline), butane or propane lanterns, kerosene table lamps, barn lanterns, and railroad lamps use combustible fuels. These light sources require extreme care in use. Even if you are familiar with the operation and maintenance of these lamps and lanterns, if they are accidentally knocked over, they can and probably will start a fire. Be careful, and never attempt to use or fuel a pressurized gas lantern inside your home. Flame-dependant lighting is strictly prohibited in commercial structures. You should have the same rule in your home as well.

Spots and Floodlights

Spots and floodlights are usually 6- or 12-volt lights used by fire departments, railroads, and utility crews. They tend to be heavy but very bright, and the batteries are long lasting. Some smaller versions of these "professional" lights are now showing up in the retail market. One of the best in the "professional" league is manufactured by Streamlight and sold by police/fire supply companies and larger hardware and outdoor outlets. The Streamlight power fail model comes with a 110-volt charger base and a 12-volt DC mobile charger base. When using the 110-volt AC charger base, if the power goes off, the light comes on. These lights are an excellent choice for the workplace as power fail lights in critical areas. Plus, you can remove the light from the charger base and carry it with you. You have three lamp options, flood, spot, and a fairly new flood/spot combination model. They cost around $100, but if you need a tough dependable light, look no further.

Emergency Power

The subject of emergency power could itself fill an entire book. We'll spend a bit of time on portable electric generators because they are an emergency supply item that remains in high demand. As with any mechanical equipment, you must exercise good safety habits and understand the equipment, as well as potential risks from improper operation.

Whether your needs for a generator are of the "homeowners" variety with a capacity of one to five thousand watts, or a backup power plant with several million watts of capacity, some common decisions must be made before you go shopping. They are (1) What size do I need and what can I afford? (2) Will this be a portable or installed generator? (3) What fuel type do I plan to use?, and (4) How can I get the emergency power to the devices I plan to operate?

All portable and backup generators have an engine, which requires fuel. This fuel can be gasoline, propane, natural gas, or diesel fuel. The vast majority of smaller generators are gasoline powered, but propane and diesel are becoming more popular. The alternative "non-gasoline" fuels are safer to store, handle, and in the case of propane and natural gas, are cleaner burning.

WARNING

Never use a generator indoors, no matter how small it is. When using a generator outside of your home or office, be absolutely sure it is sitting well away from air intakes and any doors or windows that have been opened to permit the use of drop-cords or cables. Carbon monoxide, an invisible, odor-less, and toxic gas, can seep indoors and cause illness or even death. Never operate a generator or other gas-powered engine under your home, in the basement, or in your garage. Carbon monoxide can easily fill an enclosed area. You'll nod off to sleep and very possibly die if carbon monoxide seeps into your home. Put generators outside!

The electrical output of most portable generators runs anywhere from 300 to 15,000 watts for generators sold through home improvement and hardware stores. Prices range from around $500 to a couple of thousand.

A relatively new entry in the portable generator market is the "inverter generator." These units combine the functionality of a portable generator and the "clean power" output of a UPS best. These hybrids generate AC voltage, which is then converted to DC, and then reconverted back into AC voltage by an onboard voltage inverter. The inverter generator is an excellent choice when using power-sensitive electronics such as servers, switches, routers, and communications equipment.

Regardless of the size or type of generator you purchase, always read the instruction manual and follow the manufacturer's operation recommendations. This includes grounding the generator before starting. This is probably one of the most overlooked safety steps by homeowners. Also protect the generator from flood water, rain, or other environmental hazards. Read the instruction manual.

Large commercial generators that can power an entire office complex or industrial operation, operate on the same basic principle as their smaller cousins (an engine turns an alternator to make electricity), but of course cost much more and require special engineering, installation, and maintenance. These larger generator installations generally use diesel fuel. Permanently installed generators for homes and small-to-medium busi-nesses tend to use natural gas for simplicity of fuel delivery/storage issues. Prices includ-ing installation start around $4,000 for a home version up to many hundreds of thousands of dollars for a backup power plant with multiple generators and related equipment for commercial applications.

How much emergency power do you need? The simplest method is to use one of the many power sizing charts available online or at retail outlets. A portable generator in the range of 3,500 to 5,000 watts is a good fit for most homeowners to keep things running.

If you require a generator above 10,000 watts, will it be permanently installed or transportable? This certainly has a bearing on fuel type and the connection to your "load" (stuff to be powered). One of the most overlooked issues for generators (large or small) is how to get the electricity to the devices you want to power. In other words, where do you plug it in?

You have only two choices. First, and by far the best option, is an automatic or manual transfer switch. This device disconnects commercial power and easily (and safely) connects your "load" (home, office, or manufacturing facility) to the generator. Automatic switches sense when commercial power has stopped, starts the generator, and then switches the load to the generator. A manual switch requires human intervention to start the generator and then flip the switch to begin using the power. As you might expect, the automatic switches are expensive but worth the investment if power failure is not an option. All permanently installed generators require a transfer switch. Some small manual transfer switches are designed for residential use, allowing a single connection between the generator and the breaker panel. These cost a few hundred dollars and allow you to choose the area of the home to power while safely disconnecting from the commercial power supply.

TIP

Hire an electrician. A professional will be able to advise you on the best and safest method of installing a generator and power transfer switch for home or commercial use. This is serious stuff and mistakes can cost many more times the amount paid for professional consultation and installation.

The second option (and most used) is to utilize individual power cables or drop cords connected between the generator and your equipment or appliances. For smaller generators and home use for powering only a few items, the drop-cord solution is fine.

WARNING

Be extremely cautious when running drop cords into your home so that you do not allow carbon monoxide gas to enter as well. If using a window or door for cord entrance, be sure to make the access opening as small as possible and keep the generator well away. Use tape or weather stripping to make the entrance as air-tight as possible.

UPS and Battery Backup

An excellent way to keep critical equipment running during commercial power failures is a UPS power supply. These devices operate much like the automatic transfer switch and generator combination mentioned earlier except that they have no moving parts and are thus safe and simple to operate for indoor and home use. You'll probably find some of these near PCs and servers at the office.

The UPS contains one or more batteries that are kept charged by an onboard charging circuit that uses normal commercial power and an inverter to produce 110 volts of AC from battery power. A power sensing circuit monitors the commercial power source for quality and consistency. If the unit detects a low-/no power or high-voltage condition, (in the blink on an eye) it disconnects commercial power and supplies electricity to any equipment plugged into its outlets. These devices also filter the commercial power source and remove voltage spikes and ripples, which can damage sensitive equipment. They are available in various sizes depending on how much current you need and the length of time you want to operate the protected equipment when the commercial power goes away.

With a large UPS, the main consideration is how much time you need, want, or can afford before the batteries run out of power and no longer provide sufficient current to power the inverters. Most large commercial installations provide enough battery capacity to allow a generator sufficient time to start and rev up to operating speed to supply enough power to begin charging the batteries once again.

Portable 12-Volt Inverters

A reliable source of emergency power is sitting right out in your driveway. Your automobile and its 12-volt DC power system can provide plenty of power for charging cellular phones (you probably have a cigarette lighter adapter or "12-volt power cord" now anyway) and for producing limited (a couple of hundred watts) amounts of AC power with a DC inverter. As mentioned earlier, an inverter converts DC current into AC for the operation of lights, laptops, battery charging, and small power tools (this does not include hair dryers or toaster ovens). The inverters simply plug into the cigarette lighter socket of your automobile and provide a clean and quite safe source of voltage. They, however, cannot operate continuously and must be used intermittently. Larger inverters are available but require direct connection to the vehicle battery,

Solid-state inverter generators are marketed as "generators" but are in fact a large 12-volt battery or array of batteries, a DC inverter, and a container with 12-volt DC and 110 AC outlets. The smaller units work well for limited power use and for jump starting your vehicle if needed. Since there are no moving parts, they are quiet and can be safely used indoors. They can be recharged from a 12-volt DC power source or the supplied battery charger. These inverters are available in a number of sizes and weights (the batteries are heavy) from around 20 pounds up to several hundred pounds.

Larger permanently installed inverters can power an entire small business or home for extended periods of time. Many homeowners living in remote locations depend on large inverters with a battery array to supply AC voltage for some of their power needs. The batteries can be charged using one of the alternative power sources mentioned in the next section.

Alternative Power Sources

Wind, running water, and thermal and solar energy are all "alternative power" sources. While these may appear to be out of the financial reach of most homes and businesses, portable solar panels that can recharge cellular phones and laptops are becoming mainstream and affordable. As we move deeper into the twenty-first century, the "alternative" sources that become cost effective and dependable will find market share quickly. Portable solar cells in neat fold-up cases are available for $60 to $100 in many electronics and "road warrior" catalogs. Expect a good one to charge your cellular phone in several hours of bright sunlight. Larger "portable panels" can provide the power to charge and maintain satellite phones and other equipment requiring more current. Large solar panels for providing heat and electricity for homes is commonplace in many areas of the country, and these panels capable of supplying the needs of an entire home have dropped in price while gaining efficiency and market share. Solar-powered street lights, web cams, and traffic signs, while expensive, have an attractive return on investment.

Fuel cells are now finding their way into more common use. As environmental pressure increases, these "chemical generators" will become more cost-effective. While the technology is exciting, so is the cost. For the present, this technology is out of the reach of most individuals and companies for routine use.

Staying in Touch

I cannot overstate the importance of communications and how critical staying in touch will be for you and your family in a disaster or other crisis situation. (Under normal conditions, that's easy now since everyone has a cellular phone and "on-hip" Internet access and e-mail.) However, when the lights go out along with the infra-structure we depend on to make our normal communications effortless, we must have a "plan B."

Remember when there was no Internet? Close your eyes for a moment and pretend we've been transported back to a time when there is no e-mail and no browsing the World Wide Web for information and current updates on breaking news. There is no cellular service, no voice mail, fax, and no easy and reliable tele-phone service for that matter. It's a bit hard to imagine, isn't it? Really, it wasn't that long ago (about 50 years) that basic telephone service was considered a rare com-modity. Even 15 years ago, the Internet was something that most people believed involved fishing.

Fifteen years ago, cellular phones were the size of bricks, service was limited to metropolitan areas, and the phones were used by the very few and the well-to-do.

Think back to those times and try to imagine how you would stay in touch with your family, customers, and the office. Your little investment in a daydream may pay big dividends in your future, for as soon as tomorrow, next week, or next month, we may be left without some, or most, of our modern communications infrastructure.

As a society, we are so dependant on our communications infrastructure that it makes a tempting (and sometimes very soft) target for those who would do our way-of-life harm. Turn off communications and you can no longer visit an ATM machine to withdraw cash. Businesses can't receive or fill orders; our transportation, finance, utilities, and even law enforcement depend on reliable and uninterruptible communi-cations links to conduct normal operations.

Our communications infrastructure is designed for routine network capacity and normal traffic patterns. An event that destroys infrastructure and disrupts these "normal patterns" can overload surviving infrastructure and cause failures in com-munications networks. A "fast busy signal" is the first sign of trouble. How can you stay in touch when our normal communications services and systems fail or are taken away?

The first and most important radio you can own is a "SAME" all hazards alert radio. SAME is an acronym for "Specific Area Message Encoding." It naturally is a U.S. government term, but we can overlook that because the technology and system are so important. These radios, which can be purchased at any home electronics store or from numerous sources online, alert you to impending dangerous weather or other life-threatening incidents in your community. These include tornadoes, hurricanes, hazardous materials incidents, terrorism, and other civil emergencies.

The SAME alert radio has an audio alert tone, an alphanumeric display, and a speaker so you can receive audio information from your local NOAA (National Oceanic and Atmospheric Administration) office. Yes, this alerting service is provided by the National Weather Service but this is not just your old reliable weather forecast. NOAA has partnered with local, state, and national emergency management agencies and the Office of Homeland Security to provide emergency information for *any* emergency situation.

After purchasing, you simply program the SAME receiver with your community's unique alert code. Every city, county, and community has a unique code. When an emergency alert or warning is issued for your community, an alert tone sounds and the receiver's audio is turned on to inform you of what action is necessary. The alerts provided are *official information*, not someone's opinion based on second- or thirdhand reports.

Now, I'm sure you may be thinking that with CNN and the Internet, why bother? Unless you sleep with one eye on CNN or have someone at home or work monitoring local emergency response agencies around the clock, you need this radio. While CNN and other media reports are usually accurate, they are not "official" sources of information. The SAME all hazards radio is.

Several ideas and programs are in the works for an improved national alerting network, but for now the SAME radio is a dependable solution for quickly alerting the population of dangers at any time of the day or night. I urge you to purchase one for your home and workplace. Does your school have one of these? If not, make sure they do very soon. Cost varies from $30 to around $80. Most radios include a battery so the radio continues to work even if the power is off. By the way, once you purchase the radio, there is no monthly charge for this vital service.

TIP

The SAME alert radio is as important to your safety as your smoke alarm, and just like your smoke alarm, it may save your life.

Dynamo Radios

Dynamo (emergency) radios are now marketed in numerous places and come in a variety of colors, including camouflage. I don't have a clue why, but they do look cool. They cover the AM, FM, shortwave, and/or weather bands. Most include a small light for finding your way, and some include an outlet for charging your cell phone.

An onboard dynamo or "generator" produces power by turning a small crank. This action produces direct current which charges an internal battery supplying power to the radio. You can store this radio for years and "crank it up" when you need it.

FRS Radios

FRS is yet another acronym, this one for "Family Radio Service." These two-way radios are the inexpensive pairs of "walkie-talkies" advertised in most of the sporting goods and electronics stores. They allow license-free family communication over distances of a half mile or so. They are extremely valuable for emergency communications in and around the neighborhood when nothing else works.

Ham Radio

When disaster strikes, ham (amateur) radio operators provide invaluable communications services to local, state, and federal authorities, the military, and the general public. These volunteer operators provide their own equipment, training, and electrical power to keep emergency information flowing when other communications facilities are out of service. It's their hobby, and they do this important service for free.

If you know a ham radio operator in your community, ask about his or her ability to get messages into and out of disaster areas. One day you may have need to get information about a loved one or family member in a disaster area, or you may need to send word that "we're OK." And while you're at it, you may just discover that you have an interest in getting involved in this fascinating hobby.

The "POTS" Line

We have access to so many cool communications technologies today that it's astounding. VoIP (Voice over Internet Protocol), personal satellite phones that fit into a coat pocket, cellular, and cordless phones with range that allows us to carry them with us when we visit neighbors. Remember that if the power goes off, so do most of our communications. While many cordless phones in our homes have backup batteries, the majority do not. However, the "Plain Old Telephone System" (POTS) operates on DC voltage supplied by the telephone company central office. Having a simple "plain old telephone" to plug in and use during these times will allow you to stay in touch.

Summary

In this chapter, we've covered a great deal of information related to your preparedness at work and at home for unexpected emergencies and disasters. If there is one single rule to remember, it is that all of us must be prepared mentally, physically, and emotionally for the next catastrophic event that may disrupt not only our lives, but also the lives of our family, friends, and coworkers. Having a plan, basic supplies, and the knowledge that we can and will get through it together will make us all stronger as individuals and as a nation.

Index

A

Advanced Local Emergency
    Response Team (ALERT), 233
American National Standards Institute
    (ANSI), 210
Ammonium Nitrate and Fuel Oil
    (ANFO), 243
Animal Liberation Front (ALF), 236
attack techniques, in SCADA systems
    key-logger software, 183
    Man-In-The-Middle Attacks
        (MITM), 182
Awareness intra-preneur, 162

B

battery-operated lights
    handheld lights, 306–307
    headlamps, 307–308
    illumination lamps, 308
    spots and floodlights, 309
BHMA/ANSI Standards
    for auxiliary locks, 210
    for high security locks, 210–211
    for security locks, 201–202
    transformation of convention lock, 203
    156.30 version
        deficiencies, 214–215
        destructive testing, 213
        key control, 213
        surreptitious entry resistance tests, 214
Bilevel®, 200
BiLock®, 199
biometric authentication systems,
        SCADA security
    comparison parameters, 258–260
    description of, 255–256
    factors for authentication, 257
    measurement tools
        DNA sampling, 262
        facial recognition, 261–262
        fingerprints analysis, 263
        parameters used, 257–258
        voice analysis, 262–263
    minutia measurement, 271–272
    vulnerabilities
        device tricking, 266–268
        electronic manipulation,
            268–269
        identity theft, 269–272
biometric signature, 269–270
blasting caps, 241–242
bomb threat planning
    explosive device components
        container, 240
        initiator, 241–242
        main charge, 242–243
        power source, 240
        switch, 241
    target hardening
        delivery, 246
        employee identification, 246
        interior doors, 246–247
        mail rooms, 247
        outside of work environment, 245
        using camera, 246
    terrorist profiles
        domestic terror targets, 236
        formalized terror groups, 237
        International terror targets, 236–237
    terror target classification
        commercial and transportation
            targets, 239

bomb threat planning (*Continued*)
  infrastructure target, 238
  statement target, 237–238
British Columbia Institute of Technology
  (BCIT), 174–175
Builders Hardware Manufacturers
  Association (BHMA), 210
business defense plan, 288–289

C
Charlotte Fire Department (CFD), 233
communication protocols, in SCADA,
  70–71
conventional pin tumbler lock
  components of, 193
  essentials for design, 196–197
  mechanism of, 192
  security enhancements
    anti-bumping pins, 197
    bitting design, 199–200
    design of key, 200
    keyways, 199
    security pins, 198
  vs. high security lock, 202–204
covert entry, 192
Crime deterrent technique, 244
Critical Infrastructure Information
  (CII) Act of 2002, 99–100

D
"data breaches,", 139, 142
data matrix, 153, 157
Diamant®, 201
distributed control system (DCS), 66–67
double-detainer locking theory, 195

E
Egyptian pin tumbler lock, 194–195
electronic manipulation authentication,
  268–269

emergency planning
  communication
    dynamo radio, 315
    family radio service (FRS) radio, 316
    ham radio, 316
    plain old telephone system
      (POTS) line, 317
    specific area message encoding (SAME)
      alert radio, 314–315
  cooking, 300–301
  family
    communication, 292–293
    community shelter, 294–295
    evacuation bag, 295
    fire plan, 293
    ready kit, 302–304
    testing, 301–302
  lighting
    candles and other sources, 304–305
    flashlight, 305
    handheld lights, 306–307
    headlamps, 307–308
    illumination lamps, 308–309
    light sticks, 305
    spots and floodlights, 309
  pantry
    food, 296–299
    water, 299–300
  personal
    escape packs, 285–287
    safety, 283–285
  power
    alternative power sources, 313–314
    inverter generator, 310–311
    portable and backup electric
      generators, 309
    portable 12-volt inverters, 312–313
    UPS and battery backup, 312
  threats, 280–283
  workforce

business defense plan, 288–289
evacuation, 290–292
first-aid kits, 292
Environmental Liberation Front (ELF), 236
event loggers, 67–68

F
facial recognition technology, 261–262
fear-uncertainty-doubt (FUD) factor, 103
firewall architectures
application-level gateway, 85–86
circuit-level gateway, 84–85
deep packet inspection firewall, 88
intrusion prevention system (IPS), 87
stateful packet filtering, 83
static packet filter, 82–83
unified threat management (UTM), 89
firewall security infrastructure, 85–86

G
generic pin tumbler mechanism, 192
Gramm-Leach-Bliley Act, 159

H
hand geometry biometric system, 263
Health Insurance Portability and
Accessibility Act (HIPAA), 272
Human Machine Interface (HMI), 66, 173
hybrid controllers, 67

I
IDS/IPS devices, 181
Improvised Explosive Device (IED), 239,
243
Information delivery channels, 146
Information security awareness program
Awareness Standard, 150–151
business plan presentations, 147–148
and communication failure, 157
company intranet, 154

designing, 143–145
financial (money) source for, 148–149
implementation of, 155–156
importance, 140–141
information delivery channels, 146
internal consultants, 161
Manager's Quick Reference Guide, 158
materials for, 155
online orientation program, 154
program measurement
awareness quotient survey, 165
progress of program, 166
quality management process, 164
Quick Reference Guide
key topics, 152
post-acceptance package, 157
sensitive information, 153
stopgap solution, 147
Information Security Web site, 154
Insider information theft, 234
Instakey®, 199
Internal and external Security Incidents, 174
International Engineering Consortium
(IEC), 66
Internet protocol Ethernet, 177
Intrusion Protection Devise (IPS), 175, 181

K
Kaba Peaks®, 199
Keso®, 197
key-logger software, 183
keystroke readers, 28–31
Kwikset, 197

L
Letter of Authorization (LOA), 120
locks, in SCADA systems
Abus Diskus No. 24 lock, 9–10
key control, 3–4
lock-picking equipment, 13–15

locks, in SCADA systems (*Continued*)
  operation of, 4–5
  pin tumbler Master brand padlock, 7
  Sargent & Greenleaf 8077AD, 10–12
  warded padlock, 8

M

Manager's Quick Reference Guide, 158
Man-In-The-Middle Attacks (MITM), 182
Medeco®, 197
modern pin tumbler lock
  essentials for design, 196–197
  shear line and pins, 195
  vs. Egyptian lock, 194–195

N

National Institute of Standards and
    Technology (NIST), 98
National Security Agency (NSA), 97
NERC Critical Infrastructure Protection
    (CIP) Standards, 99
North American Electric Reliability
    Council (NERC), 97, 99
NSA INFOSEC Assessment Methodology
    (IAM), 97, 124
NSA INFOSEC Evaluation Methodology
    (IEM), 97, 124, 127

O

Organizational Information Criticality
    Matrix (OICM), 110
organizational vulnerabilities
  documentation review and interviews, 123
  system demonstrations and
      observations, 124
Organization for Optimal Power Supply
    (OOPS)
  business description and mission
      statement, 108
  critical information, 109

critical systems/networks, 113–116
impact considerations, 110
OICM, 112–113
organizational criticality, 113

P

physical security, in SCADA systems
  dumpster diving process, 18–20
  key control in locks, 3–4
  operation of locks, 4–5
  social engineering skills
    corporate/agency phonebooks, 23–24
    drop ceilings, 28
    employee badges, 20–21
    for internal auditor, 40
    keystroke readers, 28–31
    in Manholes, 37–39
    motion-sensing light controls, 33–34
    private branch exchange (PBX), 31–32
    tailgating technique, 21, 24
    video security logs, 32–33
piggybacking. *See* tailgating technique
pin stack, 195
pin tumbler lock
  components of, 193–194
  conventional cylinder, 197
  design of key, 200
  essentials for design, 196–197
  mechanism of, 192
  modern, 194–195
Pipe bombs, 244
Programmable Logic Controllers (PLC)
  continuous control applications, 65–66
  discrete control applications, 65

Q

Quick Reference Guide
  key topics, 152
  post-acceptance package, 157
  sensitive information, 153

R

Remote Terminal Units (RTUs), 65, 178
retinal scan technology, 263

S

SCADA security
  biometric authentication systems
    biometric signature, 269–270
    comparison parameters, 258–260
    device tricking, 266–268
    DNA sampling, 262
    electronic manipulation, 268–269
    facial recognition, 261–262
    fingerprint analysis, 263
    minutia measurement, 271–272
    voice analysis, 262–263
  information protection requirements,
    98–100
  logical flow diagram, 100
  on-site assessment process
    NSA baseline INFOSEC classes and
      categories, 123
    organizational vulnerabilities, 123–124
    technical vulnerabilities, 124–127
  post assessment process
    conducting analysis, 127–128
    final report creation, 128
  pre-assessment process
    assessment plan
      components, 120–122
    critical information, 107–109
    critical systems/networks, 113–116
    impact considerations, 109–110
    information criticality matrix, 110–113
    legal authorization, 120
    logical and physical boundaries, 117
    organizational mission, 107
    rules of engagement, customer
      concerns, and constraints, 117–120
  pre-project process

baseline/repeated assessment, 106
  gaining management, 102–103
  regulatory and policy
    requirements, 105
  researching organization, 104
  vetting assessment request, 102
  primary phases, 101
  resources, 129
Schlage Everest®, 199
Secure network management
  business partner links, 180
  configured firewalls, 180
  corporate VPNs, 179
  database links, 179–180
  network access control, 176
  RTU, dial-up access, 178
  secure wide area network
    perimeter, 175
  transmitting non-routable protocol,
    176–177
  two-factor authentication, 176
  vendor support agreements, 178
  wide area network perimeter, 175
Security Event Management System
    (SEMS), 180–181
security pins, 198
security vulnerabilities, 126
Sequel Query Language
    (SQL), 180
Six Sigma quality management process
  awareness quotient chart, 165
  paper mailer survey, 164
  progress of program, 166
Slurries and ditching charges, 243
sound amplification devices
  amplified listening device, 35
  radioshack amplified listener, 36
Supervisory Control and Data Acquisition
    (SCADA) systems, 238
  applications for, 63–64

Supervisory Control and Data Acquisition
(SCADA) systems (*Continued*)
attack techniques
key-logger software, 183
Man-In-The-Middle Attacks
(MITM), 182
backup and recovery of, 176
challenges of, 173
communication protocols, 70–71
components
distributed control system
(DCS), 66–67
event loggers, 67–68
hybrid controllers, 67
Programmable Logic Controllers (PLC),
65–66
Remote Terminal Unit (RTU), 65
components and functions of, 173
controlling access, 177
firewall architectures
application-level gateway, 85–86
circuit-level gateway, 84–85
deep packet inspection firewall, 88
intrusion prevention system (IPS), 87
stateful packet filtering, 83
static packet filter, 82–83
unified threat management (UTM), 89
firewall tool
definition, 78
multi-network
connectivity, 79–80
positive and negative security
models, 79
reactive and proactive
solutions, 80–81
internal and external security incidents,
174
law enforcement on, 172–183
network architecture, 68–70
risk determination

active scanning, 75–76
passive scanning, 76
risk mitigation, 76–78
roles in industries, 62
security issues
British Columbia Institute of
Technology (BCIT)
report, 71–72
disadvantages, 75
high-level weaknesses, 74
security policy, 77–78
TCP/IP error handling, 73
vs. distributed control systems, 67

T
tailgating technique, 21
technical security, in
SCADA systems
destroyed disk drive, 16–17
digital Shredder device, 15–16
EDR's disk destroyer, 18
sound amplification devices, 35–36
technical vulnerabilities, 124
customer communication, 127
enumeration activities, 125
tools for IEM baseline activities, 127
vulnerability identification activities,
125–126
terror targets, classification
commercial and transportation
targets, 239
infrastructure target, 238
statement target, 237–238
touch point communications, 156
3T2R rule, 211

U
U-Change®, 199
UL (Underwriters Laboratories) 437
Standards

deficiencies
  bump key attacks, 207
  decoding attacks, 208
  forced entry resistance test, 206
  key control, 208–209
  mechanical bypass, 209
  picking and impressioning
    techniques, 205–206
  test by criminals, 204–205
 for security locks, 201–202
 transformation of convention
    lock, 203
unified threat management (UTM)
 in firewall SCADA systems, 89
 reactive signature-based
    systems, 81

V

Virtual Private Networks (VPN), 174,
    178–179

W

Water Infrastructure Security
    Enhancement (WISE), 99
workforce continuity
 definition, 282, 288
 planning, 282
World Trade Center,
    234–235, 237, 239

Y

Yale pin tumbler lock. *See* modern pin
    tumbler lock

Printed and bound by CPI Group (UK) Ltd, Croydon, CR0 4YY

03/10/2024

01040340-0002